The King of the Norfolk Poachers
His Life & Times

A Biography of the Author
of
I Walked by Night

The King of the Norfolk Poachers
His Life and Times

A Biography of the Author
of
I Walked by Night

CHARLOTTE PATON

Old Pond Publishing

Published by
Old Pond Publishing Ltd
Dencora Business Centre
36 White House Road
Ipswich, IP1 5LT
United Kingdom

Cover design by Liz Whatling
Maps and family tree by John Gilkes
Typesetting by Galleon Typesetting, Ipswich
Printed in Malta

To all my family
past, present and those still to come

Acknowledgements

My very grateful thanks to the following: Bertram Akhurst, Saul Arnold, Andrew Baldry, Fred Bayfield, Toby Beadle, Arthur Bedwell, Margaret Benson, Mandy Bilverstone, Mr and Mrs Clifford Bird, Robin Bix, David Blakesley, Alec Boast, Mike Bott, Boydell and Brewer Group Ltd., Allan Bradley, John Bromily, Pauline Brunton, Mr and Mrs Colin Buck, Gordon Buckley, Brian Bulman, Val Byatt, David Carter, Peter Catling, Barry Colvin, Terry Coppin, Charles Cunningham, Richard Denyer, Geoffrey Earl, Liz Fenwick, Taff Gillingham, John Gray, David Grimes, Colin Hancy, Tony Hancy, Les Harrison, Mrs Hart, Frank Honeywood, Keith and Shirley Howell, Ivan Howlett, the staff at King's Lynn Library, Pam Kirby, Les Knowles, Gwen Luker, David Mason, Bob Moulton, Stuart Nairn, Lawrie Nicholls, Rita Norton, Nick Patrick, Charles Patrick, John Pearson, Kim Puyenbroek, Terry Reeve, Mr and Mrs Herbert Revell, Cath Rolfe, Mr and Mrs David Rolfe and family, Kay Rose, Harry Skipper, Keith Skipper, Sue Smalley, Nell Steele, Steele & Co., Diss, John Timpson, Greta Towler, Elsie Treanor, University of Reading Library Archive, Madelaine Watson, Paulette Webb, Ian Whittle, Derek Whyte, Joy Williams, Sue and Andy Willis, J.J. Wright (photographer) and David Wing.

In particular I thank Nada Cheyne for permission to reproduce extracts from *I Walked by Night* and the Trustees of the Bungay Museum for allowing me free use of Emily's manuscript. Also, Peter Billingham, John Mason and Peter Pilgram, curators of the Norfolk Constabulary Historical Collection.

Special thanks go to Brian who bore it all very patiently, and to Chris Reeve and Steve Caple whose encouragement kept me going. Without the help of these three, this book would have never have been completed.

Illustration section sources and acknowledgements

(1) author; (2) King's Lynn and West Norfolk Borough Council; (4) Mandy Bilverstone; (5) Norfolk Museum and Archaeology Service; (7) author; (8) Barbara Taylor and Lynn Library; (9) Norfolk Museums and Archaeology Service; (10) Barry Colvin; (11) Shirley Howell; (12) Geoffrey Earl; (13) Brian Bulman; (14) Dr Barnardo's; (15) Catherine Rolfe; (16) author; (17) Bungay Museum; (18) author; (19) Pauline Brunton and family; (20) Frank Honeywood; (21) John Reeve; (22) Bungay Museum; (23) Bungay Museum; (26) Bungay Museum; (27) Richard Denyer ; (29) photo by Peter Hodges; (30) Boydell and Brewer Group Ltd, University of Reading Archive; (31) Mr and Mrs C Buck; (32) Photo by Peter Hodges.

The front cover painting was photographed by Robert Fuller:
www.robertfullerassociates.co.uk

Contents

Introduction

In 2002, when my husband Brian and I finally paid off the mortgage on our West Norfolk cottage, a fat bundle of deeds arrived from the bank, which looked intriguing. After supper we settled down on the floor in front of the fire and started to read through them. They informed us that the West Bilney Estate, of which our cottage was a part, had covered over 2,366 acres and was described in the particulars when it was sold in 1924 as a typical Norfolk Sporting Property, '. . . comprising of extensive woods and a warren with a capital trout stream and marshlands where first-class shooting may be enjoyed over the property in great variety'. At that time it was being sold by a syndicate, one of whom was Marianne Catherine Cabrera de Morella of Wentworth – very posh!

We had always understood that our cottage was the gatehouse to West Bilney Hall, but lot 25 in the sales particulars, our property, was described as an attractive bungalow villa, erected of carrstone under a slate roof, and now in the ownership of Mr Boddy, a gamekeeper. We had never realised that it had been a gamekeeper's cottage, and as we chatted about our finds I was reminded of a book called *I Walked by Night* by The King of The Norfolk Poachers. Edited by Lilias Rider Haggard and published in 1935, it is an autobiography. I remembered, among other things, it telling of poaching, the countryside, rural deprivation, love and the poacher's determination not to be beholden to the gentry.

I went to the bookshelves and pulled it down, dusty and untouched since Christmas 1976 when, according to the note on the fly leaf, Mum had given it to me because she thought it might be of interest to me as it was in part about Bungay, Suffolk where I grew up. It was edited by Lilias Rider Haggard and published in 1935.

I poured myself a glass of wine and started to reread it. My memory had been correct; the poacher did say he lived in a lodge when he was, for a short period, a gamekeeper:

> When I was Keepering I lived in a lodge

I read on, and completed the book and the bottle of wine in one sitting. *I Walked By Night* is much as he originally wrote it, with Lilias Rider Haggard revising the manuscript as little as possible when she edited it. I was completely spellbound – it is a wonderful book, and he was an intriguing man; I wondered if he still had relatives living locally and whether I could find out anything else about him.

There were lots of clues in the book which led me to believe that he really might have lived in our house and I was determined to see if I could find out if it was true. However, the poacher never reveals his real name, and without knowing that I felt I could make no progress.

By happy coincidence, soon afterwards I heard the Radio 4 programme, 'Making History', where listeners write in about historical matters that puzzle them, or to discover more about the past. I decided to get in touch to see if they could tell me the name of my poacher. While I waited for their response, I started to ferret about. The author had also written:

> Were I was Keeper we had a verry large Warren beside the road running from Wormagay. One day the warriners were digging at the botom of a large hill were Oliver Cromwell was suposed to have planted his guns wen he destroyed Pentney Abby

I started by researching what Cromwell was doing in Pentney and also the history of the abbey. Established by Robert de Vaux in the twelfth century, it became a large and prestigious Augustinian priory. After a turbulent period of squabbling between Clerical and Secular, the monks settled down to good works and in 1492 were visited by Archdeacon Goldwell, who seems to have been the Inspector of Priories. He gave them a glowing report. Other inspections followed but then in 1514, the Prior's slackness was complained of. In 1520, after further complaints, the residents were spoken to separately, but all was found to be well. However, by 1532 the abbey was in a state of disrepair and then in 1536 the Prior and five canons admitted to affairs with the nuns from Marham Nunnery. The Abbess was subsequently fined and the nunnery closed.

In 1535, the dissolution of the monasteries had begun and by the end of 1536 the abbey was stripped and empty. What a disaster this must have been for the local community. The monks had run a school and offered hospitality to travellers and pilgrims crossing the river on their way to Walsingham. In addition, a large number of people were employed to feed and care for the monks and their guests.

Then Oliver Cromwell came and almost completely flattened the abbey. As M. de Bootman says in his pamphlet about the abbey:

> *Cromwell sometime in the Civil War floated flat-bottomed sloops from King's Lynn to Pentney, where he and his men had a bit of target practice at the Priory buildings reducing them to rubble. The remains were then used as a convenient quarry for building material. Priory stone can be seen in many old houses in Pentney.*

I have tried unsuccessfully to find out why Cromwell was at King's Lynn. The Fen people were some of the first to take his side, so perhaps he simply felt safe enough to come here for an 'away' day and a spot of laddish behaviour!

'Making History' got in contact to tell me that the poacher's name was Frederick Rolfe. They invited me to appear on Radio 4 to talk about what I was trying to do, and this led to several offers of help in my quest for more information. I spoke to a very interesting man, who told me that Fred (how familiar of me) lived in Nethergate Street, Bungay, about a quarter of a mile from where I was brought up. He told me that he understood that Fred had come to an unhappy end and that there had been disturbing gossip over the years about why he had. I hoped what he said was not true and it was at this point that I realised I might be uncovering a hornets' nest.

From then on, I became completely obsessed with finding out all I could about The King of the Norfolk Poachers and six years later, to my amazement I have gathered enough information to write this book. Intriguingly, much of what I discovered was at variance with the tale told by The Poacher himself.

CHARLOTTE PATON
The Old Lodge
West Bilney
2009

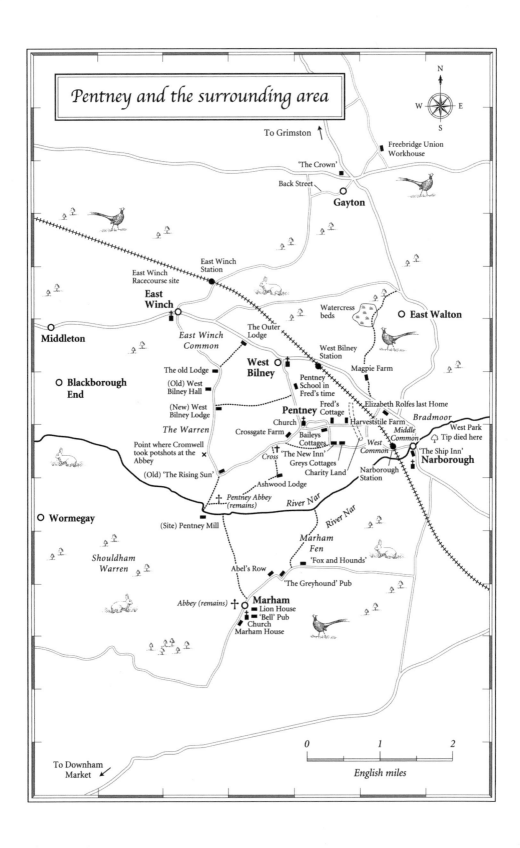

Pentney and the surrounding area

N
W · E
S

To Grimston

Freebridge Union
Workhouse

'The Crown'

Back Street

Gayton

East Winch
Station

East Winch
Racecourse site

**East
Winch**

○ **Middleton**

*East Winch
Common*

Watercress
beds

○ **East Walton**

The Outer
Lodge

West Bilney
Station

The old Lodge

**West
Bilney** ○

Magpie Farm

○ **Blackborough
End**

(Old) West
Bilney Hall

Pentney
School in
Fred's time

Elizabeth Rolfes last Home

(New) West
Bilney Lodge

Fred's
Cottage

Bradmoor

The Warren

Pentney

Harveststile Farm

West Park
⌂ Tip died here

Church

*Middle
Common*

Crossgate Farm

Baileys
Cottages

*West
Common*

'The Ship Inn'

Point where Cromwell
took potshots at the
Abbey ✕

Cross

'The New Inn'

Narborough

(Old) 'The Rising Sun'

Greys Cottages

Charity Land

Narborough
Station

Ashwood Lodge

✝ *Pentney Abbey
(remains)*

River Nar

○ **Wormegay**

(Site) Pentney Mill

River Nar

*Marham
Fen*

'Fox and Hounds'

*Shouldham
Warren*

Abel's Row

'The Greyhound' Pub

Abbey (remains) ✝

Marham
■ Lion House
✝ 'Bell' Pub
Church
Marham House

0   1   2

To Downham
Market ↙

English miles

CHAPTER 1

1862 Birth and Before

Frederick Rolfe was born in Pentney, a poor rural parish deep in the heart of the Norfolk countryside, on 28 February 1862. He was the only child of John and Elizabeth Rolfe. Beside the entry in the Pentney Parish Records showing he was baptised on 18 March 1862 are the words, 'Brought into Church the 6th April 1862', so it would seem likely that he had been baptised at home. Perhaps this meant he was a sickly child and thought unlikely to survive. Mortality rates for infants in West Norfolk were 143 in 1,000 at the time, so this was a common occurrence.

Both of Fred's parents had been married before. His mother had already lost two children in infancy during her first marriage. After her husband's death she was reduced to living as a pauper with her surviving daughter, Maria aged 7. Being classified a pauper meant that she and Maria depended on the parish for support. The Relieving Officer from the Workhouse decided she could survive in the community with an allowance – an option much favoured by the Board of Guardians for the Poor House because it was cheaper than taking the destitute in as inmates. It was a grim existence. George Ewart Evans (1909–88), who travelled East Anglia recording oral histories, wrote of a conversation with James Seeley about his impoverished childhood in Norfolk. Although Seeley recalls a time later in the nineteenth century, he tells of the tough time had by those reliant on handouts.

James Seeley was the eldest of five and aged about 9 when his father died. His mother would turn her hand to anything to earn money, including taking in washing, to keep her children, he recalled. Every morning before school, the older children had to pump sufficient water for their mother to do the day's laundry. The children all took bread and jam to school to eat at dinnertime, but to supplement this, they would scramble into the fields to steal a turnip or swede. This, they would nibble on raw as they walked the mile and a half to school. Sheep were sometimes fed locust beans, which the children also stole, thinking them a great treat.

Despite her hard work, Mrs Seeley was still forced to turn to the parish for help. The Board of Guardians allowed her 3/6d a week (an agricultural labourer earned about 12/- a week at that time). The Board said she was fit and able, so she could work to support her family. To make sure she did not keep her three eldest children away from school to work, each Saturday morning they had to present their school attendance record to the Relieving Officer to prove they had been at school all week. James remembered that they were always hungry, but that was normal – everyone who was part of a large family struggled to find enough to eat and sometimes there was nothing to eat at all.

Elizabeth may have been able to raise a little extra cash using the skills picked up from her mother. Later, Fred devoted a whole chapter of *I Walked by Night* to the witchcraft, cures and hedgerow remedies that he heard his grandmother talking about.

> My old Granny was a bit of a quack Doctor, and the People used to come to her with all there ills. She was a mid Wife beside, and one to help with the layen out of Boddies. She told me all the Charms and such like that I know . . .
>
> Then there was a charm for anyone trubbled with bleeding from the nose. They should get a skein of silk, and get nine Maids each to tie a knot in the skein, and then the sufferer must wear it round his neck. That was a shure cure for Nose bleed. The cure for Head acke was to get the skin of the Viper and sew it in to the lining of the hat . . .

Born in Pentney, Elizabeth was baptised on 24 June 1827, the third of the eight children born to Thomas and Ursula Shafto (some-times recorded on documents as Shaftoe). In 1792, Thomas was born in Castle Acre, Norfolk, while Ursula Barrett was born in Setchey, Norfolk, in 1804. They married in Pentney church on 18 November 1821.

Only one of their children appears to have died young. Baptismal records show that at least four of Elizabeth's siblings married in Pentney and lived locally. Between them, they had a large number of children, but Fred never mentions his aunts, uncles and cousins in *I Walked by Night*.

The 26-year-old Elizabeth married her first husband, George Powley of West Bilney, Norfolk, at Pentney church on 20 November 1853. He was 24 and his trade was listed as husbandman. They had three children, two of whom died young. Maria was born before their marriage, on 4 October 1853, and registered as Maria Shaftoe. However, following her baptism in Pentney church, on 1 February 1854, she was named Maria Powley, for by then Elizabeth and George had married. Hannah was baptised at Pentney on 27 June 1855. At 7 weeks old she died, having had 'debility' from birth. Robert was born in 1856 and died shortly after his birth. He was buried at Pentney church on 29 August 1856.

After just seven years of marriage, George died of pneumonia in Pentney aged 31. His death certificate records that he suffered for nine days and endured pulmonary apoplexy for an hour before he died. Elizabeth was present at his death on 27 September 1860. He was then listed as an agricultural labourer.

Workhouse records do not reveal whether Elizabeth was ever admitted, or appealed for out relief while George was alive. If he was too ill to support them, she may have done so. Many men struggled on, trying to keep their families long after they were far too ill to do so.

Research into the Powley family proved difficult. Their names appeared in Church records, but I could find no trace in secular documents. Common sense led to the belief that they would have remained in the area, but research into the surrounding villages and workhouses shed no light on the whereabouts of Elizabeth and her daughter after George's death. However, the 1861 census revealed that living next to John Rolfe was a widowed pauper, Elizabeth Stacey, and her 7-year-old daughter Maria, whose details exactly matched those of Elizabeth and Maria Powley.

Further investigation revealed Elizabeth's first husband was born in 1929 to a Miss Mary Powley and christened George Powley. In 1931, Mary married John Stacey. Thereafter George was known as George Stacey (sometimes Stacy), although the Church did not recognise the change in name. John and Mary Stacey went on to have seven more children and lived at Magpie Cottages, West Bilney.

When George came to marry Elizabeth, he had to marry her in the name he was christened with (Powley), but they called themselves Mr and Mrs Stacey. This was confirmed by the discovery of a birth certificate for their daughter Hannah, who was entered into the

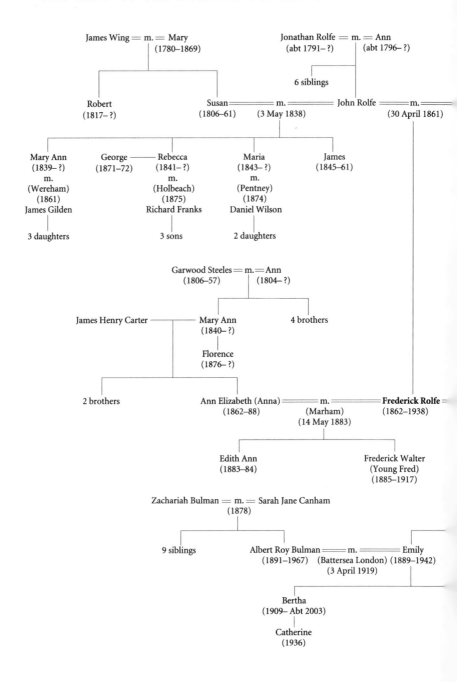

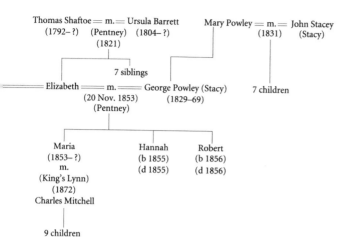

Thomas Shaftoe = m. = Ursula Barrett
(1792–?)   (Pentney)   (1804–?)
(1821)

Mary Powley = m. = John Stacey
(1831)   (Stacy)

7 siblings

Elizabeth = m. = George Powley (Stacy)
(20 Nov. 1853)   (1829–69)
(Pentney)

7 children

Maria
(1853–?)
m.
(King's Lynn)
(1872)
Charles Mitchell

Hannah
(b 1855)
(d 1855)

Robert
(b 1856)
(d 1856)

9 children

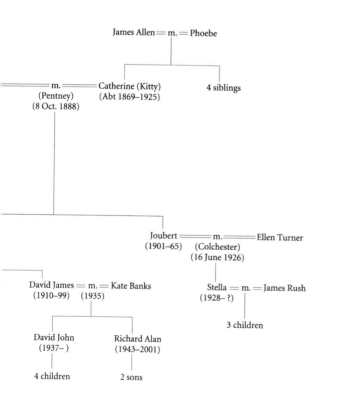

James Allen = m. = Phoebe

m. = Catherine (Kitty)
(Pentney)   (Abt 1869–1925)
(8 Oct. 1888)

4 siblings

Joubert = m. = Ellen Turner
(1901–65)   (Colchester)
(16 June 1926)

David James = m. = Kate Banks
(1910–99)   (1935)

Stella = m. = James Rush
(1928–?)

3 children

David John
(1937–)

Richard Alan
(1943–2001)

4 children

2 sons

baptismal register as Hannah Powley, although her birth certificate is in the name of Stacy. The dates match and the mother is listed as Elizabeth Stacey, formerly Shaftoe. Three years before George and Elizabeth married, they were witnesses at Elizabeth's brother James's marriage to Eliza Warren, signing the register George Stacy and Elizabeth Shafto. This leads to the assumption that they were courting for some years and Maria was George's daughter, although his name does not appear on her birth certificate.

Fred's Father, John, was born in 1813, almost certainly in Bradenham, a village about eight miles east of Pentney. He was the son of Jonathan and Ann Rolfe. The squire at the time was William Meybolm Rider. A flamboyant barrister and forceful, opinionated man, for many years he sat as a Justice on the Swaffham bench. His eighth child, Henry Rider Haggard, was born in 1856. William was convinced Henry wouldn't amount to much. Despairing of his academic ability and lack of ambition, he sent him to Africa – a move that proved an enormous inspiration for his upcoming literary career. By the end of the nineteenth century he became a successful writer, penning such popular works as *King Solomon's Mines* and *She*. Henry married Marianna Louisa Margitson (always referred to as Louisa) and lived at Ditchingham Hall on the Norfolk and Suffolk border. His fourth child was Lilias Rider Haggard.

It would have been impossible for young John Rolfe, an illiterate labourer, to imagine that his son and the squire's granddaughter would one day collaborate on the much-loved *I Walked by Night*.

What motivates people can be quite strange. Fred's grandfather Jonathan was always prepared to give up a day's work to watch a hanging. Later, with the advent of the railways, special trains were laid on at excursion rates for such events:

> The harts of the People were much more callous than to day – my Grandfather walked from my home to Norwich, a distance of thirty miles to see Bloomfield Rush the Murderer hung on Castle Hill, and there were thousands of people there. I think it was the last time any one were hung in Publick at the Castle. They had been tryen him for days and days, and the whole County wanted to se the end of him, and most of them as could do so got there one way and another, even if they had to walk.

The background to this particular case was that 59-year-old Isaac Jermy, a Recorder in the Court at Norwich, his son Isaac Junior and daughter-in-law Sophia, and Isaac's 13-year-old daughter Isabella had just finished dinner in their Elizabethan home, Stanfield Hall near Wymondham, on 28 November 1848 when Isaac and his son were shot dead by an intruder. Sophia was maimed for life and her maid crippled; only Isabella was spared, following the quick actions of the cook. Despite his disguise of a mask and a woman's wig, the culprit was recognised by the servants.

James Blomfield Rush was arrested and found to have a motive. In a complex and slightly shady deal, Isaac Jermy had lent him money to purchase a farm and it transpired that Jermy was set to foreclose on the £5,000 mortgage in two days' time.

On 29 March 1849, Rush defended himself at the trial by trying to lay the blame on others who had brushed with Jermy in financial dealings. The Victorians hung onto every word of the case, which was reported at length, and caused a sensation. Even Charles Dickens visited the scene of the crime. Drama increased when Sophia's crippled maid was carried into court on a specially devised bed to give evidence. Rush's mistress Emily Sandford, governess to his nine children, gave evidence for the prosecution, heightening the excitement. It took fourteen hours for Rush to sum up and just ten minutes for the jury to find him guilty.

Passing the death sentence, the judge remarked that he 'saw the hand of God at work' in an act of retribution for Rush's failure to make an honest woman of his mistress: 'If you had performed to that unfortunate girl the promises you made her, to make her your wife, the policy of the law which seals the lips of a wife in any proceedings against her husband would have permitted you to go unpunished.'

Protesting his innocence to the last, Rush was hanged on 21 April 1849, on the bridge over the moat at Norwich Castle. Thousands flocking there found stalls selling pottery figures of the principle characters, which were bought in large numbers. There were food stalls and drink flowed. A good time was had by all, except Rush. In fact, gala – a festive occasion – comes from the word gallows because everyone went on a jolly to see a hanging!

In Pentney church, Fred's father John (25) married his first wife Susan Wing (33) on 5 March 1839. Susan was born to James and Mary Wing from Pentney in 1804. The couple had four children: Mary Ann (1839), Rebecca (1841), Maria (1842) and James (1845). It was confusing to read in the 1851 census that John and Susan had four daughters, the youngest being Jane, but by the 1861 census Jane had reverted to James. Presumably the enumerator must have mis-heard in 1851 and as neither John nor Susan could read or write (both marked their marriage certificate with a cross), they would never have known. In the 1861 census only Mary Ann (21) and James (16) were still at home. Rebecca (20) was a servant at Church Farmhouse, Pentney, while Maria (19) was at the nearby village of Middleton, working as housemaid to Thomas Mathews, a farmer.

Mary Ann was acting housekeeper for John, because on 17 Febru-ary 1861, Susan had died aged 57. She suffered gastric fever for four weeks and dysenteric diarrhoea for three weeks. Meanwhile, Elizabeth Stacey and her only surviving child, Maria, were living next door.

CHAPTER 2

1862–82 Growing Up

Elizabeth married John Rolfe on 30 April 1861, just 71 days after Susan's death, when she was 34 and John was 48. *I Walked by Night* describes Fred's father as a difficult, bigoted man, so one wonders what the attraction was. Did she marry him to keep a roof over her head, because life as a widow with a daughter to care for was a terrible struggle? Perhaps Mary Ann did not want to continue living at home with her peppery father, so he needed a housekeeper, for men in those days did not fend for themselves.

The author Flora Thompson (1876–1947) wrote in her book, *Lark Rise to Candleford*:

> *Patty was not a native of these parts but had come there only a few years before as housekeeper to an elderly man whose wife had died. As was the custom when no relative was available, he applied to the board of Guardians for a housekeeper, and Patty had been selected as the most suitable inmate of the Workhouse at the time.*

In *Arcady for Better or Worse*, a book written by a clergyman, Augustus Jessopp, about rural Norfolk in the late nineteenth century, the following tale is related:

> *An habitual drunk, Dick's first wife died and left him with two children, the eldest three years old. Dick had such a bad character that no one would be his housekeeper, the neighbours 'did for the children'. Within ten days of his wife's death Dick's patience was exhausted. Off he walked to the Workhouse, got admission on some pretext to the women's ward, and gave out that he wanted a wife and wouldn't go until he got one. An eager crowd of females offered themselves. He picked out the prettiest.*
>
> *"What's your name?"*
> *"Polly Beck."*

"How many children?"
"Three!"
"Who's the father?"
"Don't know! I had two by Jack the butcher, they died. T'other three ain't so big."

In less than an hour Dick, Polly and the three little ones marched out together happily. At the Registrars office, within a month, Polly became Mrs Styles and turned out not such a bad wife.

Whatever their reasons, John and Elizabeth married, and ten months later Fred was born. The children of John's first marriage were almost off his hands. James is listed in the 1861 census as a 16-year-agricultural labourer and would probably have been on half wages as a half man, but he would still have been bringing money in. With only Fred and Maria to bring up, the family would have been better off than most.

In the mid–1800s village life in England was hard, the average wage being 10/- (about 50p) and the well fed bought about a stone of flour for two each week, each stone costing 2/6d. The principal groceries were cheese, yeast, sugar, paraffin wax candles (used from mid–1800s), tea, tobacco for the head of the household, with a few coppers left over for beer. Groceries were purchased from John Sare, the Pentney grocer, or from the post office, which also served as a butchers and general shop. Meat was rarely eaten, while herrings and fat bacon (when families could afford them) were saved for father and any working boys so they had the strength to work, as it was imperative to keep the wage earners well. Prosperity was seen as the ability to have one meal that included meat a day.

In 1880 a loaf weighing a pound cost 1d, milk was a penny a pint (skimmed, a farthing). Tea was an expensive luxury, coal cost 25/- a ton, sheep's heads were a penny and doctor's fees ranged between 2/- and 6/6d. The average number of children in a family was between five and six. They survived largely on bread and dripping, porridge and root crops boiled into a stew.

Sadly, any happiness the Rolfes shared must have been short-lived, for while Fred was a toddler, his step-brother James died in King's Lynn Hospital on 19 December 1863 of General Deposit of Tubercular Exhaustion.

Known as the 'White Plague', tuberculosis killed almost everyone who caught it. It was found in the bones of Egyptian mummies and there was no hope of a cure until the germ was identified in 1882. The disease reached epidemic proportions in the 1600s when one in five died of it and there was a real fear it would wipe out whole cities.

Following an outbreak of cholera in 1833, the good men of King's Lynn decided the town must have a hospital and so they purchased Gallows Pasture, a meadow where criminals and pirates had been hanged in the 1600s. King's Lynn Hospital was opened in 1835 and extended twice more, due to the generosity of two local benefactors, so by the time poor James arrived, there were beds for fifty-two patients. The downstairs wards were reserved for patients who had had accidents, a common occurrence in a rural port. This was to spare them the ordeal of the stairs. Upstairs, the acute surgical and medical wards were mixed. Every care and comfort was given. Great importance was attached to the need for lots of fresh air – 'bad air' was thought to harbour germs. The wards were heated with open fires, which must have made cleaning difficult, for everything was scrubbed each day. It was not at all Spartan, though: there were fresh flowers and pictures on the walls, plus toys for child patients.

In 1863, the year James died, the hospital admitted 344, mostly accidents, with a high rate of recovery after surgery. A year later, B.W. Richardson, MA MD, an authority on pulmonary tuberculosis, came to King's Lynn. He found a 'fine hospital giving free treatment to the poor'. The locals dug deep into their pockets and gave generously to support the hospital and feed good nourishing food to the patients. Richardson's only criticism was of the food – too much carbohydrate and not enough protein (he made no mention of the need for fruit and vegetables).

There is no record of how long James Rolfe was a patient, but it is doubtful he would have had many visitors. The ten miles into King's Lynn was a long way to walk, particularly in winter, even if the family could afford a day off work, assuming their employer would allow this. Trains would have been expensive and presumably they did not know how long James would linger. Postal services had been running for about twenty years (Robinson Crusoe was Postmaster at Lynn). Would someone from the hospital have written or used the Telegraph system, which began in 1845, to send a telegram to John and Elizabeth to tell them the sad news? As neither could read, who would have read it out to them?

However his parents received the news, James's body must have been borne back to the village by train or over the muddy roads by cart in the late December half-light. What followed must have been a pitiful but common sight as the little funeral procession made its way to Pentney churchyard, either on foot as a 'walking funeral', or possibly in a cart lent by a generous farmer, washed down and filled with straw. James and his father are both listed in the census as agricultural workers, but it is not known on which farms. Not for James the plumed horses, the family dressed in black, the draped crepe, the mutes and all the outward signs of grief beloved by the Victorians.

James's funeral would have been very much as described in *Candleford Green* by Flora Thompson:

> *The women would follow the coffin, in decent if shabby and unfashionable mourning often borrowed in parts from neighbours, and men with black crepe bands around their hats and sleeves. The village carpenter, who had made the coffin, acted as undertaker, but £3 or £4 was covered by life insurance. Flowers were often placed inside the coffin, but there were seldom wreaths, the fashion for those came later.*
>
> *A meal to follow the funeral was almost certainly provided, and the food then consumed was the best the bereaved could obtain. These funeral meals for the poor have been much misunderstood and misrepresented. By the country poor and probably for the majority of the poor in towns they were not provided in any spirit of ostentation, but because it was an urgent necessity that a meal should be partaken of by the mourners as soon as possible after a funeral. Very little food could be eaten in a tiny cottage while the dead remained there; evidence of human mortality would be too near and too pervasive. Married children and other relatives coming from a distance might have eaten nothing since breakfast. So a ham or part of a ham was provided, not in order to be able to boast 'we buried 'im with 'am', but because it was a ready prepared dish which was both easily obtained and appetising.*
>
> *These funeral meals have appeared to some more pathetic than amusing. The return of the mourners after the final parting and their immediate outbursts of pent-up grief, then, as they grew calmer, the gentle persuasion of those less afflicted than the widow or widower or the bereaved parents, for the sake of the living still left to them, should take some nourishment. Then their gradual revival as they ate and drank. Tears would still be wiped away furtively, but a few sad smiles would break through, until, at the table a sober cheerfulness would prevail.*

For John and Elizabeth this sad tableau would have been enacted all too frequently, both their spouses having made the final journey to the churchyard at Pentney within recent years.

As a child Fred loved to spend time with his maternal grandparents, who lived close by:

> They were a dear old cupple, and I was verry fond of them and they of me, and would never hear any thing rong of me.
>
> . . . and I used to sit and listen by the hour. I never herd any thing like that at home from my Father, even if he knew any thing. He would never tell me a tale except about religon, I got plenty of that – much good it done.
>
> Wen my Father got to hear that he was tellen me those tales he forbid me goen to see the Old People, but I always managed to get to them some way or another.
>
> . . . I used to hear a lot about the horrors of tranceportation. I often think that the old People of the Eighteen Centuary, used the tales of tranceportation as a Bogey man to frighten there sons. The young generationn now would not even know what it means to be tranceported.
>
> I had an Uncle tranceported some where round about that time for Sheep Stealing, and Grandfather have told me many a time about it. He was a Shepperd and lived at West Acre. It was the time that Amerricca was asken for Emergrants to go out, and he stole the sheep to get the money to go there. They told me he got twenty years sentence, and was sent as a convict to Australia.

After a few years of working for the Government, Fred's uncle was released. He was then free to work where he liked, so long as he did not leave the country. *I Walked by Night* goes on to describe how he carried on his trade as a shepherd, saved money, married and settled. When he died, he owned eleven square miles of land, and 40,000 sheep. Certainly, he was able to send money home to his parents. Lilias Rider Haggard added a footnote to the book to say Transportation was looked on as a terrible fate, mainly because the lack of communication and very isolated nature of English villages made the distance even more terrifying.

She also recorded that a bottle of the prisoner's urine was corked securely and hung up in his old home, then anyone would know how he was getting on. If the urine got cloudy, he was ill; if it wasted, he was dead and the family went into mourning.

25

Prisons at that time were not for holding convicted prisoners and periods of imprisonment were not a sentencing option; they were used solely to hold those on remand. Once their case was heard, either they were sent to the gallows, transported, whipped, pilloried, put in the stocks or fined. There were Houses of Correction, such as the Bridewell at Walsingham that housed tramps and vagabonds, if they were not considered to be the deserving poor. Originally intended to train inmates to lead useful lives and learn a trade, they became prisons in all but name. Magistrates decided whether the tramps should be aided or punished, and punishment was harsh: they would do the most unpleasant of tasks to earn food, and could be whipped or be pierced through the ears with a red-hot iron.

Juries were beginning to feel uncomfortable about passing the death sentence for less serious offences and so fewer verdicts of guilty were passed. One way round this was to offer a pardon to criminals if they agreed to enter the Army or Navy, or to order transportation.

When transportation to America ceased in 1776, serious over-crowding in prisons led to the use of hulks as floating prisons. To ease this problem, a fleet of convict ships left for New South Wales in 1787. The first ships were desperately overcrowded and the prisoner treatment and conditions appalling; many died on the journey. Inhumane treatment continued while they served their sentence but once free, they could carve out new lives for themselves, or find a way to return home.

With the introduction of punishment by imprisonment in 1853, transportations lessened and by 1868 it had ceased altogether. Between 1787 and 1868, 160,000 convicts were transported to Australia. Four thousand were from Norfolk and most of these were held in Norwich Castle until they left. Men and women were not segregated. While in prison, Henry Cabell and Susannah Holmes had a child. Sadly, by the time the baby was born the rules were tightened and the sexes separated, so Henry rarely saw his child, though he was said to have developed a remarkable fondness for it. Eventually trans-ported in the first fleet to go to Australia, all three were reunited and became one of the colony's founding families.

Fred's grandparents also told him tales of smugglers, who like poachers worked as a defiance and a necessity. His Grandfather recalled boats coming in from Holland and Germany with cargoes of spirits and silks. Large quantities of contraband were moved under the cover of darkness. In November 1829, a 39 ft galley was captured

26

at Breydon, with a cargo of 283 half ambers of proof brandy and about 6,000 lb tobacco. November 1832 saw 5,565 lb tobacco and about 650 gallons brandy and geneva (gin) seized from a large tub-boat and lodged in the Custom House at Wells next-the Sea.

These boats were met by luggers out in the Wash and some of the contraband brought across Terrington Marshes to Marham Fen, where the goods were hidden until they could be moved on down the Green roads for dispersal. Undoubtedly, these tales must have coloured Fred's views on breaking the law.

In 1871, Rebecca, John's second daughter and Fred's stepsister, left her employment at Church Farm, Pentney as she was pregnant. John George was born on 2 November 1871 in Gayton, possibly at the Workhouse. On 17 September 1872, the baby died of chronic diarrhoea and exhaustion. Hustler Shaftoe was present at his death. Another illegitimate child and another infant death, it was common at that time but nonetheless very sad.

It may be that Rebecca went home to her father and Elizabeth to have her baby because in the 1871 census they were living in Back Street, Gayton, where John's occupation is listed as farm bailiff, although Fred recounts in *I Walked by Night* that his father:

> worked forty year on one farm as a Labourer, and never got any higher.

There does not appear to be anyone farming in both Pentney and Gayton, so why was John there, and why, ten years later on the 1881 census, was he back in Greys Cottages, Pentney, listed as an agricultural labourer? At every census John and Elizabeth had moved, so presumably John was not in tied accommodation.

The Census Act was passed in 1800 and the first official census held on 10 March 1801. Held every ten years since, except in 1941 when World War II was taking place, it was the first recording of the English population since the Doomsday Book in 1086. The census becomes open for public perusal after 100 years.

This country had previously resisted a formal count with church-goers believing it to be sacrilegious, quoting the terrible plague that struck in Biblical times when a census was ordered by King David.

An 1827 map of Gayton shows that the layout of the cottages and the shape of the village are surprisingly similar to how the village is now, but it is not possible to work out which cottage might have been John and Elizabeth's, as the census does not appear to run logically. Also, as recently as 1906, half of Back Street was called Willow Lane.

Interestingly, *Harrods Directory* notes that in 1871 a Petty Sessions was held in the Crown Inn on the first Monday of every month. Presumably this ceased when the courthouse in Grimston, the next village, was built in 1881 – a place with which 9-year-old Fred would later become familiar. In those days, he would almost certainly have attended the school in Gayton that was built in 1851, although his name does not appear in the Minutes or Punishment Book.

Sadly, the records for Pentney School are missing for the period when Fred was there, after the family returned, but he recounts in *I Walked by Night* how he was always up to mischief as a child:

> So one day we turned the Master out of school and locked him out. The School was maniged by two of the Farmers and the Clergyman. They came down and stood outside, and promised to lett us off and forgiv us if we would come out. We would not at first, but of cors we had to come out in the end to go home, and wen we did they began on us and we on them. We had aranged to get out by the back way, so we got to the road befor they knew that we were there. There were plenty of stones in the Road, and we verry sone shewed that we could throw them all rite.
>
> Well the end of that was that they turned about six of the worst of us out of school for good, and forbid us to go there anymore, so that was the end of my lerning. A lot we cared as there was plenty of work for Boys in them days.

1870 saw the first legislation about school attendance. At the time, all children were forced to go school, but it was not free. The 1880 School Act compelled education until 14 unless pupils could pass the Labour certificate earlier, proving they had reached an acceptable standard of education. Sadly this meant that bright children who would have enjoyed and benefited from school left early, leaving their duller friends to struggle on until 14.

The introduction of the Act placed schoolteachers in a terrible dilemma. Farmers, who were often on the Board of Managers at the school, were keen to pay low wages because of the Agricultural Depression and this they could do to children, who were capable of stone picking, beet thinning, bird scaring, potato planting, etc. Parents were desperately poor, so they were eager for their children to work and so the schoolmaster had to allow the law to be broken. After the harvest, parents also kept the children home for gleaning (the gathering of stray ears of corn) and what they collected became an important supplement to the winter larder. Children also stayed at home to pick acorns, which they sold to the gamekeeper as feed for his pheasants. Girls particularly were kept at home to look after younger siblings while their mother had yet more, or went out to work to supplement the family income.

In *I Walked by Night* Fred tells of a young vicar who came to the parish and took a great interest in the village lads, organising a night school and games to keep them occupied. He himself was reluctant to go, fearing he might be preached at:

> But I did go in the end and I do not think he ever gave me a word of that sort, just treated me kindly. True he wold some times talk to me for my good, and some People thought I was getten better and quieter, but I am sorry to say I was some thing like the Smugglers and the Self rightus People; I was working in the dark as much as possible.

The vicar was John Samuel Broad, MA, who took over from the Revd. St John Mitchell in 1875, when Fred would have been 13. A new man, full of zeal to win over his flock, it was with his encouragement that Fred gained a love of reading and writing.

Fred's first job at the age of 13 was with farmer Thomas Paul, of Ashwood Lodge, Pentney, as the 'copper hole Jack' or 'back'us [back house] boy'. Paul owned 850 acres and employed twenty-six labourers and nine boys on the land. Fred's role was to light fires, carry wood and generally run errands issued from the back door. Paul was churchwarden at Pentney for fifty-six years; his wife and daughters were regular worshippers and pillars of the community. Fred was sure he got the job (perhaps the vicar asked Paul and his family to take him under their wing?), so they could keep an eye on him, but mostly his eyes were elsewhere.

Already he had been poaching since the age of 9. Despite a flogging from his father when he showed him a hare that he had snared, he had caught the bug. Now he poached whenever he could, selling hares to the fish hawker, who took them through to Lynn Market that he attended twice a week.

But Fred was unable to settle to the life that many of his fellow villagers were content with, staying all their lives in the same place with one job, marrying locally and perhaps venturing to King's Lynn only once or twice a year. He wanted excitement and soon tired of being under the watchful eyes of Farmer Paul's spinster daughters, so he took a job as pageboy to a shepherd. This was much more to his liking, for there he could poach to his heart's content. During times when he was not required by the shepherd, he was put to work cutting turnips and working in the fields; there he watched and listened, and perfected the art of poaching. Whether he became cocksure or careless is debatable, but inevitably the long arm of the law eventually caught up with him.

CHAPTER 3

1882 Prison

Game Trespass – Frederick Rolfe labourer, Pentney was summonsed by John Bell, Gamekeeper, Narborough with trespassing in the day time on Pentney middle common, in search of game, on 21st October. – Bell stated that he saw defendant on the common with a pair of rabbits, each of which had a snare round its neck. Some snares had been set near to where defendant was standing. Defendant threw the rabbits away upon p.c. Flint approaching him, and also ran away, but was caught by the officer. – Flint stated that at 5.45 a.m. on the day in question he was with Bell on the common. Saw defendant going to a rabbit snare which was set. He approached witness within 5 or 6 yards, and witness spoke to him, whereupon he ran away. He had a rabbit in each hand, which he threw away. Each rabbit had a snare on its neck. Witness called out to him, and he said: "As long as you know it is me it is no use my running away." He then returned and took a snare out of his pocket.

Defendant was fined 10/- and 13/- costs, and in default he was sent to Norwich castle for 14 days.

Grimston Petty Sessions, 6 November 1882, report from the *Lynn Advertiser*.

The Docking Divisional Court records and prison entries show that Prisoner 8901 Frederick Rolfe served his time with hard labour in lieu of payment of a fine of £1 15s 6d, which is at variance with the press report. If the second figure is correct, then his fine and costs would have amounted to about three and a half week's wages. Fred's education was listed as Imp., presumably meaning it was imperfect; he was 5 ft 4½ in tall, with brown eyes and his religion was entered as Church of England. He was released on 19 November 1882.

More importantly, this shows that Fred was 20 when he first went to prison. The court record (1882) shows he had no previous offences. Devotees of *I Walked by Night* will know this is much older than he led them to believe; in the book, Fred refers to himself as a lad and a boy, but in fact does not give his age. However, the blurb on the back of some editions states that he went to prison for the first time at the age of 12. How and when this inaccuracy came about is uncertain, but it has until now gone down as fact and is regularly quoted in historical records, books and academic papers as an example of the treatment of child prisoners.

An entire chapter of *I Walked by Night* is devoted to Fred's time in prison and the daily routine and food are described in great detail:

> Then came diner, wich was one pint and a half of stirabout, composed of one pint of oatmeal, and half a pint of maze meal put in the oven and baked.

He also recalls the system of rewards-marks for which prisoners could earn money and the very hard work of being on the treadmill from 9am to 12 noon and from 1pm to 4pm. Incidentally, the word 'Screw' (meaning a prison warder) comes from how tightly the screw was turned on the treadmill; the tighter it was, the harder the prisoner had to push as he walked on endlessly. Following this, oakum was picked until bed at 8 pm. Fred states that food improved after the first fortnight. This may well be an inaccurate recollection because he says that he was inside for a month when in fact it was only fourteen days. The fear and feeling of humiliation were certainly seared into his memory and he remembers much of the detail, including his cell, the suit covered all over with a broad arrow, the kindness of his turnkey (prison warder) and the role of the Church in trying to reform prisoners. In Fred's case, prison did not reform him for he came to hate authority and made a vow that he would be as black as they painted him.

Norwich Castle is on a site that has housed prisoners since 1165. From the fourteenth century, its importance as a military building declined and prisoners were kept in the increasingly tumbledown keep. By 1698, there were complaints about the bad state of repair, which made it easy for prisoners to escape. Repairs costing £1,303 0s 1d were put in hand in 1707, the battlements being removed to provide stone for the repairs. The money to finance this was raised from the rates of the Norfolk Hundreds.

Originally, groups of people were literally gathered in hundreds and formed into administrative areas with their own court; even today we still have administrative areas known as 'Hundreds'. By the latter part of the eighteenth century, a brick building was built within the four walls of the castle for felons and debtors. This included a bathhouse, a hospital and a chapel with a pump house in the yard for the prisoners' use.

Over the next 160 years, in keeping with society's changing ideas, various reformers tried to make prisons more humane. During this period the head gaoler paid the County to hold the post; he then earned his living by selling provisions, including wine, to inmates. Families of prisoners were allowed to bring food in, which was fine for those with loved ones and money to support them, but others less fortunate were reduced to begging at the gates and living on donated scraps. The expression 'life on a shoe string' came about because debtors used to beg from upper windows by lowering their boots by the laces for people to put coins in. Additional money could be earned from various tasks, such as making laces, garters, purses, nets, etc. At one stage spinning wheels were provided for the prisoners, and gaolers shared any resulting profits. Gaolers also made money from the discharge fee required from those on remand who were found not guilty. They required a fee to release them from irons, so some innocents remained until the money could be raised to pay for their freedom. Gaolers also charged a fee for the curious to go and peer at condemned men and women.

During the nineteenth century prisoners began to be kept by the State, thus they no longer needed daily access to their families and isolation was considered a suitable way for them to reflect on their wrongdoing and to improve discipline. In some prisons this was taken to extremes with prisoners not being allowed to see or speak to each other. However, this was in part stopped when prisoners started to deteriorate mentally.

With the introduction of the treadmill some advocated that the very pointlessness of the task was to make the prisoners reflect, but at Norwich the treadmill ground flour for a local miller, who paid for this service. After 1844, no women or children under 14 were allowed to go on the treadmill, when it was found that pregnant women were miscarrying while walking the endless steps. It is said that the maximum height a prisoner could climb on the treadmill in one day was 12,000 feet, almost the equivalent of the Matterhorn. Prisoners who could not, or would not do this, were given bread and water and kept in their cells, but it was found they were better nourished than those being fed regular meals and then stepping ever onward for six hours a day.

During this period, improvements to all gaols were carried out, but Norwich Castle posed particular problems because of the constraints of the castle building itself. In 1832, the women were moved to Wymondham. Until then both sexes were housed together, which was found difficult to police. In 1887, it was found that whatever alterations were made at the castle, they were still inadequate to house prisoners in humane conditions and the New Prison was subsequently built on Mousehold Heath.

Many years later, Fred wrote:

> It is a long time since those days but many is the time I have walked through the Beautifful rooms of Norwich Castle, now that it is a Museum and thought of the weeks I spent there in Prisson, and all of the missery and sufferen that have been endured inside the Walls of that Historick Building.

How amazed he would have been to find that a tape recording plays in the castle of someone reading his description of his time there, using it as an illustration of how cruelly children were treated in those days, even though the museum have not authenticated his true age. The experience certainly left an indelible message and embittered him.

Fred also remembered that on his return to Pentney he was shown no kindness or pity. Had that happened, life might have turned out very differently; instead, villagers gave him dark looks and jeered at him. He recalls meeting John Broad, the same vicar who had encouraged him earlier, on the road soon after he was released:

> He stopped me and wanted to know how I liked Prisson. It seamed to me he asked it with a sneer, any how I knew I cut him off pretty quick, and I never entered his Church again.

He also found it difficult to get work:

> ... they wisper to a Master 'He have been in Prisson' and blite all his good resilutions.

On Fred's release from prison, exasperated by his feckless behaviour and the shame he had brought on the family, his father threw him out. As a good churchman, John had relentlessly drilled right from wrong into Fred, or so he thought. Fred took a cottage of his own. It is no longer there, but rubble and brick showing through the soil when the field is ploughed clearly indicate where it stood. Set back a little from the main street, it has, as Fred describes in his book, easy access to the fields and footpaths leading away from the village.

Throughout this time Fred was poaching and while his father may have disapproved, others in the village did not. 'Hollow meat' is a term used for poached meat and rather in the way of the highwayman, poor families would occasionally find it discreetly tucked out of view on their doorstep. For the mid-Victorian rural poor who could seldom afford to buy meat, this was a rare treat. Because of this, and the way that they flouted the rules, taking only in the main from the rich, poachers were held in some regard. One of Fred's finest boasts was that he never killed a pheasant with someone's name on its tail.

Ted Bradfield, poacher turned gamekeeper in Hunstanton Park, offers a rather different explanation: 'When moonlit nights came round during the winter months, it was no good – I had to go on the prowl. I never did earn my living out of poaching, but all the same I used to earn a hell of a lot of pocket money.' He also revealed, '. . . poachers have often told me that they mostly take game for the excitement rather than on account of pecuniary benefit, and that the poacher stood alone in the hierarchy of the village.' Whatever the reason, poaching was rife and certainly not frowned on by ordinary folk.

Many labourers asked a tailor to put a poacher's pocket inside their sleeved 'weskits' so that any rabbits or game they were lucky enough to kill while working in the fields could be carried home in complete secrecy. Poachers had a loop stitched at the top of the pocket on the inside of their coats which held the barrel of a gun, the butt resting in the bottom of the pocket. Usually, poachers' coats were usually made of velveteen, which was often green.

Catapults were often used to poach and frozen blackberries made excellent bullets as they were eaten, or melted away and left no evidence. Poachers used to produce the game for the first day of the season, as it was not possible in reality to kill them legitimately and ship them to the poulterers in time for the great and good to have them on their dinner tables on the day shooting started. One story goes that a London butcher had scrupulous customers, who would not eat game slaughtered before the official date so the poulterer had live birds poached and sent to him. Immediately after midnight on the first day the season began, he shot them and everybody was happy.

Another tale was of a poacher returning with his night's takings when he saw a policeman coming towards him, some way away. The postman came right up behind the poacher on his bike and quick as you like, the game was under the parcels and the postie rode past the policeman whistling. The poacher followed on with a cheery, 'Good morning!'

Victorian women often helped poachers by moving game about under their voluminous skirts, some going so far as to have a specially constructed 'crinoline' frame made. Strung about the waist, this harness meant the kill could be hung from the contraption in complete secrecy. Sometimes, too, hooks were placed on the underside of well covers, a cool and secret place to hide ill-gotten gains. Certainly, the poacher was ingenious.

In *60 Years a Fenman* (1966), Arthur Randall lets us into some of his secrets: he made 'hingles' consisting of long pieces of twine to which horsehair nooses were tied at 3in intervals. The twine was placed on the ground and seed scattered to attract larks, which coming down to feed were entrapped in the horsehair. He did not say whether they were to be sold as singing birds or food, probably the latter. Think how many you would need for larks tongue pie!

In a very old copy of *Mrs Beeton's Book of Household Management*, first published in 1859, there are three recipes using larks. One for a pie requires nine whole larks which have been plucked, gutted and cleaned. How on earth do you pluck such tiny things, never mind truss them, as the second recipe demands? Larks were considered excellent and a great delicacy, either roasted for fifteen minutes over a clear fire, or broiled for ten and served on toast as an entrée. From Michaelmas to February, they were sent to London by the basket, having been netted in vast numbers on the stubble.

Larger hingles, with a single loop on top of a long stick, were used for slipping over a pheasant's neck as it roosted at night. The very deft could reach up and catch a bird, but here the risk was that if it was not swiftly caught and silenced immediately, it might make a noise and draw the gamekeeper's attention. Gypsies were reputed to be very good at 'silent poaching'. Larger hingles were used to catch pheasants: while seeking corn, brandy-soaked raisins or dried peas spread out to tempt them, the birds would put their heads through the hingle, which then jerked up, being on a finely balanced bent wand of hazel.

Boys, many of them spending all day in the fields scaring crows and tending animals to earn a pitifully small wage, were not averse to a little poaching. Ingenuity was the name of the game: lying quietly in a ditch bottom sometimes proved lucky for them, as a rabbit ventured by. Another trick was to take a very prickly bramble stalk and push it down a hole, where you knew a rabbit was hiding. The briar was then turned round and round until the rabbit's fur was well and truly tangled in the thorns and then it could be gingerly pulled out. Birds were also trapped for the collector and to save damaging any of the plumage, the boys killed their victims by forcing open their beaks and cutting the throat from the inside. They also trapped linnets, goldfinches and male nightingales to be sold as caged songbirds.

Snares were an effective way to catch rabbits, but the problem was that if the gamekeeper spotted the snare, he could then keep watch to see who came back to check on it.

Poachers always cut the buttons off their clothing so they did not become snagged on their nets as they dealt with them quickly in the dark. These were long nets, either a bagged net which was placed along a field edge and had rabbits driven into it, or gate nets covering the gate, usually held on by pebbles resting on top of the gate. A dog was used to drive hares towards the gate and as they reached the net, the stones were disturbed and the net dropped, entangling the hare.

One gamekeeper had two thousand stakes made, each with a twist of barbed wire on the top. These he drove into the ground, so the poachers snagged their nets as they dragged the fields at night for partridges.

In *I Walked by Night*, Fred recounts how his father disowned him and they did not speak for many years. John and Elizabeth must have been so disappointed in him; each had lost a son of their own, and perhaps placed undue pressure on him to be the model son they so desired. Model son he was not, though. Not only did he disgrace the family with his criminal ways, but he had also got a local girl pregnant.

CHAPTER 4

1882–86 Anna

Anna Carter was born on 21 March 1862 at Marham, a village about two miles across the fen from Pentney. There, she was christened Ann Elizabeth. In legal documents as an adult she usually called herself Anna, so as this was obviously her preferred name, she will be called Anna in this book.

Her mother Mary Ann was a Marham girl, having been born in the village in 1840, the fifth child and only daughter of Ann and Garwood Steeles. They were a large and respectable family in the area, being wheelwrights, blacksmiths, beer retailers and carriers, travelling to and from Marham to the Maids Head, King's Lynn, on Tuesdays and Saturdays. Later they were coachbuilders. After Mary Ann's marriage to James Henry Carter, a journeyman shipwright, she lived in Woolwich, Kent. How the couple met is unknown: perhaps she went into service and met him there or he may have come up the River Nar on one of the lighters (barges). These flat-bottomed boats brought bone for the bone factory, where it was ground down for fertiliser. They also hauled coal inland from King's Lynn; having arrived from northern England, this was loaded onto the lighters for distribution along the Ouse and its tributaries.

Mary Ann must have come home for the birth or been visiting her family when Anna was born. The railway had arrived at Narborough (the station serving Marham and Pentney) in 1845, so the journey from Woolwich — if that's how Mary Ann travelled — would not have been difficult, although expensive for a working family. She registered her new daughter on 2 April 1862, twelve days after the birth, so one assumes it must have been a normal delivery. Across the fields, three weeks earlier Elizabeth Rolfe had given birth to her sickly baby, Fred.

Marham is an odd village, now overwhelmed by the RAF camp. Without a pub, it seems to have no heart and the church is neglected and unkempt. Even in Fred's time it would have been unusual in that it stretched for over two miles almost entirely on a single road.

White's Directory of 1845 records:

> *Marham or Cherry Marham is a long village with several good houses, 7 miles west of Swaffham and 8 miles north east of Downham. Its parish contains 817 inhabitants, and about 4000 acres of land, a great portion of which is in large open fields, having perhaps the finest grass-turf in the county, and is remarkable for large hares, said to be the best runners in the kingdom.*

In the village and surrounding area, hare coursing went on right up until 2005 when it was officially banned, but from the number of rumours heard, and the court appearances reported in the local press, it is still a regular feature today.

> *Marham was formerly noted for its great abundance of cherries and walnuts; but most of the trees of the latter fruit were cut down during the late war [Napoleonic] and sold to the gun-makers, some of the largest for as much as £100 each tree.*

After Anna's birth, Mary Ann and James went on to have two boys: James Henry in 1864 and Edward in 1866. On the 1871 census young James is recorded as living with Granny Steeles and two cousins in Marham; of the rest of the family, there is no certain trace. In the 1881 census all three children are living with Granny Steeles and their uncle William, who was a wheelwright.

Mary Ann, 35, by then a widow, was also living close by in the village with a daughter, Florence, who was born on 21 April 1876, with no father named on her birth certificate. Anna, then 19, is listed in the 1881 census as a domestic servant.

In his description of their courtship in *I Walked by Night*, Fred said Anna was an orphan:

> It was perhaps a fellow feeling as drew us together in the beginning, as she poor girl was as much persequted as I had been. She was a servant up at a Gentleman Farmers not so far away from were I was liven, and of corse she had her night out like other servants. She was just eighteen years old, the same age as myself wen I got to know her and she started bein friendly with me.
>
> As soon as it was known that she and I was palling up, those that

she worked with, and others, tried by every means in there power to stop her, thinken no doubt that I was no proper compney for her, she haven no parents, and no one to go to. But it was all to no purpose, she would have her way.

Clearly, however, Anna was not an orphan, her mother being close by in the village. Nor does it seem she was living in as a servant, but rather still residing with uncle William, Grandma and her brothers, so it was not a question of being allowed her night out from the big house, but more likely escaping from Grandma's beady eye to spend time with Fred. At the time Fred, who had not yet served his first prison sentence, was living in the middle of a row of five dwellings known as Greys Cottages, Pentney, with his mother and father and Granny Shaftoe, who was by now a widow.

Wen ever I went to meet her I used to take my dogs with me if the night was rite – or my gun. Many and many a night she came out with me, for she was no hindrence to the game. She could run and Jump as well as me and there was few could beat me at running wen I was a Young man. She could carry as many Birds to – and carryen Birds is no light Job. Many a hare have she carried under her coat for me, and many a Phesant. As it was all Cuntry round that part we had some good sport.

Well I supose that tale got about, and wen they found that they could not stop her from me, they gave her notice to leave her place. There was sevrell Ladies round about who was intrested in her, and put themselves about to get her a place in London at good wages so she should be out of my way. But no she stayed, and stuck to me through thick and thin, wich she could do as she had no parents, and no one to controwl her, so she went what way she wanted.

Having taken his own cottage on his return from prison, Fred recalled:

As I have rote befor, I had a home of my owen to take her to, as sone as she was ready to come, and after a bit she did come, and shared it with me for about four years or more.

Old maps fail to reveal where the pound to which Fred refers was once situated.

Just at the back of the Cottage was a round wall called the Old Pound, were years befor they used to put strayen cattle. That was done away with a long time ago, but the pound came in useful as it aforded us good cover to get home many a night wen we had been out on the Job.

Unless the baby was very premature, Anna must have already been in the early stages of pregnancy when Fred went to serve his prison sentence in November 1882. The couple were married on Monday, 14 May 1883, only just within the three months required by law following the reading of the banns. Both were just 21. According to parish records, the banns were read on 25 February, 4 March and 11 March 1883.

The requirement for banns to be read came about to regularise weddings and do away with common-law marriages. It was enacted in Hardwickes Marriage Act of 1754. Prior to this, the situation had been in disarray with clandestine marriages and young people being married inappropriately or without their parents' consent. The new law stated that a marriage could only be solemnised in a parish church or public chapel after three readings of the banns, or by licence from the Bishop of the Diocese.

The 1754 Act forbade people under the age of 21 from marrying before they came of age without parental consent. As the law only covered England and Wales, it began the habit of minors wishing to marry without consent to flee across the Scottish border to marry in Gretna Green.

Banns giving the names of the couple are read to the congregation by the clergyman in the parishes where the bride and groom live, and if that is different, in the parish in which they are to marry. They must be read on three Sundays within the three months running up to the marriage, but are usually read on three consecutive weeks. This provides an opportunity for anyone to put forward any legal reasons why a couple may not marry.

Fred and Anna were well enough educated to sign the register, Anna with a practised hand and Fred with fine flourishes, so why did they wait until only two weeks before the baby's birth? Was it because of parental objections and they needed to wait until they were both 21? Anna's own mother was hardly in a position to criticise, having given birth to an illegitimate child five years earlier, but Granny Steeles might have been a different matter. It would seem she took all her grandchildren under her wing from time to time, but the fact that Anna, Henry and Edward were living with her while her daughter was

41

living in another home in the village with little Florence suggests she was disapproving of her daughter's behaviour, for it seems she was always left with grandchildren to support. Perhaps Mary Ann felt that as she herself had managed to raise an illegitimate child alone, that might be a better option for her daughter than marriage to Fred.

The marriage certificate shows that both the witnesses came from Anna's side: a cousin and a lodger, who lived with Anna and her brothers at Granny Steele's. It also stated that Fred resided in Norwich, which is odd and unexplained.

At the time, premarital sex was commonplace and rural Norfolk had the fourth highest illegitimacy rate in the country (10.8 per 1,000), but with as many as 25 per cent of brides being pregnant at the time of marriage, it is more likely the family objected to Fred rather than the horror felt in middle-class Victorian society of a 'base born' child. It is thought that some girls hoped to catch their man by becoming pregnant but alternatively, it is argued that men wanted to be sure their partner was fruitful before they married.

Did Anna want to marry Fred, or was she persuaded to do so? Was Fred coerced into marrying her or was he afraid of the Bastardy Laws? Whatever the circumstances, the marriage can hardly have been the stuff of dreams.

The 1876 *Magisterial Formulist* shows that there was plenty of legislation to catch fathers of illegitimate children, twenty-five pages in all, containing thirty-five different charges under section 6 of the Bastardy Laws Amendment Act 1873. Women could go to the local court and ask for support during pregnancy, and after the child was born. The Workhouse could chase a man for support if the new mother was staying there. There were laws enabling distress warrants to be issued and laws to make the father pay funeral and other incidental costs if the child died. Also, laws to bring him to court if the orders were disobeyed, and finally a Warrant of commitment to prison, if all else failed.

There are two different charges outlined in the *Magisterial Formulist*, one to be enacted if the father fails to support the mother and child, and one if he owes upkeep to the Union Workhouse, which has been keeping them. The wording is similar and full of the majesty of the Law:

> . . . *by two justices of the peace acting for the said division (and having jurisdiction for the said Union)* ~~~~~ *was adjudged to be the*

putative father of a bastard child, born of the body of ~~~~~~, a
single woman, was brought before us to show why the same should not
be paid, that no sufficient distress can be laid upon his goods and chattels
.......Convey the said ~~~~~~ to the common goal there to remain
without bail or mainprise for the term of ~~~~~ unless such sum and
costs, together with the costs and charges of attending the commitment
and conveying of the said ~~~~~~ to the common goal, and of the
persons employed to convey him thither, amounting to the further sum
of ~~~~~ to be paid and satisfied.

In 1849, George Batchelor was ordered to pay Depwade Union
2/9d a week for seven years to support his daughter, plus arrears of
£1 4s 6d.

Lots of women were simply deserted – the men just skipped town
and were untraceable.

Fred wrote:

> The days went on till the time come for her confinement, wen to my
> great sorrow she died. Young as I was then it was the hardest blow I
> have ever had to bear in all my life, the more so because it came so
> sudden, and there was no reason I knew it should all end like that,
> and no warning. She did not want to go and I had lost a dear pall as
> well as a loven wife, and she left me with a new born baby – for the
> child, a boy, lived.

For those who have read *I Walked by Night* and so enjoyed the
romance Fred describes between himself and Anna, it will come as a
revelation that Anna did not die in childbirth or have a boy.

Fred talks with such love and warmth of their courtship and marriage. Here is a little of what he wrote:

> After about three years things fell out so that it became Imperitive that
> we got married . . . I have no need to tell why. She was one of the best
> pals that a man ever had, and the best wife any man could want. Do
> not think dear Reader that I am telling a love story, but it is true that I
> loved her more than anything else on this earth and she loved me the
> same. It was not only me that loved her neither, for it always seam
> she had a way with her with all live things, and pets and birds.

Edith Ann was born on 25 May 1883 in Marham. It is unclear
whether Anna went home to her family to have the baby or whether
she and Fred were living in Marham at the time. Fred was working as

an agricultural worker, so it fell to Anna to stop Doctor Steele from Downham Market to proudly register her baby daughter. At the time, the doctor was also the local Registrar and he carried the registers with him in a leather satchel as he rode about visiting the sick, so that people in the remote villages were spared the ten-mile journey to Downham Market to register their child, as had been compulsory since 1837.

Lord Chancellor Thomas Cromwell introduced the first formal system of registering the population in the reign of Henry VIII. Every clergyman in 1538 was ordered to keep a book in which to record details of all baptisms, marriages and burials at which they officiated. In 1597, in the reign of Elizabeth I, each parish was ordered to purchase a special book in which to record details and from this to make an annual transcript to be lodged with the diocesan registrar. This led to improvements, but records were still incomplete.

The Burial Act (1768) decreed all corpses must be buried in a wool shroud to aid the coffers of the government as there was a tax levied on wool. After each burial an oath had to be taken to confirm the Act had been obeyed.

Eventually, in 1837 two Acts came into being: The Registration Act and the Marriage Act. The General Registrar was appointed to administer, at local level, the civil registration of births (not baptisms), marriages and deaths, and to allow a system for civil marriages. Medical statistician William Farr pressed for the cause of death to be included on certificates so that records could be kept to follow medical patterns.

There is no record to be found that Edith was christened, something that might have helped reconcile Fred with his father. He went on seeing his mother, so she may have seen the baby, but Anna would have been denied the chance to defiantly show off her new husband and baby before the villagers, cutting a dash in a flattering outfit, including a new hat.

Fred was listed again as a labourer on Edith's death certificate when he registered the child's death aged 8 months, on 16 January 1883. He is recorded as being with Edith when she died, it would seem they were living in Pentney at the time.

Edith's death certificate records her cause of death as marasmus. The *Collins Dictionary* definition is wasting of the body, with most cases due to inadequate calorific intake. Clinically there is a failure to gain weight, followed by weight loss and emaciation. The medical description goes on to describe symptoms similar to those seen on television film footage of harrowing scenes from famine areas of Africa. Poor little thing, she just starved to death.

In the 1860s mills had come into use that ground corn into refined white flour, removing the valuable wheat germ. It was much the same health issue as today: brown wholemeal bread versus refined white. By the 1870s, this was available in the remotest of shops and most likely Anna, like all the forward thinking girls of her time, thought it modern and labour saving, so the bread she baked would not be very nutritious. This she would have fed crumbled into milk to her child, a form of baby food known as 'pap'.

Along with the rest of the labourers' families in the village, almost certainly the only milk Anna would have been able to buy would be the skimmed version from the local farm. Skimmed, because the cream would be removed to churn into butter; it was known as 'blue milk' because of its colour. Probably after Anna stopped feeding Edith herself, she weaned her on to pap, which had insufficient nourishment and so her daughter slowly faded away.

In Henry Rider Haggard's book *A Farmers Year*, which he wrote after giving up writing adventure stories and turned to farming and good works, he recounts:

Never shall I forget my early experiences of Heckingham Workhouse. Having been elected a guardian I attended the Board in due course, and, as is so often my fortune, at the very first meeting fell into controversy. At that date all the children in the house, including infants, were fed upon skimmed milk. Owing to some illness, however, the Doctor ordered them a ration of fresh milk, which ration the master had neglected to discontinue when the sickness passed. Consequently there arose trouble, and with the Doctor he was brought up before the board to be reprimanded. Thereon, with the courage of inexperience, I rose and announced boldly that I considered new milk to be a necessity to infants and that, if I could find a seconder, I would propose that the allowance should be continued to them until they reached the age of nine years. Somewhat to my astonishment a worthy clergyman, now long dead, seconded the motion, and there followed a great debate. Soon we found it would be absolutely hopeless to carry the innovation in its original form, and were obliged to reduce the age limit from nine to five years.

The argument of the opposition was that the children were not fed upon new milk in their own homes, to which I replied that even if they starved at home, it was no reason why they should be starved when in the public charge. Ultimately the Board divided, and to my surprise I carried the motion by a majority of one vote, so that henceforth the infants at Heckingham were rationed with fresh milk instead of 'blue skim'.

Within eight months, Anna had become a wife and mother, and she now stood beside a tiny grave grieving for her child, the weather as bitter and raw as her emotions must have been. Fred described his wife as a woman fond of animals and wildlife, and it would seem the death of her child was from ignorance rather than neglect. In *I Walked by Night*, Fred recalls that she cared for Fred's working dogs, and one of her own, Tip, with much care and affection:

My wife thought the world of Tip, and I often used to say to her in fun, you think more of the dog than you do of me. She looked after them all, but he was always the first to have a hot drink and a rub down wen we came in from a night's work. He would lie at her feet and look at her, and she would talk to him as she would have talked to a child, and I beleve he knew what she said as well as I did. Perhaps her feeling the way she did for that dog had something to do with what hapened after.

The months went by and it came to about three months befor her time. She had to give up going out with me as she always had done, as she could not get about as well as she used because of the child that was comen. So I went out alone one night and took Tip with me and lost him. Of corse I did not pay much regard to that, as dogs often miss there Master at night, but are shure to find him or go home on there owen.

Wen I got home to her in the morning time the first thing she said to me was 'Where is Tip, you have not brought him back with you?' I said no, and told her that I had missed him some were, but she need not fret as he would be home on his owen befor long. Then she said 'No, he will not come home any more, he is dead and lay on Narborough park at the foot of a tree – I saw him hit the tree'.

Well of corse I pooed that and told her she must have been dreaming, but she said no, she had never been asleep all night but lyen and waiting for me to come home.

Well as the dog did not come back I went to look for him, and shure enough after a bit I found him as she had said layen at the foot of a large oak Tree. He had made to kill at a rabbitt and struck his head on the bole of the tree, and broke his neck.

After military service, local man Les Harrison came to Narborough (the next village to Pentney) in about 1953, when he must have been in his early 20s. He lived in a cottage on the Narborough Hall Park. One day, while sheltering from the rain under a large oak tree in the park, he was joined by Albert Coggles, the elderly gamekeeper for the estate then owned by the Ash family. As they stood beneath the dripping leaves, Mr Coggles remarked that they were under the tree where the Norfolk Poacher had hanged his dog.

Mr Harrison recalls, 'I think it was only when it was mentioned this summer, when a friend and I were talking in the cricket pavilion and someone brought up the poacher who used to take game from the park where the pavilion now stands, that I thought of it again. I have never spoken to anyone, not even my wife and children, about the incident. I remember I thought it awful at the time.' He has never read *I Walked by Night*, so he has no knowledge of the facts in the book.

When told that Fred had said his dog broke its neck on the tree chasing a rabbit, Harrison said, 'I know dogs – I can't believe a dog would do that. I think what the gamekeeper told me, that the dog was hanged, is more likely right. Whether the dog was no good, or Fred lost his temper, I don't know.' He also recollects hearing, though he can't remember the source, that one night the poacher took pheasants home and hid them under his pregnant wife's bed. When police arrived to search the house, the dog indicated the pheasants' whereabouts by sniffing round the bed and this led to Fred being charged with poaching. It was suggested this might have been his motivation in killing the dog. 'That does not tie up,' said Harrison, 'he would have been taken straight off to the lock-up, not left to take out his ill humour on the dog.'

Tip – Anna's dog – was a cross between a Smithfield sheepdog and a greyhound. Not handsome but very efficient, they were crossed to combine the speed of a sight dog with the intelligence of the sheepdog. Their coats took on the characteristics of either breed, but looks were not important, ability was what counted. Smithfields are no longer a distinct breed but the lurcher, another favourite of the poaching fraternity, is still much prized in East Anglia. Their biddable nature and high intelligence mean they are easy to train.

In *I Walked by Night*, Fred gives a detailed explanation of the training methods used to get the ideal poacher's dog. Gamekeepers reckoned it took a poacher a year to train up a good dog so to deprive one of his dog gave the keepers some respite. The methods used were brutal and cruel. Fred mentions sweeping the yard around where his dogs were chained up to stop the keepers leaving poisoned meat unnoticed. Gamekeepers also used a vicious device called a dog spear. An iron spear, about 3 in long and usually barbed, was placed over a hare run. If the dog chased a hare, the hare was able to pass under the spear, but the dog was impaled upon it, often with fatal results. To teach a young dog not to maul game, their trainers inserted two spikes diagonally through the carcass into a newly dead bird: this was supposed to instantly cure any desire the dog had to eat the game.

If a poacher lost his dog it was not unknown for him to 'borrow' one. It would be found, exhausted, back in its usual place in the morning. In addition, poachers certainly 'borrowed' dogs they liked the look of and mated them with their bitches.

In his autobiography, *Fourscore Years* (1943), G.G. Coulton – who was raised in Pentney during the 1870s and 80s – made two references to Fred:

> *Mr Paul, the gentleman farmer under whom Rolfe the poacher worked as a boy, to whose kind treatment he pays a tribute, but from whose pigeon cote later on, he took as heavy toll as from my mother's peahens. . . .*
>
> *Rolfe, who deserves international fame, for his freak biography is a precious human document, which I am able to verify in every important particular.*

I Walked by Night links these two stories:

> Then something hapened wich made them verry careful how they handled me. A Farmer lost some Turkeys, and they took me and my pall and locked us up on suspicion. They took me first and then they went after him, and said that I had told them everything. Wen he came to the lock up he asked me what I had told them. Of corse I said nothing as I knew nothing about the Turkeys.
>
> Well they took us befor the Magerstrates and remanded us for eight days to se what they could make out. Just befor we were to apear again they found the Turkeys under a straw stack that had fallen over. They let us out with a lot of Apologies but that did not sute me. I went to a Lawyer to know what redress I could get. I put the case in his hands and he got £5 each for us for rongful arrest.

> That tale had a finish to it. A Game Dealer at Lynn wanted to know if I could get some Pea Fowl, or eggs. I had noticed this same Lawyer had a lot of them Birds – they used to sit and lay about the place. I took a dark lantern one night, and hunted round and came acros a bird sitten on some eggs. I put the old bird in a bag and the eggs in my shirt. Then I come acros another bird with young ones, they too went in the bag, and I got them safley to the Dealers and made a good days work out of them.

The lawyer was J.J. Coulton, father of G.G. Coulton, the author.

J.J. Coulton was an eminent King's Lynn solicitor, who moved to Little Ketlam, Pentney, in 1871 with his wife and five children. Coulton relished the austere, declining to wear a coat in the coldest weather and becoming a vegetarian. Clerk to the Guardians and Rural Sanitary Authority, King's Lynn Union, he was also superintendant registrar and gave a great deal of his time to local charities and societies around Pentney.

In his book, Coulton tells of another Pentney poacher who lived in a cabin on some wild land at the edge of the village called Bradmoor. He had no job, but always carried a half crown in his pocket lest any policeman charge him with having no visible means of subsistence. A common crime in those times, a fine was usually imposed which of course could not be paid, so the accused was punished with a week in prison with hard labour in lieu.

Coulton also wrote that at some time in the 1880s, in a hard frost on King's Lynn High Street on market day, a man fell heavily. A poacher, he had left his gun hidden within his clothes in such a way that the force of his fall activated it, discharging both barrels into his body.

Another instance he remembered from further afield involved a fight between poachers and gamekeepers. In the scuffle a gun went off and shot one of the poachers in the thigh. The police being summoned, they followed a trail of blood until they found the poacher holed up in a barn, where his comrades had carried him and plugged the gaping wound with straw. He survived and as he was carried on a litter into his trial at the Assizes, looking at the double row of policemen, he remarked, 'I should like to get a day's shootin' among ye all.' His sentence is not recorded.

Coulton also recounts in his book that as children, he and his sister were invited by Benjamin Young, their farmer neighbour, to go into his garden and help themselves to the fruit he grew there. It was a sad indictment of the time that the farmer would indulge the middle-class children next door, but let the labourer's children in the cottages close by exist half-starved, denying them even a rabbit. This is illustrated by the following press report.

Game Trespass – Frederick Roofe [sic]

Labourer Pentney was charged on remand with trespassing in search of game on Land at Pentney on 31st August 1884 since which time the defendant had absconded. Hardiman Morton said he saw the defendant on Mr Benjamin Young's land between 6 and 7 o'clock on the Sunday morning in question. He was beating a turnip field and fired a gun.

Witness was behind a high hedge and could not see what defendant shot. Witness got over the fence and ran after defendant who crossed the plank over the river and pulled it after him thus preventing witness from following. Defendant was further charged with a like offence on land of Mr G. Goddard on the 13th September 1884. Morton stated that about 6.30a.m. that day he saw defendant shoot some birds; he was not more than 10 yards from the defendant.

Grimston Petty Sessions report by the *Lynn News*, 2 July 1888

Village constable Hardiman Morton was a neighbour of Fred's when he lived at Greys Cottages. The land on which Fred was caught was within a mile of home. He seemed to have no thought as to whether he would be caught – perhaps the excitement of pitting his wits against officialdom had made him careless, for clearly he would be recognised and easily found:

> I had got such a liken for the Game I was past stoppin. Poaching is something like drug taking, – once begun no goen back, it get hold of you. The life of a Poacher is anything but a happy one, still it is exciting at times, and the excitement go a long way to sothe his concience if it trubble him.

Cornered and unable to flee one night, Fred was badly beaten up by four keepers:

> . . . they got a cart from the farm near by, and took me to the lock up and left me.
> The next morning I was nearly Dead, so bad that the Police had to send for the Doctor, and wen he had looked at me he ordered me to

> be taken to Lynn Ospitall. I had a verry bad cut head and a Brused
> Boddy.
>   I stayed there for a fortnight . . .

Charges for the crimes committed in 1884 were laid against Fred
in 1888, although they took place four years earlier. On a later occasion in 1884, Fred – having just won a gun at a pigeon shoot – was
coming home with his pals in high spirits when they started to pot at
pheasants in a wood, making a lot of noise. The keepers were soon
after them. A fight ensued and Fred laid out a keeper, who was one of
those who had assaulted him on the earlier occasion:

> I did not stop to think or lose the chance of payen some of the score
> back that I owed.

Fearing the man was badly hurt, Fred fled to the nearest town,
probably King's Lynn, from where he took a train to Manchester. By
then Anna was pregnant again When Fred left that night to save his
own skin, it seems he thought very little of his wife's, for there is no
record that the two ever met again.

It is not perhaps surprising that Lilias Rider Haggard writes in the
preface to *I Walked by Night* that it was only with the greatest reluc-
tance that Fred talked about his much-loved first wife – he must have
been deciding which fib to tell next!

CHAPTER 5

1886–88 Manchester

Over forty years later, when Fred was writing *I Walked by Night*, he remembered with great clarity his time in Manchester, much of which is verifiable. Certainly the places he mentions are correct, if spelt incorrectly. What he appears to have forgotten is that he had a wife back in Norfolk. Clearly he could not mention this in the book for he had already told readers that Anna was dead. Not only was she very much alive, but pregnant too.

Fred says that as a warrant was out for his arrest he adopted a false name and corresponded with his mother via a friend. Why did Anna not join him? Perhaps he did not ask her to go, or perhaps she could not afford to go – although Fred had found the money easily enough when he chose to flee. One wonders if Anna had had enough of his reckless lifestyle. Whatever the reason, when she gave birth to a boy, on 22 February 1885 in Marham, she named him Frederick Walter, so possibly she still loved her husband and hoped for his return. In this book he will be known as Young Fred to differentiate him from his father.

Postal orders had been introduced in January 1881 so Fred could have sent Anna money from time to time, but did he? According to *I Walked by Night*, a great deal of his spare time seems to have been spent participating in sport, mainly pigeon and sparrow shooting and whippet racing. He proclaimed he was good at these and often won; also he admitted his wages were good, but he did not save money as there was a lot to spend it on.

When Fred first arrived in Manchester he got work with a horse dealer. Part of the job entailed going to Ireland to bring horses back to England. These were principally used as carriage horses. Crossing Irish draught with thoroughbreds made the right combination for the horses needed. At the end of the 1800s, horses were big business: in London alone there were some 15,000 hansom cabs, 22,000 horses were owned by the London Omnibus Company, while the railway owned 6,000. Carriers had another 19,000, 1,500 cleared rubbish from the city streets, 3,000 drew brewers' wagons, 8,000 hauled coal and 700 hearses.

Fred enjoyed the company of the Irish, saying they were:

ever corteous to a Stranger.

He describes an Irish fair, saying that unlike English fairs with merry-go-rounds, gambling was the main entertainment, other than drinking and fighting. In addition, he talks about prick the garter, a trick of slight of hand. This involved looping a piece of ribbon and asking the punter to pin it to the table so the loops remained intact when the end of the ribbon was tugged. The art was to loop it in such a way that the ribbon could be pulled to its full extent, so the fraudster always won. A century earlier, to be caught conning the public in this way was an offence punishable by death.

During the latter part of his time in Manchester, he took a job at a mill at Bowker Bank, which he recollected as 'Booker Bank'. Photographs of the area show that when Fred was there, it was largely farmland, the mill being the only building in the vicinity. The view from Middleton Road, where he went shooting with men from the Three Arrows pub, is of agricultural land, with tree-lined field edges so his change from rural to urban was not as great as might have been expected.

All the places Fred mentions in the chapter about Manchester are within a small area to the north of the city centre. He began as the horse trader's assistant behind Strangeways prison and then, venturing further north, he went to Crumpsall, where the mill was located. To reach it, he would have travelled through Cheetham, which he recollected as 'Cheetmill'. There, he used to stop at a public house to meet up with a sporting crowd. He found their northern ways very different to those in Norfolk, but having got to know them, he found them honest and good-natured.

Cheetham Hill had a big part to play in his future for it was there that Catherine Allen (known to her family as Kitty), the girl who was to become his second wife, lived. Thankfully a document exists outlining Kitty's life in great detail. Written by Emily, the daughter of Kitty and Fred, here is the opening extract:

PREFACE

Dear reader, I am the daughter of the man who wrote the story "I Walked by Night" after reading it I am inspired to write my mother's life story, she was orphaned at eight years of age, and had many ups and downs like we all do, but I hope none are as badly used nowadays as she was. I will now let her tell her story in her own words.

AN ORPHAN'S LIFE STORY

TOLD BY HERSELF TO HER DAUGHTER

Happy Childhood

I began life very happily as the daughter of a coal miner in Staffordshire. We were a happy family, consisting of father and mother, a boy and three girls. Till I was six I was the third child. Then my mother presented us with another little baby brother, making five children altogether. But she never seemed to get well, and when baby Jim was a month old she slipped away from us. One afternoon I came home from school and went up to her room and found her lying down, she said, "Kitty take the baby and see if you can quiet him, he is so cross today, and I am so tired, maybe I can sleep a little then."

I took the baby downstairs, where sister Lizzie, she was twelve then, was trying to get supper for us all. I carried the baby for a little while and he soon went to sleep. My father earned good wages, he was a foreman, and my brother earned a little too, so we were well fed and well clothed. Soon supper was ready and my father came home. After having his usual bath, he always came home as did all miners, black as the coal he worked with. He went upstairs to see how mother was, I had told him she said she was tired, I little knew how tired she meant. My father came running down the stairs, crying, "Run for the doctor, Seth, I'm afraid your mother is very ill."

When the doctor arrived he could do nothing my mother was already beyond all human aid. My father was nearly wild, he was devoted to my mother, and she dearly loved him. And everything was so unexpected. After the funeral my eldest sister tried to take Mother's place, but she was only twelve but a neighbour used to come in and help with the baby, I tried to help some too, I could nurse the baby and get him to sleep too. He was so sweet and good.

Left an Orphan

When he was two years old my father came home with a bad cold one night. If he had stayed home from work he might have had a better chance, but of course he went to work, after using a few home made remedies, mustard plaster on his chest, and eating onion gruel going to bed, it seemed to do no good, he just got worse and worse. At last he had to stay home, but the dreaded lung fever (called now pneumonia) had set in, the doctor came and sent us a nurse, but he became unconscious and kept calling Phoebe (that was our mothers name) in less than a week he went home to mother, he died with her name on his lips.

Now we were orphans indeed. His sister came and took the baby, he cried pitifully but she seemed to do just as she liked. We tried to get along, but our little money was soon gone. My brother then 16 ran off and joined the army. He hated the coal mine, but stayed at it while father lived, just to please him. A miner came courting my sister she was a big girl for her years. And she soon married.

A woman came who claimed to be our aunt. Goodness knows she didn't act like one, but the authorities, if there were any never interfered and she took my little sister Emma and me home with her. She seemed to be a widow, she had no children she soon put us to work. She made little cakes to sell at three a penny, and forced me and little sister to peddle them from door to door, and dared us to come home without selling them, she would not give us any of the money, nor no food till they were sold. Then she would give us a slice of bread and lard each and send us to bed. Our bed was a mere bundle of rags in an attic.

One day my little sister cried so with hunger, all the cakes were sold except three. I thought she would not miss one penny, so I gave my sister two, and ate one myself. When we got home she counted the money then inquired very harshly for her other penny, I told her we had eaten three cakes. I said "beat me if you like but please spare little Emmie." She had beaten me before when I had lost a halfpenny. It had been a perishing cold day, snowing and we were poorly clothed, I might say in rags, she had never bought us anything and we had gone home a little earlier, most people were kind and bought a few cakes from the orphans, we told them how we made our living. Down came the strap again until we were both a mass of weals and bruises, little sister fainted and I screamed. A man passing pushed open the door with the words "What in the world is going on here?" Our aunt replied "None of your business. I'll teach these brats to steal and eat my cakes." "Oh will you?" says he, "tell me your story little one" turning to me. I gasped out between my sobs, how she had taken us from our home some miles away, when we were left orphaned by our father's death, saying she was going to raise her sister's children as her own and finally how she had used us.

Life in an Orphanage
The man took us to the nearest clergyman, and we were placed the next day in the Stafford County refuge. We were bathed and dressed by a kind looking woman in a nurse's uniform. Our heads combed and then sent to a large dining room with a lot more children more pitiful little orphans, some blind, some imbeciles, some sensible, some deaf and dumb. All mixed together, on the whole we were not ill treated, but we got very little schooling, an hour every afternoon. If we were over eight years old we were taught to scrub floors, wash, do dishes, and other general housework, but the food was terrible. Most of the food might have been good, had the cook taken the trouble to cook it. Our Monday dinner supposed to be meat pie, we christened smashed horse, with raw 'tatters' and a bit of duff stuck around it. And the breakfast porridge often had cockroaches cooked in it. One poor little blind girl always sat next to me. She used to ask me if there was any beetles

in her porridge, poor little kid. Some of the other children would put them on her plate knowing she couldn't see, then roar with laughter if she got one in her mouth.

They used to teach us carols to sing at Xmas, also old songs, I learnt several old songs there; some of the children seemed to know some sad old things. Some lively adventurous ones, I learned When You and I Were Young Maggie, I'll take you Home Again Kathleen, Go and Leave me if you Wish it, and some which I found out were from Thomas Moore's Irish melodies.

The matron said I had a sweet treble voice and wanted me to sing outside her door on Christmas morning. I sang Good King Wenceslas for her, and I'll Take You Home Again Kathleen. Also the Gypsy's Warning. Christmas time ladies used to come and bring us sweets, fruit, nuts and toys, also to adopt us if suited. The second Christmas I was there, I was now a big girl of ten. A woman took a fancy to me, she said she wanted a girl to take home as her own to be a companion to her little girl about the same age as me. She was allowed to take me away with her. My little sister cried to go with me, but to my great sorrow, I had to leave her behind. I never saw her or any of my family again.

A New Home

After travelling from Stafford to Dudley town, I found I had arrived at my new home, and soon found out I was to be a servant as well as a companion to her little girl, who was an ill mannered youngster who would do nothing for herself.

There were three boys as well as the girl and the woman and man. They certainly were wild children as I will tell as I go along. I tried my best to please them all, I wasn't very tall and used to have to stand on a stool to do the washing, my mistress used to call me up on a Monday morning at 4 o'clock to start the copper fire, to wash with. It used to take me all day to get it done if any article did not seem clean enough for her, back it would come into the tub to scrub again. One day I was straining the potatoes and the lid came off the pot and I dropped the *potatoes in the sink. She was so mad, she jabbed a steel table fork into my arms in four places.* (Editor's note – she bore the marks all her life.) *Several times when she went out the boys would drag me around the kitchen by the hair of my head. Their sister thought it great fun. One morning I overslept and was a little late getting the breakfast ready. My mistress beat me over the head with a stick.*

At last I decided to run away I had put up with it for two years, I never got any money or any clothes only what the girl left off, I never was allowed out on the street. And only got the scraps from their table for food. I got up early one morning, and succeeded in getting out of the house without awakening anyone, it was just breaking day. I took a loaf of bread and a piece of cheese out of the pantry and trudged off into the country, it was a beautiful day in late autumn, and the country was green and far different to the coalfields with their blackness everywhere. I stopped when I got hungry and ate some bread and cheese, got a drink out of a wayside brook, and trudged on again. I slept under a tree that night, I got a little food at some of the cottages I passed, I was trying to get to another town. I soon became exhausted, and I laid down to weary to care. I had no food for two days and nights, some man came along with a cart and gave me a lift, and some food. He left me at a Police Station in the next town. Here I was tried and put into jail for a week, for wandering around with no means of subsisting namely = a vagabond.

A kind old clergyman visited me there, I told him my story, he said, "Well my poor child, that's a terrible hard story, but I think I can help you." I said, "I would be so glad if you would Sir." "Well," he said, "how would you like to go to my sister in Manchester? She needs a maid and will pay you wages. I will pay your fare". The next day I was let out under his care. He put me on the train to Manchester.

A Little Happiness Comes Along
After a few hours journey I reached Manchester it was a large manufacturing town. And the porter told me which

tram to take, when I got to Cheethem Hill, I was very
kindly welcomed by a woman about 50 years old who
proved to be a very kind mistress, she gave me some decent
clothes for a start, I was very happy with her doing the
housework and she did her own cooking, she used to take
me everywhere she went, which wasn't far, to church or
marketing or a walk in the park. It seemed she had
stayed at home with her mother till she died, thus
romance had passed her by. I sang cheerfully about my
tasks, all the old songs I knew, she taught me another one
with a sad haunting melody.

Go and Leave Me if You Wish it
CHORUS
Go and leave me if you wish it,
I would never cross your mind
If you think me so unworthy
Go and leave me never mind

1st VERSE
Once I loved with fond affection
All his thoughts they were for me
Until a dark girl did persuade him
Then he thought no more of me.
Now he's happy with another
One that hath bright gold in store
Tis him that caused my feet to wander
I'm left alone because I'm poor

2nd VERSE
Many a day with him I rambled
Many a happy hour I spent
I thought his heart was mine forever
But I proved twas only lent
My heart has failed and I know it
The heart that fondly beats for thee
I could never tell another
Tales of love I told to thee

3rd VERSE
Many a night when you are sleeping
Taking of your sweet repose
While I poor girl lie broken hearted
Listening to the wind that blows
Farewell friends and kind relations
Farewell to you, my false young man
Tis you that caused my feet to wander
Never to return again

Romance
One day my mistress got the sad news her brother the
Clergyman who sent me to her was very ill.
She said to me "What will I do Kitty, I can't leave you
here alone" "Oh yes you can" said I "I'll be alright, you
go to your brother". After a little more argument, and
leaving me various instructions she departed. She also left
word at the Police Station to have the man on the beat
give an eye to the place in case of burglars. I busied
myself with the house cleaning, it was spring time, also I
had some sewing to do for myself. The third evening I was
alone, a young policeman knocked at the front door. He
said "Pardon me miss, but I think I saw a man go into
your back yard" "Oh! Oh!" said I "you'd better come
through and catch him I am alone here" He came in but
could not find anyone. After that he called every night,
and I would make him some cocoa, and give him some
supper. He was an orphan like myself. By the time my
mistress came back we were great friends. Her brother had
died and she had stayed for the funeral. Now she said she
had no one left to care for her but me. When I told her
about my sweetheart she was pleased that I was having a
little more happiness in my life. And allowed him to come
in when he pleased in the evening. I also used to go out
to the theatre or for walks with him when he was off duty.
Soon Tom wanted me to get married, now much as I
cared for him, I didn't want to leave my dear Miss Mary
alone. I asked her what I should do, she was the only
friend I had. Of course she did not deny us our happiness,
she said we could live in part of her house, and I could

still attend to her few wants which Tom consented for me to do. We set the date for our wedding. We were both very young. I was seventeen and Tom twenty two. The wedding day was set for the 10th of December. Miss Mary was to go with me to St John's Church at 11 o'clock. Tom was to bring a friend arriving a few minutes later. The night before the 10th we were so very happy and when he kissed me goodbye I never thought what would happen before morning. He had to go on duty that night. Next day Miss Mary and I went to the church, me attired in a simple blue suit and hat, Miss Mary in grey. The clergyman was there waiting but no Tom, we waited an hour. Still he never came. Miss Mary and I went to the Police Station to inquire for him. I seemed to know something dreadful had happened.

They told us, his body had just been found in a side lane, he had been killed the night before by some night prowler. I was prostrated with grief for several days I never left my bed. Miss Mary poor soul did all she could for me. She did everything to rouse me to take some interest in life again. I soon found for my foolish moment of the night of the 9th November I was to pay the usual penalty, a baby, how I lived for its coming it seemed all I had left of Tom.

What I was going to do after it came I did not stop to think. My kind mistress though she hated to see me go thought I had better go away for a while till it was over as she didn't want the neighbours to know. So I left and found a person in the country who I paid to take care of me till after my baby should come. At last the time came, when I must go down into the shadows to bring back another life. My darling baby was the image of Tom how I loved him while he was spared to me. I left him with the kind motherly woman for a day and went to ask Miss Mary's advice as to what to do next. To my utter surprise the house was closed and empty. She had been found dead two weeks before my baby came. My life was again saddened by sorrow, she had been a real Mother to me. I did not know where to turn now but knowing my money would soon be gone I went back to the country and got

61

the women to keep my baby for me. That she gladly did. I secured a job in a cotton mill so I could go home at night to my baby. He was now my only joy. But alas! He was to be taken from me also. He took diphtheria at three months and went away. I kept on at the factory for over a year.

A New Friend

A young man working in the factory started to notice me, he was handsome in a rugged sort of way, he wanted me to keep company with him. I didn't know hardly what to do, as I was very lonely, although I could never forget Tom, it was no use brooding over his loss, and I didn't have anyone to ask advice of now. He was totally unlike Tom being short and fair, Tom was tall and dark. But I was still very young only nineteen. After we had kept company for six months, I forgot to say he came from the country, his mother sent for him to go home. He went I thought it would be the end, but no he wrote for me to follow him and we would get married. Needless to say I went.

It has not been possible to substantiate the story Emily tells of her mother's early life. Despite searching the census records and births, marriages and deaths, there are no positive finds to prove definitely where the family came from or who they were. Researching local papers of the time, and checking police records does not produce any evidence of the murder of a policeman, and as the banns books for St John's Church, Cheetham are no longer in existence, it cannot be proved that a marriage had been planned. This does not mean that the tale is untrue; simply that being retold second-hand many years after Emily heard the stories from her mother, there may be small inaccuracies that make research very difficult.

The songs Kitty learnt at Dudley Workhouse and sang to her family have clearly stayed with them all their life. She replicates them in her manuscript to emulate the style of *I Walked by Night*.

What is clear is that Kitty Allen left Manchester to follow Fred into rural Norfolk, without knowing what she was letting herself in for.

CHAPTER 6

1888 Fred Marries Again

While Fred was in Manchester, life had not gone well for Anna. Her health deteriorated, and on 17 April 1888 she died of phthisis (consumption) in All Hallows Hospital, Ditchingham, many miles from Marham, on the far side of Norfolk.

She had no family around her. The death certificate states that Anna was the wife of Frederick Rolfe, a labourer of Pentney. Had she defended him to the end, or was she too ashamed to admit that her husband had deserted her?

Why did she leave Young Fred, the child born in 1885, with her family in Marham? He would only have been 3 years old. Was the family afraid they would catch consumption? Poor Anna, she died miles from home, at 26, after a very short marriage – fourteen months in all. Already she had lost one child when Fred left and was expecting their second; you can imagine the tittle-tattle and the gossip. Why she was at All Hallows Hospital remains a mystery.

All Hallows started life as a penitentiary for fallen women in Ship-meadow, Suffolk. Under the supervision of Lavinia Crosse (daughter of John Crosse, a famous Norwich surgeon), the dedicated group of women who cared for the prostitutes soon formed themselves into a Roman Catholic sisterhood. The committee for the establishment was deeply shocked and Church of England chaplain Revd. Suckling resigned. With Miss Crosse as Mother, All Hallows was reopened in better premises on their present site in Ditchingham on St Michaels Day, 1859. A cottage was utilised as an orphanage and bigger premises built in 1862.

An extract from the All Hallows *Archives* shows what a grim existence it could be:

> *The Life in the home was strict and tough by modern standards. Usually girls spent two years there, but some of the younger entrants*

stayed as long as 4 years. A girl who came when she was 14 remem-
bered rising at 6 a.m. and spending a good many hours in the laundry,
which was a commercial one. She recalled wooden tubs full of soiled
linen, from greasy men's working gear to the finest ladies' underwear
arranged around the walls. Upstairs a circle of irons wedged in by a
supporting rail heating up on the top of a large stove. A laundry girl was
trained to wash and iron up to the highest standards. She would polish
starched shirts with a polishing iron, and smooth the inner circle of the
Sister's caps with a crowner. This particular girl became head laundry
girl, and despite the hard work, the heat and perspiration, loved it. All
the girls were trained in domestic chores, but the stronger and more intel-
ligent worked in the laundry, and while all mended their own clothes, a
few worked in the sewing room, the more skilful graduating from plain
sewing to the finest stitches on delicate underwear, trousseaux and baby
linen.

A system of reward and punishment was introduced. A girl started
with sixty marks to her credit, but bad behaviour or shoddy work could
reduce them. Outrageous behaviour could land a girl in the punishment
room on bread and water for a day, but sustained efforts to improve were
rewarded with the coveted St Michael's badge. Treats were few. Girls
could buy sweets with the little money they earned at weekends, and once
a year, usually at Michaelmas or on some national event such as Queen
Victoria's Jubilee in 1887 a day without rules and a picnic either in the
Convent or in the Orphanage grounds made a welcome change from
routine.

Obviously the nuns were keen to encourage spirituality and if a
girl showed an interest in taking Holy Orders, she was welcomed
into the Order of Repentance. Over in the Orphanage, girls over
10 were charged £33 a year for their keep (under 10s cost £28) –
presumably relatives or charities footed the bill.

Things were not much better in the orphanage. The better-class
girls were trained as governesses, while poor cottage girls were taught
the skills necessary to become domestic servants. It was a harsh and
dreary upbringing. Fallen women were kept strictly apart from the
children.

In 1872, the hospital opened. *Kelly's Directory* for 1888 records it
was capable of holding twenty patients, who were admitted without
restriction from any practicable distance for a small weekly payment.
Incurables, convalescents and female patients were also received, the

latter at an increased charge, because they were about to be confined.

The nuns had Missions in both Norwich and Ipswich, and sent food from a farm they had in Ditchingham to a kitchen in St James Parish, Norwich to provide cheap dinners for the poor. They also set up a maternity fund to help provide nightwear for expectant mums and clothes for their babies. As the Convent was set up principally to care for fallen women it may be that Anna was reduced to prostitution to survive, or perhaps she was pregnant.

For the first fifteen years after the house opened, girls and young women from Norfolk and Suffolk were sent there through the Church Penitentiary Association either as 'fallen women' or 'women in moral danger'. The nuns also opened a home in Norwich, much as an assessment centre would be today; girls stayed there for three months until suitable accommodation was found, or it was shown they could not cope with the restrictive regime and left. Sister Lavinia also became aware that provision for sick girls was required and a special lock-in section was started to treat mainly cases of venereal disease. After 1876 the regime seems to have softened once they moved to the improved premises and more room was available.

James Rolfe, Fred's stepbrother, had been treated for consumption at the hospital in King's Lynn back in 1863 (the doctor there was a specialist in tubercular diseases), so why did Anna go to Ditchingham?

Fred recounts in *I Walked by Night* how he returned from Manchester after six years. His mother had written to tell him that his father's health was failing and as one of the gamekeepers with whom he had trouble was dead and the other gone away, it was safe for him to return. This information is incorrect in a number of ways: first, although John Rolfe may have been in ill health, he did not die until 1897, so it is much more likely Fred heard that Anna's health was failing or that she had died. He was not away for the time he states; from the evidence of press reports he seems to have been away at most from September 1884, when he absconded, until 2 July 1888, when he was convicted of the two offences at Grimston Court, for which he fled in 1884. He received twenty-one days with hard labour for each offence, in lieu of fines of £3 0s 9d. It is not clear whether he was arrested or gave himself up, more likely the former because he never made life easy for the keepers and constables.

Fred must have had time to gain employment before he went to prison because he is listed in court records as being a bricklayer's labourer. He spent this period of imprisonment in the new prison on Mousehold Heath, Norwich, which opened in 1887. *In I Walked by Night*, he tells how he found his treatment there a great deal more humane than the time spent in Norwich Castle as a young man.

Samuel Daws, who was sentenced on the same day for stealing two dogs, got fourteen days. At 70, this can't have been easy, but at least he did not go hungry and it might have staved off the day when the workhouse was his only option. Samuel Day, also of Pentney, was awarded one month for killing game without a licence. The difference between Samuel and Fred was that Fred was convicted of poaching (killing rabbits, vermin and so on). Killing game such as hares, pheasants and partridge was regarded as a more serious offence. Game could be killed with a licence, but these were only awarded to the great and the good. It was an even more serious matter to be charged with poaching for anything at night, and there were additional charges if you were caught on a Sunday.

Huge numbers of rabbits were killed legitimately by warreners and sent to the towns and cities. One winter in the early 1870s, from October to March almost 1 million rabbits were sold in Birmingham. The by-product was fur. For the poacher, as well as the legitimate dealers, it was big business. Traders bought the rabbit skins fresh or dried; the poachers, if possible, sold them on fresh, not wanting to leave any evidence around.

Traders used to put their bicycles on the train and go out into the countryside, then ride around villages buying skins before they returned by train with their purchases hung on a pole attached to the frame of the bike. Some journeyed by foot. Other dealers would send empty hampers to those who sent a postcard saying they had collected enough skins.

As a perk, cooks at the big houses were allowed to sell skins from the back door. They were also able to sell dripping and fat scraped from the sides of washing-up bowls, before the maggots got in, for soap making; they also dealt in bones and feathers. Not all mistresses would allow the money made to be kept, insisting it should be spent on ornaments and the like to cheer up the servants' hall. That is why rag and bone men always carried trinkets to swap for goods.

Rabbit skins made their way to factories such as one in Brandon, which started in 1791. The skin trade began there because of its proximity to the Breckland Warrens, where rabbits have been 'farmed' for many centuries. Initially in the 1700s the skins were processed in the homes of the outworkers described as 'bunny pluckers'. After being sorted into colour and quality, the fur was plucked by hand but by the time Fred's skins would have arrived, the trade became automated in two factories in the town: S. & P. Lingwoods Ltd and W. Rought Ltd. There, the skins – if they arrived 'wet' or fresh – were strung up high, away from vermin to dry. Once dry, pelts were then wetted again to make them pliable, the grease removed and they were cut to lie flat.

The fur was then pulled. The machines took off the longer, delightfully soft hairs, which were used to fill cushions, mattresses and so on. The remainder was felted for the manufacture of hats. Pelts were treated chemically, originally with mercury, a highly poisonous metal, which caused dreadful health problems including senility – hence the term 'as mad as a hatter'. Mercury was brushed into the fur using a formula that optimised the speed at which the remaining fur felted when removed from the skin. The process was later mechanised, and there are photographs of women standing at the pulling machines.

It was hard and dangerous work as the knives removing the fur were extremely sharp and revolved very quickly. It must have been a foul, smelly way to earn a living! The shredded skins were then sold for glue, size and even used in the sweet-making industry. The Lingwood factory processed between 100,000 and 150,000 dozen skins a year, enough to make approximately a quarter of a million hats annually.

After World War I there were not enough local rabbit skins to satisfy demand so they were imported as well, English skins then fetching as much as a shilling each. The death knell of the industry came with the popularisation of the motorcar, when hats were no longer necessary and they ceased to be fashionable.

The rabbit is not indigenous to the British Isles; it was introduced from southern Europe in the twelfth century to produce both fur and meat. At that time known as a 'coney' (from the Latin *cuniculus*), rabbit was originally only the name for the young. It was not naturally a burrower and suffered initially from predators and cold winters thus the medieval rabbit was much prized. In her book *Norfolk Life* Lilias Rider Haggard quotes an account book, which tells of eight thousand rabbit skins being an item of cargo exported from Blakeney in 1587.

Warreners were employed mostly by ecclesiastical landlords to breed rabbits to feed the monks, many in the Brecklands because of the dry sandy soil and low rainfall. They constructed artificial mounds for the rabbits to shelter in and fed them chopped furze and hay during the winter. Warreners acted as gamekeepers to keep predators, stoats, weasels, foxes and polecats away. Rabbits were culled in the autumn when their fur was at its finest. The meat was considered a delicacy: Samuel Pepys talked of hashed rabbit. Squeezing the jaw indicated whether the rabbit was young and tender – if it cracked, it was good to eat.

There were also recipes where the joints were covered in silver, wine and blades of mace. In one recipe the meat was covered in a sauce made of egg yolks and grape juice. The rabbit was especially useful to monastic communities over many centuries because the unborn foetus, known as laurices, was not considered meat and could therefore be eaten on Fridays and during Lent when meat was forbidden.

Rabbit was also used to designate wealth and rank. Henry IV liked black rabbit fur for his undergarments. In her book, *Clothes and the Child*, Anne Buck mentions that in 1556, Lady Petre's account book had an entry for furring a gown. At 14, Thomasine Petre had a cassock and gown of cloth furred with black coney skins and a furred worsted gown. Her younger sister Katherine had a furred night-gown. Clothes were often lined with rabbit fur and the linings were of such value that they were bequeathed in family wills. Think back!

> *Bye, baby bunting*
> *Daddy's gone a- hunting*
> *Gone to get a rabbit skin*
> *To wrap the baby bunting in.*

'Bunting' was a term of endearment.

Inevitably some rabbits escaped and, having learnt to survive doing what rabbits do best, they soon became abundant. Where there were rabbits, poachers would always be found, whether this was just one man taking enough to feed his family, or a large armed gang ready to do battle with warreners and gamekeepers.

The prison on Mousehold Heath where Fred did his second stint is a typically solid Victorian building, still in use as a prison today. It was originally symmetrical, but over the years there have been many additions to house offices, etc., but the fine brickwork can still be seen. It does not appear intimidating, with plenty of windows and lots of chimneys, which suggests it must have been warm. Certainly Fred approved, and this is what he said:

> Of the New Prisson I have nothing to say here, but that I should prefere that to the Poor Law Institution if I had to Choose. The food is more fit for human Beins now, the Cells are comfortable and evry man have a better Chance. By industry and if he want to he may get a good Job. They have five acres of garden, and lots of the men are engaged working in them. The work is much more intresting, and the prisners have conserts evry other Sunday and lectures on week nights, and evry one can atend them. A Prisner have a knife and fork to get his food with, and bread and butter for his breckfast, and tea or a pint of cocoa for each meal.
>
> The Discipline is kept up but in a much more human way. A Prisner may shave twice a week, and is alowed to have his own safety raysor if he have one.

Inside, it was light and spacious, although from the cells it was only possible to see the sky. There were thirty-two cells on a landing and four landings altogether; there were proper washhouses too. The cells where condemned prisoners were held are still there, as is the place of execution, but it is now the kitchen and canteen area.

On 12 August 1888, Fred was released. Kitty's document suggests that it must have been soon afterwards that he asked her to join him:

> On arriving at the station, it was two hundred miles from Manchester, I found I had to walk about four miles through dark country lanes alone as no one was there to meet me. Such a change after the lights of the city.
>
> I got directions from the station master which way to go, I left my trunks and carried my small handbag with me, I stumbled on through the dark, it wouldn't have been so dark, but there was woods on one side of the road most of the way, and no houses near the road for the first mile and a half, then as I was passing what I found afterwards to be a grand gentlemans estate I saw a woman near the gate on the inside. I called out to her, "Come out and keep me company". Turning again there was no one to be seen. What did I see? I had now come to a district rich in ghost stories. The fen district of East Anglia.

69

I walked a mile or so further to four crossways not knowing which way to take I knocked at a cottage door. To my surprise I heard a rough woman's voice say "You aint a comen in here tonight" It struck me as funny, I burst out laughing, the woman opened the door, she said, "Well and who may you be and where do you come from?" I answered her, "Could you tell me where Mr so and so lives?" "Why yes" she said "go up that lane straight in front of you, turn to the right and you will see some cottages on the left, they live in the fust one" and shut the door. So I again walked on, it seemed about ten miles to me. I was tired enough with my all day journey without prowling round the country half the night.

<u>Life in the Country</u>

I knocked several times on the door, I just began to think no one was going to answer when a window was flung open above, a head came out and a deep voice spoke, "Hello, what do yer want?" I said, "Is Fred there?" "Of course and fast asleep Why?" "Well wake him up" says I "and tell him Kitty is here". He was soon downstairs, it seemed my letter had not been received, it came the next day, so you see it wasn't his fault I had the long walk alone.

They soon had a fire going and made me some tea, and gave me the best they had. I think we talked most of the night, my husbands mother thought I must have seen a ghost. But I said "Oh nonsense, one of the young ladies out for a breath of fresh air." I was certainly more afraid of the living than the dead, how could a dead person hurt anybody? They hadn't much accommodation for me, but they did the best they could, me sleeping with Fred's mother, and him sleeping with his Dad. Well next day we went to the Parson and put up the banns. They had to be published three Sundays before we could be married.

A few days later I went with some more women to the harvest field, first time I had ever seen one, we used to take the men's dinner to them. It was quite a novelty to me. They used to have beer too in the fields and some of them took too much. I noticed a big rough looking fellow *come lurching towards us. To my utter surprise he seized me by the shoulders and kissed me, a perfect stranger. I was stunned for a moment. His sister came up and shoved him away, she said "get out of this yer drunken fool, she belongs to Fred and he'd kill you for that if he knew." With that she begged me not to tell him, telling me my husband to be had an awful temper. I agreed as he had done me no harm, only given me a scare.*

Some months afterwards I was sorry I never told, for such things will come out, it was an awful place for gossip. My husband's mother made my wedding dress. I had brought a length of soft grey stuff with me. We were married in the village church on a Sunday morning early in October.

At the time Kitty travelled, the railway fare would have been about 1d a mile in third class, so it must have cost her a week's wages and a great deal of courage. The stationmaster to whom she spoke well have been Nebuchanezzar Ayres, who was in charge around that time.

The station is not four miles from Pentney, more likely a mile and a half, but as in Kitty's day the route is mostly down an uninhabited wooded, narrow lane. For a city girl, with her dainty shoes and no doubt a natty outfit to impress Fred and the in-laws, it must have seemed very scary indeed, particularly as she did not know if she would be welcome when she found Fred.

Happily she was, and they were married in St Mary Magdalene, the parish church in Pentney, on Sunday, 8 October 1888. Revd Augustus Speed was now there – a fact that may have softened Fred's refusal to enter the church after Revd Broad's comments on his return from prison, although Revd Broad would have performed any service held for his first child Edith's funeral, which must have been a bitter pill for Fred to swallow.

The 1881 census shows there were 538 people in Pentney, more than half (279) had actually been born in the village, only twenty-one were not born in Norfolk and just ten were not from East Anglia. With her strange accent, her ignorance of the countryside and as Fred's future wife, Kitty must have stood out and been the object of endless gossip and intrigue.

So now Kitty can be added to the list of women Fred charmed.

Anna, it seems, was persuaded to go against her family's wishes and endure his criminality and feckless disregard for the outcome of his actions. Clearly Fred possessed a sharp mind, although he could have used this to better effect, perhaps. It was difficult to rise above your station but people did manage to do so, as might Fred have done – except he seemed driven by the thrill of getting one over the system.

Kitty had been persuaded to leave everything she had ever known, so what was it about Fred that so appealed to women?

CHAPTER 7

1888–94 West Norfolk

Kitty's biography gives a detailed account of life with Fred:

We lived on with his parents for about a year. His mother used to go out as a midwife as his father was unable to work. But he could use his tongue alright. He had some peculiar expressions. He'd say when he would come home and find me busy washing "Hi there Kitty, you're as busy as the d- in a high wind today". And if anyone paid a visit around supper time, and it began to rain as it often did he'd say "You'd better be getting home hadn't you, nearer the night the wuss the weather".

After we'd been married about three months my husband came home in a towering rage" Whatever's the matter" I said "I'll soon larn yer" he says and taking off his belt that he always wore he thrashed me until I fainted. His mother came running saying "what do you think you are doing you d — what has she done any way". Well it seemed the man who kissed me in the harvest field had told his side of the story. When Fred was told the true facts of the case, he was very sorry and humbly apologised.

He was a good husband in lots of ways, he brought me home all he earned only keeping a shilling for tobacco, which he could not do without. I hated the country with its gossiping people and found it very hard to settle down. I got along fairly well with his people, his Dad loved to hear me sing in the evenings. Fred who had a strong baritone voice used to sing with me. He could sing the Gipsy's Warning verse for verse with me. But I think Dad liked When you and I were young Maggie the best

73

I wander today to the hills, Maggie
To watch the scene below
The creek and the creaking old mills, Maggie
Are the same as they were long ago
I was there when the birds used to sing, Maggie
And join in the song that we sung
We sang just as gaily as they, Maggie
When you and I were young.

Our Own Home

When we had been married a year a baby girl came to bless our home. My husband was overjoyed, and so was I. I had something definite to think of and work for. She was a big healthy baby weighing 14 lbs at birth. My husband got everything for me that I wanted. He could find eggs, apples and nuts where no one else knew they grew. He could also snare or shoot a rabbit, pheasant or hare with the best of them. He has told all about it in his book "I Walked by Night". We never wanted for anything, but his parents didn't like it, as they were afraid of the law. But I thought like him, wildlife was for those who could get it.

Soon after my girl came we left the old people and got a place of our own. My husbands pay as a labourer wasn't enough to live on, so he found a market for game. He used to go out nights with his dog and gun and net and walk miles and carry home game of all kinds, but although it added to our income I used to lay sleepless nights when he was out. I was always scared he would be caught. He would come home in the early hours of the morning, I always had to leave the door so he could get in. The latch string was always out.

Some nights he would burst in all out of wind, throw the hares or birds some of them still alive in the pantry. He had run from keepers. He got caught a few times, but as long as he could pay the fines we didn't mind.

We arrived with our furniture at Marhamton, there my husband had secured a job as shepherd, he loved animals except horses. He earned a little more money but still not any too much.

We lived beside a particularly spiteful neighbour here,

she was very hard up having a large family to feed and her husband only earning 10 shillings a week. She was always borrowing stuff from me and not paying it back. My husband often gave them a rabbit to help them, but I think the more we gave her the uglier and worse tempered she got. She got so jealous of our success she went and told the police that she saw our dog catch a hare on a Sunday afternoon. Of course he was well known to be a poacher. So he had to appear before the Magistrate at Downham. They never found no hare, there wasn't any to find, it was a lie all through but he was convicted and sent to jail for six weeks.

It happened in the spring of the year. But no one would employ me, even my little girl who was going to school came in for her share of abuse from her school mates. It was certainly no joke to be a poacher's wife and child. But I hit on a plan to get a living, it kept us going till Fred came home. I gathered water cress out of running streams and bunched it up and sold it a halfpenny a bunch, I had to walk to distant villages too. Sometimes when we were walking along the old dog would come along with a rabbit in his mouth and lay it at our feet. So we did not fare so badly.

Fred and Kitty's daughter Emily, the author of the manuscript, was born in 1889 so she would have remembered the mid-1890s. Her recollections of the stories and songs her mother told her must have remained with her all her life, for the document was not written until 1936.

Poor Kitty, she was probably very lonely and spent a great deal of time talking to her daughter of her past life for want of anyone else. Her great granddaughter remembers being told that Kitty heard voices telling her to go back to Manchester, which she ignored and always regretted. Where could she have gone? She had no contact with her family and no money.

Men interviewed about poaching often talked of gathering primroses in hedge bottoms, the significance of which Frank Callum revealed in *Both Sides of the Fence* (1987). As a child:

. . . when I was sent primrosing – which was a cover-up. All the banks on the hedgerows were covered with primroses, which gave good

camouflage for my nesting expeditions. I had to find any pheasants' eggs in the hedgerows and mark their position so that I could find the nest later. Very often I had the keepers accost me, thinking I was birds nesting, kick my backside and send me home. I had to relate to my Dad all my findings and my markings and when it was dark he found the nests that were not being sat on and took the eggs. He had a special trilby hat with a torch inside which pinpointed the markings, and subsequently the nests. Two villages away he had a contact who purchased all the eggs.

The following extract is from *A Farmer's Year Being His Commonplace Book for 1898* (1899) by Henry Rider Haggard, chairman of the Bungay Magistrates Bench for many years:

Today at the Bench we tried one of the egg-stealing cases, which are always plentiful at this time of year. The defendant, a 'marine dealer', was accused of sending a box of 251 partridge eggs (twenty dozen small, eleven reds, i.e. French partridge according to his own invoice found in the box) to another 'marine dealer' in a neighbouring town.

This second gentleman, by the way, was recently fined £31 10s being 1 shilling an egg for 630 stolen eggs. The case against the defendant today was clear, and he also was fined a shilling an egg and costs, with the alternative of two months in prison.

I know it is commonly said that magistrates are severe upon this class of case, and very ready to convict upon slight evidence. This is not at all my experience. On the contrary, the fact that most of them are sportsmen tends to make them very careful, and I have on several occasions seen poaching cases dismissed when the evidence would have been thought sufficient to ensure conviction in most classes of offences. It is extraordinary what an amount of false sentiment is wasted in certain quarters upon poachers who, for the most part, are very cowardly villains recruited from among the worst characters in the neighbourhood. When some friends and I hired the shooting at Bradenham, one of our keepers, a very fine young fellow named Holman, interrupted a gang of poachers engaged in killing pheasants at night. He was unarmed and they were armed, and the end of it was that one of them fired a gun straight at him, the contents of which he only escaped by throwing himself behind the trunk of a small tree. The man was identified, and tried at the assizes, but as it was only 'a night poaching case' a sentence of six months was thought to be sufficient punishment for this vigorous attempt at murder.

Not a year goes by without keepers, who are merely doing the duty for which they are paid, being murdered or beaten to a pulp by these bands of thieving rascals, who are out, not for sport, but for gain. But bad as is the night poaching business the trade of the egg stealer is perhaps even more despicable, since, as I told the defendant today, not only was he himself breaking the law, but he was causing many others to break it also. It is not to be supposed that these large lots of eggs are found and thieved by one man; on the contrary a system of 'feeders' is necessary in their collection. A rascal of the stamp of our friend the 'marine dealer' is in touch with various bad characters in the villages round about who suborn labourers to find the nests in the course of their daily toil, and when they are full to bring them away at night. These in due course reach the hands of the middleman, who pays them at a certain tariff, and passes them on to some honest merchant who does a larger business. Ultimately they find their way through game dealers or by the agency of a not too scrupulous head-keeper, into the possession of the tenants of great shoots who are anxious that their bags should be big in due season, and try to increase their stock of partridges by buying eggs, not knowing of course, that they have been stolen, very frequently from the neighbours' land and sometimes from their own.

The feeders, as Rider Haggard describes them, were very harshly treated. In a case heard in Swaffham (1881) by his father, William Haggard of Bradenham Hall, two men charged with stealing three pheasant eggs were fined 3/6d for each egg, with 9/- costs. Bear in mind that wages were about 10/- a week then, so the eggs cost them two weeks' money.

Another case in the same week tells of two brothers who stole eleven pheasant eggs; the older brother tried to take all the blame, but the bench found them both guilty and fined the eldest £3 5s 3d (six and a half weeks wages) while his sibling paid 15/9d. One wonders how they found the money, for it is stated that the fines were paid into court immediately!

Fred himself was involved in one case of stealing eggs:

Dismissed

Frederick Rolfe (29) labourer, Pentney, was charged by George Clarke with trespassing in search of game on land of Mr Lewis Marriott on 1st ult. Complainant deposed that he was a vermin killer to Mr Marriott and about 5 o'clock on the morning of the day named he saw the defendant stooping down looking in the bushes as if after eggs. Witness watched him for ten minutes or quarter of an hour, and then went up to him and said "Can't you find any?" He replied that Mr Marriott's keeper employed him. For the defence, defendant said he was working on Mr Household's farm "rushing" and that he went the way he did because it was 1½ miles nearer. Case dismissed.

Grimston Petty Session, 19 May 1890

However he was often in court for other offences:

Game Case
Frederick Rolfe, Labourer, Pentney was summoned by James Harris, gamekeeper Marham for trespassing in search of game on land in the occupation of Mr Gates Green. William Chapman, farm bailiff to Mr Paul, said he was on his masters land at 4 o'clock in the afternoon on January 11th and saw defendant "driving" with another man. Defendant had a gun under his arm and went on to Marham fen. Witness followed, and watched him, and heard some birds rise near him, and saw defendant shoot. He also saw him walk about 20 yards and then stoop as if he was picking up something. Would not say positively what birds they were. Previous convictions were put in by Supt. Mash, but the Chairman told the defendant that the magistrates would give him another chance, and dismissed the case against him with a caution.

Downham Petty Session, 9 February 1891

And yet again:

Trespassing
Frederick Rolfe and Henry Back, labourers, Pentney, were charged with trespassing in search of rabbits on land at Marham, in the occupation of Mr C.R. Brasnett on 5th inst. James Holman, gamekeeper, said he saw the defendants with guns on the land at 4 o'clock in the morning. He could swear to Rolfe but was not certain as to Back. He watched them off the land, and then saw them go to on to Mr Boyce's land at Narborough. Albert Pitcher, labourer, said he was with the last witness on the morning in question and saw two men on the land. He ran one of them into a garden and lost sight of him. Witness thought by his dress and back that it was Back. The case against Back was dismissed and Rolfe, who pleaded guilty was fined 20/- and 23/- costs.

Downham Court, 13 July 1891

Docking Divisional court records of 21 December 1891 show that on 7 December, that same year, Frederick Rolfe was charged with taking two pheasants from the land of Thomas Paul at 5.30 pm at

Pentney. He was committed to one month's hard labour and bound over for one year, with two sureties of £5.

Until around this time, Fred, Kitty and Emily had been living at Bailey's Cottages Pentney, but court cases from now on show that they had moved to Marham.

Policemen must have walked miles before bicycles were invented. There are at present 101 parishes in West Norfolk, and in 1872 there were 232 policemen, so each parish had about two policemen. Constable Thomas Bocking watched over West Bilney around the time that Fred was starting out as a criminal. One of the first members of the police force on which our present-day system is based his first posting as a raw recruit, aged 20 in 1840, was a village two miles from Downham Market, on the edge of the Fens. The area was full of navvies, who were building the Ten Mile Bank, part of the system of waterways being constructed to drain the Fenlands. Bocking said they were a wild lot and gave no end of trouble, but determined to do his duty as best he could. A wonderful obituary of Tom Bocking appears in the *Lynn Advertiser, Wisbech Constitutional Gazette* and *Norfolk and Cambridgeshire Herald* in 1898:

> *In the village to which he was first assigned there were two grog shops, having taken lodgings in one of these, he was quickly summonsed to the other. On repairing thither he learnt that a burglarious entry had been affected. Of this there was sufficient indication, and before he had long been in the house he detected a movement in the old fashioned chimney.*
>
> *A thought struck him and appreciating the difficulty of dislodging his quarry from such a hiding place by aggressive means therefore he resorted to a stratagem. It was the custom of the natives in those days to smoke their bacon with turf, a plentiful supply of which was always to hand. A bundle of this commodity was accordingly deposited in the grate and set fire to, but the burglar while the smoking process elicited abundant evidence of his whereabouts, refused to succumb either to its baneful influence or to the threats and entreaties vociferated from below.*
>
> *Then the landlord ran for some gunpowder, and proposed to blow the burglar up, but Constable Bocking repelled the suggestion as alike inhuman and fraught with danger to the assembled company. There was no help for it; the chimney must come down; and while the constable guarded the grate, the host and his following went on to the tiles and actually demolished the chimneystack down to the level of the roof.*
>
> *Still no visible signs of the burglar. His laboured breathing could be*

heard and that was all. His capture was now only a matter of time, and revolving this in his mind the intruder resolved to capitulate, which he did by sliding down from the cavity over the mantelpiece. The picture of the dazed, begrimed and half-smoked burglar as he emerged from his sooty retreat was one to be remembered; but his condition evoked little pity, and he was promptly secured.

This was Constable Bocking's first arrest, and although the captures have been legion since, it is doubtful whether he applied the "bracelets" with greater satisfaction. The prisoner, when questioned showed plenty of bravado, and excused his ascent of the chimney on the plea that "any port was good enough in a storm". In order to demonstrate at once the fallacy of human confidence and the defects of his handcuffs, he broke open the latter on the first gate he came to; but the demonstration was premature, and the pair reached Downham together without further incident, the one to report his first capture and the other to be dealt with according to his desserts.

Later, when posted to Beachamwell, Norfolk, Constable Bocking had difficulty – as was usually the case for policemen – in finding lodgings. Eventually he was installed in the churchyard in an offshoot of the Parsonage:

The religious surroundings of the young constable may have had their hallowed influence, but he was not long in shaking it off, at least temporarily. At Cockley Cley, near Swaffham a village not far distant, there dwelt a quasi military publican named Denney, who divided his attention between catering for the thirsty needs of his customers and spinning yarns of what he did and saw at Waterloo. Such congenial company was not lightly to be despised, and when harvest came round and the natives perpetrated the "high jinks" normally indulged in, at that season, small wonder that the constable was induced to join them. Having once done so, he threw aside the fetters of all officialdom and self-restraint and frolicked hard and fast for three whole days. There was little or no supervision then but the facts came to the ready ear of a neighbouring J.P., who lost no time in communicating them to headquarters. Accordingly Bocking was "hauled over the coals" by his chief – who considerably regretted that he could not order him to be flogged – and was formally reprimanded and dismissed to his duty. The venue of his operations was of course changed. He was removed to a large district round Lynn, embracing East Winch, Middleton, Bilney, Runcton and Narborough.

Whilst stationed in the area he dealt with poachers and fowl stealers on innumerable occasions, and other offenders, whose appearance before the Lynn bench and subsequent transference to Walsingham or Swaffham goal was deemed necessary in the public interest. The roads and the means of location were not of the best, and casualties en route were not infrequent. On one occasion as Constable Bocking was driving a female prisoner to free board and lodgings at Walsingham Bridewell, the House of Correction, a dense fog overtook him on Massingham Heath. Unable to proceed, and nightfall coming on, he unharnessed the horse, turned the vehicle upside down and there escort and captive remained until the small hours of the morning. They reached the prison at 4 o'clock, not having met a soul on the way.

Several robberies were perpetrated on the turnpike between King's Lynn and East Winch and Bocking was told specially to put a stop to them. He seldom wore a uniform, which was almost unknown among the county constabulary. He, like many others of his class, usually walked abroad in a velveteen jacket and might have been mistaken for a gamekeeper, or anything else save a constable. This was done as a protection to the men themselves, and to enable them to appear in public without attracting notice. Bocking was invariably armed with a short, stout blackthorn stick and a brace of old single barrelled pistols, and carried the inevitable handcuffs. One night he took up his customary station on the turnpike, and waited. It was then about 8 o'clock and raining. Suddenly a couple of ruffians sprang upon him, one from behind and the other before. The latter was promptly felled with a blow from the blackthorn, and in less time than it takes to write it his companion had also been levelled. The constable fell upon them hip and thigh, and, in his own expressive words, paid them till they howled for mercy. The conqueror could afford to be generous, and believing they had been sufficiently punished, helped them onto their feet. Then the trio repaired to the roadside tavern and drank each other's health.

Historically, each community was responsible for maintaining good behaviour in their own district, but during the reign of King Alfred (871–899) a system called Frankpledge was introduced. Still based on the community, where each member of the 'tithing' (or parish) was responsible for each other, these tithings were grouped into 'Hundreds', which became part of a county or shire. A number of counties formed an Earldom.

A 'tithingman' (or 'headborough') was the officer of a Hundred and responsible to the shire reeve, later sheriff. The King appointed the sheriffs who were responsible for the policing, the military, judicial and fiscal affairs within their county. This post is still in existence today in a much more ceremonial role, although high sheriffs still sit on police and magistrates committees. The militia were very much part of policing at this time.

Sheriffs held a very powerful position (think of the Sheriff of Nottingham). In 1361 Justices of the Peace came into being, and by the fifteenth century police concerns became in part the responsibility of the magistrates. By the 1600s paid constables came into being, and in the 1700s towns paid night constables, street keepers and night watchmen. Constables were appointed in parishes and sworn in by local JPs. In times of emergency, special constables were also sworn in. Therein lay the difficulties of the cost to the parish and the lack of supervision of the constables.

After the Enclosure Acts (from 1750 onwards) and the Napoleonic Wars (1799–1815), when 400,000 men returned looking for work and homes, law and order began to break down. It is hardly surprising that ordinary folk became disgruntled. The loss of common land, a source of cheap food, grazing and fuel, caused great hardship and a loss of independence. Landowners took over total control, including tied housing, of their employees. Often agricultural workers were expected to sign agreements such as the following, quoted by George Edwards MP:

> *I, the undersigned, agree to hire the cottage in the Parish of......... the property of........... at a rental of.............. and agree to give the cottage up at a week's notice should the landlord require it for any other workman.*
>
> *I also agree not to keep any pigs or fowls without first obtaining permission from the landlord or his agent.*
>
> *I will also act as night-watchman when required, and give any information I may have that will lead to the conviction of any-one seen poaching on the estate.*
>
> *I also undertake not to harbour any of my family who may misconduct themselves in any way.*
>
> *I also agree on leaving my cottage to hand over my copper and oven to the landlord or his agent and not to disturb the bricks or to remove these utensils until the landlord or his agent have refused to purchase them.*
>
> *I will also undertake to live at peace with my neighbours and to lead an honest and respectable life.*

I will, before admitting any of my family home, apply to the landlord
or his agent for permission, giving particulars on a form provided by the
landlord, their names and ages, also if married or single, and how long
they want to stay.

Landowners argued that draining and fencing the common land
during the time of the Enclosures increased the area of agricultural
land, bringing extra work, but the price for labourers was too high.
At this time poaching really took off, not only to feed hungry families
but also to show defiance. Landlords did not make the situation any
better by paying wages in the form of tokens redeemable at approved
places or by paying in kind with milk and other produce from their
own farms, thus further demeaning the labourer.

Additionally, the Corn Laws, taxing corn coming in from abroad,
meant bread prices rose beyond the means of the ordinary rural
family and forced them to rely on the Parish for relief from the Poor
rates. This was utterly humiliating for the men, especially when the
landowners responsible for the Poor Law were keen to have as few
people as possible reliant on them. In Necton, Norfolk, this agreement was drawn up in the 1830s:

Agreement is hereby had by the Parish of Necton, in committee assem-
bled this.... Day of ... 1833 that from and after date hereof encourage-
ment shall be given to all those young men who shall abstain from
Improvident Marriages by continuing single after the age herein speci-
fied, in order that in the course of a few years the Superabundant Popu-
lation of the said Parish May be diminished, and the situation of the
labourer as well as the Owner and Occupier of Lands and Tenements,
with the blessing of God, thereby benefited.

RESOLVED FIRST – that every young man who shall continue
single till after 25 years of age, without having brought the burden of
Bastardy on society, shall at all times receive, if a good and sufficient
labourer, the highest wages given to any Labourer in the Parish
of...........; and if he stand in need, shall receive the relief-money
ordered by the Magistrates of the Hundred, with out being necessitated to
go to the Parish workhouse.

RESOLVED SECONDLY – That every young man who shall con-
tinue single till after 28 years of age, without being brought the burden of
Bastardy on society, shall at all times receive if a good and sufficient
labourer the highest wages given to any Labourer in....; and if he stand
in need shall receive 6d per week above the relief- money ordered by the

Magistrates of the Hundred with out being necessitated to go to the Parish Workhouse.

RESOLVED THIRDLY – That every young man who shall continue single after the age of 30 years, without having brought the burden of Bastardy on society, shall at all times receive, if a sufficient labourer the highest wages given in....................; and if he stand in need, shall receive 1 shilling per week above the relief money ordered by the Magistrates of the Hundred, with out being necessitated to go to the Parish Workhouse.

RESOLVED FOURTHLY – That every young woman, belonging to the Parish of Necton, who have not by Bastardy or other misconduct disgraced herself, and shall be married to a man above 28 years of age, shall receive on her marriage at the hands of the Overseers......... as a wedding largesse, and if her husband before marriage shall have completed 30 years of age; she shall then in like manner receive as a wedding largesse the sum of..........; providing in both cases, the man as well as the woman be of good report.

That every young man who shall contract marriage before he is 23 years of age shall, if he in course of time stand in need, be either sent to the Parish Workhouse, or receive 1 shilling and 6 pence less than the scale of relief usually given.

And further if any young man shall contract marriage before he is 25 years of age, if he stand in need, he shall either be sent to the Parish Workhouse, or receive 1 shilling per week less than the scale of relief usually given where parties have married according to a sound discretion.

In order to keep account of such parties, it is hereby resolved that an alphabetical Register shall be kept and handed down from one Overseer to another, wherein shall be set forth the name and time of marriage of the parties, that due record may be had ever after of such their voluntary imprudence.

Although matters were slightly improved by the 1888s, memories were long and repressed labourers remained bitter, using any means they dare to expand their income. It was against this background that Kitty not only had to endure poverty, but also loneliness and hostility. She also suffered Fred's bad temper and thieving ways and on moving to Marham (remembered as Marhamton) endured the additional unpleasantness of Anna's family, who were still living in the village. Young Fred was now living with Mary Ann, his maternal grandmother, who was acting as housekeeper to William Steeles, now a coachbuilder, and her two sons, James and Edward. Mary Ann's illegitimate daughter Florence was staying with her cousin Annie Steeles, who had married grocer and butcher Charles Clayton. They lived at Washdyke, Walpole St Peter, Cambridgeshire, about nine miles west of King's Lynn.

In *I Walked by Night*, Fred states that his mother raised his young son – he could hardly say Anna's mother was bringing him up, as he declared in the book that Anna was an orphan!

In the 1891 census John Rolfe, then aged 78, is still listed as an agricultural labourer. He received just 2/6d outdoor relief when he became too old to support himself and Elizabeth. In *I Walked by Night*, Fred describes his mother as working in the fields to supplement their income. At that time they were living in Harveststile Cottage, Pentney.

Poaching

Frederick Rolfe (29) labourer, Marham, was charged with having taken two pheasants on land in the occupation of Thomas Paw, Pentney at 5.30 pm on the 7ᵗʰ inst. Defendant who pleaded guilty was committed for a month at the expiration of which time he is to be bound in £10 and to find 2 sureties of £5 each, to be of good behaviour for 12 months.

Grimston Petty Sessions, December 1891, reported in the *Lynn Advertiser*

Despite Fred declaring from time to time that he never did any crime other than poaching, the following Court reports tells a different story:

Frederick Rolfe

Frederick Rolfe of Marham was brought up in custody charged with stealing five stone weight of engine coals on the 20ᵗʰ inst., at Marham, the property of Mr George Heading. Charles Reeve deposed that he was the farm bailiff for Mr George Heading of Thornham. Coals were kept in the yard at Marham. He had missed a quantity and marked some, and from these marks he identified the coals shown him by the police constables. Police-constable Bone said he and Police-constable Pratt were watching on the 20ᵗʰ inst and about 11.30 he saw the prisoner put some coals into a bag, which he placed on his back. Witness turned his lamp on prisoner when within two yards, and he dropped the bag and ran away. Witness and Police-constable Pratt then watched prisoners house, and about 1.30 the prisoner returned and they arrested him. His coat and hands were quite black. Police-constable Pratt corroborated last witness. Prisoner, who pleaded not quilty, was fined £1, being given 14 days to pay, but on leaving the Court was arrested on the charge of felony in another division.

Downham Petty Session, 27 February 1892 reported in the *Norfolk News*

Stealing Fowls etc.

Frederick Rolfe (29) labourer, Marham, was charged by Inspector Baldwin, with having stolen 2 hens, a blacksmiths file, a screwdriver and about ¾ lb solder, valued at 5/6d the property of Thomas Paul, farmer Pentney on 21ˢᵗ February.

James William Dye, blacksmith in the employ of Mr Paul, said the smiths shop was in the yard, about 50 yards from the dwelling house. On Saturday 20ᵗʰ ult. The witness locked up the shop at noon and took the key into the dairy, where it was always kept. On Sunday 21ˢᵗ ult. two policemen came to witnesses, and he got the key out of the dairy, unlocked the shop and went to the box where he kept his tools. It was unlocked although the witness had left it locked. Upon looking into it witness missed the three edged file produced by P.C. Pratt which he left on the box on Thursday. Witness looked round the shop and noticing the ashes on the forge, saw the marks of cord trousers, a man's knuckles and the impression of two knees. Near the ashes and above them to the right of the forge was a hole in the wall 18 inches square, and 2 feet from the ground opening into the shoeing shop. This hole was about level with the forge and over it were two bags to keep out the wind. One of these was on the ground, and the other in its place. [By the chairman] Anyone could easily lift the bags and get into the building [witness continued] On the following Monday he looked about the shop again, and missed from the box a screwdriver and the solder produced by Pratt. They were witness's master's property. He knew the file by the handle, which he had made out of a piece of alder. The screw driver, he identified he made it out of a file, and could see the file marks upon it. He knew the solder because he ran it in the scythe-back produced.

P.C. Pratt of Fincham stated that on Sunday 21ˢᵗ Ult. He was with P.C. Bone watching Rolfe's house at Marham, and saw the prisoner coming in the direction of the house from the direction of Pentney. He had a small pickling bag containing two fowls, which the witness took from him. The hens were quite warm and had their necks broken. Witness blew his whistle, and P.C. Bone came and charged Rolfe with stealing the fowls from some person unknown. Witness asked prisoner to account for the contents of the bag, when he said he did not know what was in it, and that he found it in Fen Lane

Marham where he fell over it as he was coming from Pentney. Prisoner was conveyed to Downham lockup wearing corduroy trousers the same as he now had on. Witness examined his knees and found the left one very black apparently with flue ashes. After taking prisoner to Downham witness returned to Marham to make enquiries respecting the fowls and finding no owner, went to Mr Pauls at Pentney, and showed them to Martha Stebbings who identified them.

On Monday the prisoners coat was hanging on a peg in the passage near his cell at Downham Police Station, and witness took from outside left pocket the screw driver and three pieces of solder produced. In prisoners presence witness showed them to Supt Mash when prisoner said "they're mine". P.C. Bone, Shouldham, corroborated last witness's evidence, and explained that the prisoner used the file to carry the bag on his shoulder.

P.C. Pratt (recalled) further deposed that at Downham petty sessions on the 22nd ult. The prisoner was convicted of felony and was fined £1 including costs, or one month's imprisonment, and was allowed 14 days to pay in. Martha Stebbings, formerly housekeeper to the late William Chapman, farm bailiff to Mr Paul and now living at Narborough, said she had charge of the fowls during the time she was Chapmans housekeeper. She reared and fed them and saw them every day five or six times. On Sunday 21st ult. Witness was shown two fowls produced by P.C.s Pratt and Bone. She identified them as Mr Paul's property, and believed that the other also belonged to Mr Paul. Prisoner was committed for trial at Norwich assize.

Grimston Court, Monday, 7 March 1892, reported in the *Lynn Advertiser*

Mr Paul was the farmer who employed Fred as a youngster on his farm at Ashwood Lodge. It is odd that Fred always stayed so close to home when committing crimes, as everyone knew him. He was not an unintelligent man, but all sense seems to have left him when it came to breaking the law.

Frederick Rolfe (Engine driver) was indicted for stealing two tame hens, one file, a screw driver, and 11 oz of solder, value 5/6 the property of Thomas Paul, on February 21st at Pentney. Mr F.K. North (instructed by Linay and Co.) prosecuted. Prisoner was undefended. One of Mr Pauls workmen left the things locked up in his workshop on February 20th and the next day on going to the shop he found his box opened and the tools gone. Prisoner was arrested as he came home carrying two dead fowls and some tools belonging to Mr Paul. Prisoners account was that he found the things and did not steal them.

The Judge said that if a man was found with stolen property and did not account for it satisfactorily, the presumption was that he was the thief. Prisoner was found guilty. The Judge said no human being could doubt that the prisoner stole those things. His excuse was that he was hard pushed. Unless he kept straight in the future he would not be dealt with mercifully. He must go to prison for two months and perform hard labour.

19 March 1892, *Norwich Mercury*, Press Report from the assize hearing:

This is the only occasion during the time when the family lived in Marham on which Fred went to prison. It would seem too early in the year to be the case where Kitty resorted to keeping herself and Emily by selling watercress. Perhaps a later case exists, which went unrecorded in the press.

An elderly gentleman who lives locally remembers large wicker baskets of watercress neatly stacked on Narborough railway station, ready to be taken to London. The cress was picked on East Walton common, where crystal-clear springs bubble up. Eventually this became the Trout Stream, which flows through West Bilney to Blackborough End, where it joins the River Nar. In London children of the poor, aged as young as 7 and 8, used to go to the market to buy the bundles of cress and then, from 6am to 10 am, and again in the afternoons, they would travel the suburban streets, calling, 'Cresses, four bunches a penny!' Perhaps they did the same in Manchester and this gave Kitty the idea of how to keep herself while her husband was inside.

In May 1893 the local paper reported that Frederick Rolfe of Pentney was summoned by Frank Kilburn, Inland Revenue Officer, and pleaded guilty to having kept a dog without a licence. He was fined 10/- and 7/6d costs. Then, in a further report of November 1893, he was charged on 14 November 1893 with having four pheasants and nine conies in his possession on the highway at East Winch. Fred was fined 20/-, with costs of 13/6d in default committed for one month. He must have chosen not to find the money as a note in Police records states that he was handed over to the Jailer at 8.35 pm on same date. A further note says the game was to be sold by order of the magistrates.

During this period, a farmer reported to the aforementioned PC Bocking that wood had gone missing from his log pile and so he and Bocking drilled a hole in one of the logs and placed a plug of dynamite inside. Several days later a large bang was heard in the village and part of the gable end of one of the cottages had fallen out. They had their man!

Pentney was an open Parish, meaning it had no squire, who would be the patriarch for better or worse. For better, in that those in the 'big house' tended to keep their estate cottages in better repair and kept the men in full-time work – at a price. The squire and his lady had a great deal of control over the lives of their cottagers and there are examples of the Lady from the big house giving out blankets to the poor, but insisting they were returned in the spring to be laundered and stitched into a calico bag for storage until autumn. If anyone was ill in the summer, it meant a trip to the big house for permission to unseal the calico! Clothes clubs were also run by the big house or the vicar's wife: cottagers paid into them and then received help to purchase new clothes – very philanthropic, but the catch was they would only release the money for clothes they deemed suitable.

At Marham there were several big houses, but those who worked for Henry Villebois, seemed to have been lucky in that he did care for his men's welfare:

> There was a Squire Villolas liven at the next villige, Marham it was called, and he would employ all he could. He would say to his Agent, 'Cant you find them men some work, clearing out weeds, draining or any thing, if not we shall make Poachers and thieves of them all'.

In the absence of a squire or landowner, most of the agricultural workers were hired as 'day men' (employed as and when needed), and if they were unable to give a full day's work through age or infirmity were paid half, quarter or three-quarters of a man's wages, depending on their level of fitness and ability. In the Pentney census (1881), Richard Butler aged 88 still listed his occupation as agricultural labourer. Only one man was listed as a pauper and living off any such handout thought fit by the relieving officer.

Writer G. G. Coulton said of Pentney that as an open village it was more likely to have high levels of poaching, where all the locals were involved, actively or simply by keeping quiet about what they saw. Being outside the influence of a major landowner, there were no tied cottages so there was no risk of being made homeless if anyone was caught breaking the law.

Several items in the press tell of cottages in the village being in bad repair. Lord Henry Bentinck MP promised at a Conservative meeting at the New Inn, Pentney, on 24 October 1891, to look into the matter of the cottage accommodation being bad, as raised by local labourers. Cottages tended to be owned by private individuals who each had a few properties and as rents were low, they did not see their way to repairing and maintaining them. Parish records, 3 October 1895, report that three of Crisps Cottages had only one privy between them, so out of repair that it could not be used. It was resolved that representation of the facts be made to Freebridge Lynn, Rural District Council.

Many of the village girls were in service before they married their childhood sweetheart, so they would have seen how the wealthy lived and longed to emulate them. But earth or flagstone floors, low wages, endless children and lack of running water made it hard to maintain any standards. Coal fires and endless mud made the fight against dirt an uphill struggle and even wood was hard to come by as it almost always belonged to someone.

There seemed to be very little entertainment for the women mentioned in the press – unless they went to musical soirées put on by the Church. One held in West Bilney in 1905 for church funds included Miss Sporne, who gave a whistling solo!

In the second half of the nineteenth century, there were four pubs in Pentney, although the Mill Inn was right down by the old Abbey ruin and used mostly by the lighter men (sailors), travelling up and down the river in flat-bottomed barges. At least the women must have been able to let their hair down and have fun after harvest when farmers treated their workers to a generous supper at the New Inn; the room was always cleared afterwards for dancing and singing.

For the men there were dog races, not only for pure-bred dogs, but for mongrels too, and sparrow shooting matches could also bring big rewards. One shooting match at Denver offered two geese as first prize and one goose for shooting three starlings. Quoits was also a popular pub pastime.

The highlights for the women seemed to be when the hawkers came into the villages. Not only did they have goods to sell, they brought news and gossip too. There were the men who came down from Scotland selling knitting wool and socks; there was the toffee lady on a Saturday. Once a year the Bible seller came – they checked who the newly weds were and sold them a Bible, though most could barely read. Every year thereafter, they offered to add the name of the newest child into the flyleaf for 1/-.

It seems that after the railway arrived in Pentney, houses were built nearer the station and Little Pentney, clustered around the ruin of the Abbey, fell into disrepair. There were as many as forty cottages within living memory; now all that remains of most are the garden plants running wild in the verges and apple trees, grown tall and sparse through the scrub. A few cottages, and the building that was once The Rising Sun (which closed in 1916) now remain. Once a year, Little Pentney men challenged Pentney to a cricket and football match on a pitch in Low Road, exciting huge rivalry. No doubt the women got to watch and help with the refreshments.

On 27 October 1846, the railway line opened from Lynn to Narborough. The line through to Swaffham opened a year later. Narborough was a pretty station and is now a private residence; it was built on the boundary of the village so not too far for the residents of Pentney, the next village, to walk to (the line was axed during the Beeching cutbacks of 1968). For a brief time, there was a station at West Bilney, but it was little used and closed quite quickly.

Not only was the station used commercially and for essential travel, outings for pleasure were taken as well. From 1884 to 1904 the West Norfolk Hunt ran steeplechase meetings at East Winch, three miles to the west of Pentney. They became a prestigious event, held either on Easter Monday or the Monday after. Albert, Prince of Wales, was president, but only agreed to accept the position on the understanding that the committee, '. . . would be particular about whom you admit to the club.' The Royal Family and their guests attended regularly from Sandringham close by until Queen Victoria's death in 1901. Pickpockets and tricksters plied their trade. Grimston court was filled with cases of such petty crooks after the race meeting. At its height about twelve thousand people attended Race Day, most arriving by train. Great Eastern Railway employees policed the stations along the way. Almost certainly, Fred would have enjoyed the day.

Between 1888 and 1894, Fred moved his family backwards and forwards between Pentney and Marham several times. For the first six years of her married life, Kitty somehow struggled on, baby Emily being her only pleasure, but then her luck changed.

CHAPTER 8

1894–96 Gamekeeper, West Bilney

Kitty and Fred's change of fortune is recollected by Fred in *I Walked by Night*:

> About this time a strange thing hapened, at least, considring how I got my living and the name I had, it was a strange thing to hapen to me. A Gentleman came down to Norfolk and bought an estate close to where I lived. It seam that the Farmers told him about me, and one day he sent for me to go and se him. Well I went and wen I got there what should he do but offer me the place of Game Keeper.

According to the 1912 sales particulars, the West Bilney Estate had 'first class shooting which may be enjoyed over the property in great variety. The light character of the soil is specially suited to the rearing of a large stock of pheasants and partridges. Hares are numerous, the Warren provides capital rabbit shooting and in addition the large area of marsh pasture land affords wild fowl shooting, including duck and a large number of snipe which breed on the land'.

It was to this estate that Fred moved in 1894, although to which house initially remains a mystery. There is a Gamekeepers Cottage, known as Forster's End in the sales particulars; that house is still there but is not as Fred and Kitty described their home. Two buildings on the sales particulars fit the bill as they are both called the Lodge, the name Fred refers to as his cottage. One on the main road, being the outer gatehouse, would seem unlikely to be the Lodge to which Fred refers:

> We were not much troubled with Gypsys were I was Keeper as we were some distance from the main road, but some used to camp on a comon about half a mile from my house.

East Winch Common is about half a mile away from the other Lodge and the Warren mentioned in the sales particulars is about a mile further on towards Pentney, both described by Fred in *I Walked by Night*. This second Lodge is almost certainly the one in which he lived. In the sales particulars of 1912 it was described as having 3 acres 0 rods and 17 perches of scrubland with the property, almost exactly the amount of land the Lodge had in 1972, when purchased by the author.

The then owner who asked Fred to become his Keeper was Clement Edward Royds Bentley J.P., who moved from Stratton Strawless, Norfolk to West Bilney in 1894. He became a Magistrate on the Grimston bench so would quickly have learnt of Fred and his poaching ways.

There are a number of cases where Bentley was on the other side of the bench. One is particularly memorable. In 1901, he took Jeremiah Riches, landlord of the Rising Sun, to court for placing a dead branch that had fallen from a tree on estate land in his empty cart. In court, Riches argued that as the branch was dead and unsightly he thought no harm was done by his removing the wood for a bit of kindling. The bench decided not to convict the defendant of felony, but stipulated he should pay damages and costs of 20/-.

Bentley himself appeared in the witness box in 1897 when his coachman, Robert Stevens, embezzled him. He had instructed Stevens to sell a horse carcass; this he did to the publican of the Carpenter's Arms at East Winch for 11/-. Once paid, Stevens had drinks worth 1/-, which he said Mr Bentley had told him he was allowed. He failed to give his master the other 10/-. Bentley told the bench that Stevens had mounting debts, with which he had tried to help him, but eventually they reached £30. The bench sentenced Stevens to one month's hard labour to run concurrently with a theft charge, because he had ordered goods on his master's behalf and had not paid for them.

Fred described Mrs Bentley in his book:

> She was an Australian Lady – took some pleasen some times, had been used to Black servants I suppose which made her so severe perhaps. I always managed to get on well with her, as she had one son, a weakly Boy about sixteen years old. He could not do the things most boys do, and it often fell to my lot to amuse him.
>
> The days that he could manage to get out I used to tell him about the things that I thought would intrest him. If I found a rare bird's nest such as the nest of the Crested Ren or long tailed Tit Mouse, I would

show him that. So I got on well with his Mother. The Master was not his father as the Lady had been married twice.

The 1901 census confirms Mrs Margaret Bentley was Australian, but does not show any children living at the Hall. Kitty and Fred's daughter Emily described the period:

Better Times

Now there happened to be a village just west of us, that I will call Bentley.

The gentleman who owned most of it, thought a good poacher would make a good gamekeeper, so he paid a fine for my man and gave him the job of gamekeeper on his estate, we moved to his place into a cottage surrounded by woods, it was very lonely, but we got on well there, the gentleman had married a widow who was very wealthy she had two children, a girl and a boy in their teens. They were quite friendly to me and used to take me and my little girl to the woods and we used to pick flowers and bunch them up and send them to Lynn Hospital. They used to bring my little girl toys and sweets very often and they would sit in my cottage and drink cider and eat my cakes just like one of my own. They used to give parties at Christmas and invite their tenants and their employees, we used to have a big Christmas tree and have a real swell time. They were happy times.

Emily's recollections, written over forty years later, show that the name Bentley stuck in her mind, only she remembered it as the name of the village, rather than her father's boss. Court cases of the time confirm Fred was a gamekeeper although initially he may have lived in Pentney:

Assault

Frederick Rolfe gamekeeper Pentney was charged with having assaulted and beaten Charles Hodgson, Carpenter and wheelwright of the same place, on 27th March. Defendant pleaded not guilty. Complainant deposed that he was occupied in his garden when defendant came along the road and said "What have you been saying about me, you Irish..............? Witness replied "I don't know that I have said anything; come when you are sober". Defendant repeated it several times, and wanted him to come out of the garden, but he would not, and went on with his potato sowing and said he would appeal to the magistrates. Defendant said "I don't care for all the ......; I'll shoot you, you Irish....... . I'll meet you sometime when dark".

After five minutes swearing and cursing he came into the garden. Witness held up his spade and could have struck him. Defendant "catched" him on the ear and knocked him down. Defendant's wife came and said "Come out" but he would not. Defendant said the complainant first struck at him with the spade, and afterwards got the worst of it, he only took the spade away from him.

William Riches gamekeeper deposed that complainant came with the spade and threatened to knock defendant's brains out, and defendant got hold of it, and in the struggle the complainant went down.

Fined 2/6d with costs 8/6d.

Grimston Court, 6 April 1894, reported in the *Lynn Advertiser*

Charles Hodgson lived in Webster's Cottages next to the Rising Sun public house in Pentney. It would seem Fred may have spent too long in there. Poor Kitty tried to intervene and act as peacemaker but as usual Fred's lack of judgement landed him in trouble. It seems that at one time he lived next door to the Rising Sun, probably in 1897. A recent inhabitant of the cottage had no firm evidence, but had heard this was the case. She had been told that an old chap had been known to lean out of her kitchen door (then a stable door), smoking a pipe and he was believed to be Fred; on occasions when going into her kitchen she detected a strong smell of tobacco smoke. Certainly Fred's uncle James Shaftoe and family lived there in 1881, as is shown on the census, so perhaps Fred and the family were staying with them.

Further corroboration of Fred's employment came from two more court cases:

Poaching
Frederick Chapman 19 Labourer of East Winch was charged with having trespassed in search of game and conies in land in the occupation of J. Clarke at West Bilney on Sept. 4th 1894. Frederick Rolfe, gamekeeper to Mr R Bentley deposed to seeing defendant about 7 pm with a little boy and a dog on a string. He afterwards loosed the dog and it ran two or three rabbits.
Fined 5/- and 9/6d costs.

Grimston Court, 29 September 189 reported in the *Lynn Advertiser*

Assault on a Gamekeeper
James Thomas Mitchell, 20, a labourer of Middleton, was charged by

Frederick Rolfe, gamekeeper, with having assaulted him at West Bilney on 23rd November and there was a cross summonses in which Mitchell charged Rolfe with having used threats towards him. Complainant said he met defendant and four others watering a traction engine at about 8am, and altercation ensued, and defendant said "I'll knock your .... eyes out" struck at witness, and afterwards gave him a back handed blow on the chest, "You................., you can summon me.

Witness dropped the hammers on the nipples of his gun, which was on half cock, and said to defendant: "If you hit me again, I'll put the muzzle of the gun in your face". The caps were on and the gun was loaded; he let the hammers down on the nipples for safety. The men started the row about some rabbits and a man named Chapman. The cross summons was then taken, Mitchell deposed that Rolfe first spoke, an altercation ensued, and Rolfe said "You long....... I'll put this through you: both barrels on full cock", and at same time pointed the gun at witness.

The Bench dismissed the charge of threatening, but reprimanded Rolfe for pointing the gun at Mitchell, who was fined 2/6d and cost 9/6d.

Grimston Court, 3 December 1894 reported in the *Lynn Advertiser*

Written in the margin of the police log beside this case is 'quasi criminal'. Mr Pilgram, a prosecuting police inspector in the days before the Crown Prosecution Service, who now works as curator at the Police Museum in Wymondham, Norfolk, advises that 'quasi criminal' appears quite often in the records and it would seem this was a note for Home Office statistics of cases that were not police brought; as in bastardy cases, which appear very regularly, or what we would now call 'family matters'. In the case of the altercation between Fred and Mitchell, Mr Pilgram's guess was that Mitchell pressed charges against Fred, and not the police.

Fred seems to have got rather above himself during this period. Before his elevation to gamekeeper he would not have been able to own and carry a gun openly – it would have been illegal unless he could show reason why he should have one and where he had permission to shoot with it. So it was with a swagger that he carried his gun into the Ship Inn at Narborough. Asked by the landlord to put the gun out of the way, he refused to relinquish his badge of office and an argument ensued. Finally the landlord told him that unless he put the gun aside, he would not serve him. In a fit of temper, Fred threw the gun into the corner, where it went off, causing a large hole in the ceiling.

1. The Old Lodge, West Bilney, in 2009.

2. The Bridge over the Nar at Pentney Mill, by Walter Dexter R.B.A. (1878-1958).

3. Grimston Court House built in 1881, where Fred often found himself.

4. Grey's Cottage, where Fred and his family were living in the 1881 census. This photograph was taken in 1911.

5. Norwich Prison while it was still located in the castle, as it would have looked when Fred served his first term of imprisonment.

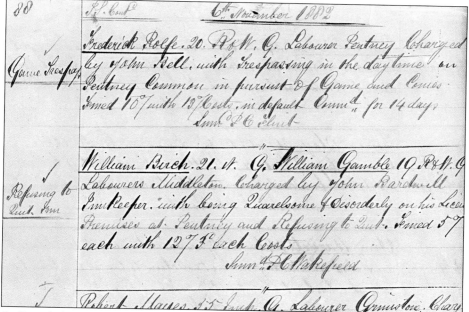

6. Record of Fred's first offence (top entry) from Docking Court Record, Grimston Court being in the Docking division.

7. The Oak tree in Narborough Park where Fred hanged his dog.

8. The Lodge in West Bilney, taken by Mr Arthur Taylor on 10 May 1892.

9. George Edwards, preaching from a wagon in East Rudham in 1918.

10. The isolated Freebridge Union Workhouse in Gayton.

11. Stibbard Memorial Cross, with the cottages where Fred lived with his family on the left. This photograph was taken in the 1920s.

12. Fred Rolfe (right) as Regimental Rat Catcher, holding a ratting stick and gin trap.

13. Roy Bulman and Emily Rolfe on their wedding day, 3 April 1919, at All Saints Church, Battersea.

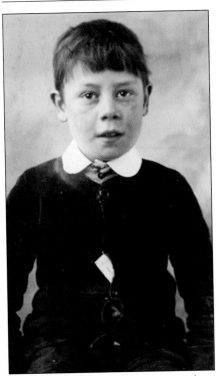

14. David Rolfe, taken when he entered Barnardo's on 20 April, 1920.

15. Bertha Rolfe, Fred's granddaughter, who lived with Fred and Kitty from birth.

16. Shipmeadow Workhouse, where Kitty died in 1925. It is now apartments.

17. Bridge Street in Bungay, as it would have been in Fred's time. His home at no. 7 is just behind the van at the end of the street. Nethergate Street is immediately to the right of the van.

18. 7 Bridge Street; the yellow cottage where the family lived in the 1920s.

19. Mrs Jessie Redgrave.

20. Clark's Yard, as it would have been when Fred lived there with Mrs Redgrave after Kitty's death.

21. Fred's home at Grammers Green, Mettingham. He lived in the lean-to with the tall chimney, originally the brew house, when he left Mrs Redgrave's home in the early 1930s. Painted by John Reeve.

22. Lilias Rider Haggard (left) with her sister Angela.

July 15. 29

The life and History
of the (King of the)
Norfolk Poachers
Riten by himself

I was Born in a small villige
in Norfolk of honest Parents that
would have scorned to do any thing
to ofend the laws of the land
I suppose there were some latent
sporting blood in me I was an
Only Child they brought me up
to Oner and obay the King and
all those put in orthourety under
him to Keep all the laws of the land
in reverence well I was sent to schue
till I was thirteen yearold but during
that time wen a boy about 9 years
Ago I was with father in the gay

23. The first page of Fred's book, *I Walked by Night*.

24. Frederick
Rolfe in
1935, when
he was
about 73.

25. Frederick Rolfe. This
was probably taken as
a publicity photograph
when the book was first
published.

Mrs. R. Bulman
Bradford R.R.3
Ontario
Canada

Feb. 27th 1956

Dear Miss Rider Haggard,

I wrote you some time ago, promising to write my mother's story. I thought maybe you could make a book out of it, sort of a companion to my father's book "I walked by night." I've written it from memories of things my mother told me about her early days. There were a few years which I don't know very much about as I was not home much from 1912 to 1918. In 1919 I came to Canada. I have also written a few of my mother's old songs that she loved to sing. Of course I don't know if you can do anything with the my manuscript or not. Maybe my father could tell you any details that I have left out.

I remain yours very sincerely
M. Emily Bulman.

26. The letter which accompanied Emily's book about Kitty's life.

27. 1 Nethergate Street, Bungay. Fred died here on Wednesday 23 March, 1938.

28. Some of Bungay's Best Snares.

29. Les Knowles, who came across Fred's body, standing with the author in front of the restored 1 Nethergate Street.

```
                         Ditchingham House
                              Bungay.
May 8th. I934.



      Received of Lilias Margitson Rider Haggard  the sum of   £20

  ( twenty pounds)  in full payment and satisfaction of all my

  rights of whatsoever description in all manuscripts in her

  possession relating to my life and experiences, and in particul

  to the book of Recollections which she is about to have

  published.


      Dated this day  9ᵗʰ of may 1934.
```

30. The document which Lilias Rider Haggard drew up for Fred to sign, giving him £20 in lieu of royalties.

31. Reverend Francis Kahn.

32. Author with David Rolfe, Fred's great-grandson, and his granddaughter Holly.

Fred and Kitty's daughter, Emily Rolfe, attended Pentney & West Bilney School. It would have been two miles to the school across the fields from West Bilney, a long walk in winter for a small girl. In one of the school record books housed at the Norwich Records Office few children are mentioned by name, but in February 1896 (when Emily was 6) the following entry appears:

Standard Children Absent by Reason of Sickness
H Butler, P Butler, Ellen Freck, and Charlotte Rix fever cases. A Wix, mouth affliction E Ramm and A Lambert other sickness.
Infants
J Parnell fever. H Wix, H. Ramm, B. Gilding and E. Rolfe other sickness.

The school log is fascinating. In it, the teacher lists the weekly topics she intends to tackle:

Pentney and West Bilney School 1896

1	28 February	A River
2	6 March	Grasses
3	13 March	Grasses and their uses
4	20 March	The Earth its shape, size etc
5	27 March	Flax culture
6	9 April	Silkworm culture
7	16 April	Silkworms
8	23 April	Pentney Abbey
9	1 May	Blacksmiths shop local visit
10	8 May	Bilney Church local visits
11	15 May	A Nettle
12	5 June	A Tree – Oak
13	12 June	Mining and mines
14		A Farm yard
15		Cast iron – smelting, wrought iron and steel
16		A sponge

The log also provides a fascinating insight into life at the time:

7 February 1896
Scarlet fever still prevails.

22 May 22 1896
Only 22 children out of a possible 124 presented themselves at the school this morning, the weather was wet and sickness being prevalent (whooping cough).

97

5 June 1896
Still whooping cough making attendance irregular, but housecleaning etc, has a little to do with the irregularity of the older children.

23 July 1896
Tues. Terrible, the children seemingly indifferent to everything. Sweltering as they sat in their desks.

27 July 1896 Diocesan Report
The children in this school passed a fairly good examination, but I could scarcely judge as to the extent of their knowledge as so many of the children were almost unavoidably absent on account of the weather. This fact possibly caused the scholars in Standard II to be a little below the mark but the paper work done by the 1st class was good as was also the repetition by the infants.
A.J. Groom Diocesan Inspector

15 July 1898
106 on books attendance 75, 30% missing. 1/3rd working in the fields, thereby contravening the Act.

3 August 1899
Several children went to Hunstanton on Monday. On Tuesday to Lynn to witness circus display; others have been engaged in the harvest fields.

August Bank Holidays used to be held on the first Monday in August so that is why the children had been to the seaside. Banker and Scientist Sir John Lubbock designed his Bank Holiday Act as a deliberate method of giving the general population, then usually working five and a half days a week, four days off each year. The bill went through Parliament easily, defining the days for England, Wales and Ireland, with slight variations for Scotland when the banks would close.

In August 1871 the first Bank Holiday took place. The response was enormous and immediate; special trains laid on failed to cope with the rush for the seaside. For most workers, paid holidays were rare at this time and the event marked the beginning of leisure time for the people of Britain, who were carried by day excursion trains to the seaside, rivers and pleasure gardens. They certainly used to have fun as races, regattas and fêtes became popular on those days.

Fred must have commenced employment on the West Bilney Estate in the spring of 1894. Traditionally, since 1752 the Lynn Mart started at 12 noon on Valentine's Day, 14 February, although the Fair preceding it began in 1203, so Fred must have been sacked in either February 1895 or February 1896.

But all happy times seem to end. My husband asked for a day off to go to Lynn Mart. He did not come back for three days, and the master got angry. I dreamed he came to the house and asked me where my man was and just as the dream foretold, so it came to pass. He came to my door the next day and I could not give him any information. He told me he would give him the sack when he came back. On the fourth day he came home and was very ill for a long time after it. He had gone into a pub for a drink and got drugged. His money was stolen and he had a bad time of it. Soon as he was able we moved back to our old home, but we only stayed a year. Then we moved to Marham.

Old newspaper reports tell of a long history of criminality at the Mart. In 1565 the Sheriff of Norfolk was informed of the 'sundry suspicious and lewde disposed persons who cutte purses, and notable thieves planning to meet at Lynne Mart'. To counter these gangs, the Corporation employed twelve male residents of the local almshouses to patrol the Mart, dressed in scarlet coats emblazoned with the town arms and carrying heavy staves. Other safeguards were also needed, and during the 1640s the Corporation posted armed men at East and South Gates and in the riverside lanes to keep out rogues and vagabonds trying to enter Lynn at Mart time. Originally it had been a market, selling all sorts of exotic goods, many brought by boat from Europe, but by Victorian times it was principally a fun fair.

On Valentine's Day the mayor and Corporation still follow the tradition that has been in place since Henry VII established the Mart with a Royal Statute and Charter: they and their guests precede the town's mace bearers from the town hall to the Tuesday Market Place and at noon the town crier clangs his handbell and cries, 'Oyez, Oyez, Oyez!' and the mayor proclaims the Mart open. Following a short speech, he concludes, '. . . and further, that all such persons as may be justly suspected of evil behaviour, do avoid this town, and the liberties there of. God Save the Queen!'

Carriers put on extra carts to bring in the villagers and many walked miles in their best bib and tucker to visit the Mart. Imagine spending almost every day in a tiny remote village and then having a chance to dress up and look at all the wonders that came to Lynn at Mart time. How amazed those simple country folk must have been at the sight of gibbering monkeys, lions and elephants. There were plenty of freak shows too, including Siamese twins, deformed animals, an India rubber man, the world's fattest lady, the smallest man, even a flea circus. It was all there in its political incorrectness. There were boxing booths and quack doctors selling remedies for absolutely everything. A girl was cased in ice as a test of endurance. There was a waxworks exhibition and stalls selling goods of every kind. What fun it must have been.

The *Lynn News* recalls that in 1845 Walker and Craddock wrote in their history of Wisbech: '. . . that the utility of the Marts and Fairs is now almost wholly superseded and those of Lynn and Wisbech have degenerated into a mere gathering of freaks of Nature, Harlotry Players' dirty exhibitions, conjurors, wild beast and ragamuffin life in all its gipseyism!'

Today, the Mart, with its gaudy flashing lights from the dodgems, the Waltzers, The Orbiter and the Meteorite, is still going strong. The amazingly painted fairground rides stem from the first merry-go-rounds made by local man Frederick Savage in his engineering works in King's Lynn.

The Mart was the first event of the showman's year and many a showmen spent the winter in Lynn, having the rides repaired and repainted. Naive country folk were easy prey for the pickpockets, conmen and gamestars, hence (if we are to believe him) Fred's coming a cropper is not all that surprising.

On the electoral registers for 1894 and 1895, there is no trace of him but in 1896 he is clearly shown as living in the Parish of West Bilney, having moved there from Pentney. The 1897 registers confirm him that he was living near the New Inn, Pentney, having moved there from West Bilney. From this, it would seem that he lasted as gamekeeper for two years at the most. At the end of the chapter describing his time as Bentley's gamekeeper, Fred recounts:

> My Master had some sort of trubble and had to sell the place and go away. It meant bad luck for me to as I was throwen out of my Job, and sorry I was for it.

Of course, this is complete fabrication. Newspaper reports show the Bentleys sold up in 1905. A consortium headed by Wyrley Edwin George Wyrley Birch bought the estate and lived at the Hall, spending a great deal of money updating the properties. The roof of the Lodge was raised and another room added to the side, making it the symmetrical and charming cottage that it is today. West Bilney Hall was demolished between 1912 and 1924 and stone was hauled from the old Hall, which had been considered outdated, to upgrade West Bilney Lodge into the principal estate residence.

Several pictures of the estate appear in a set of Victorian photographs taken by a Mr Taylor on 10 May 1892, one being the Lodge before it was improved and when the gate was still across the road. In the early 1900s Mr Taylor suddenly gave up his passion for photography and the photographic plates were thankfully bundled up and stored until they were donated to the town library where they were discovered in perfect condition.

Once more, Fred and Kitty returned to Pentney, where they remained until the end of 1898, and Fred resumed his criminal activities.

CHAPTER 9

1896–1904 Back to His Old Tricks

Initially the family moved to a cottage at the western end of the village of Pentney, next door to the Rising Sun, but by 1898 they were living in a tenement next to the New Inn, in the centre of the village. It may have been that Fred was unable to find work after he was sacked and therefore he returned to poaching to feed his family.

Theft
Frederick Rolfe (36) labourer of Marham was charged with having stolen a double barrelled gun value £1 the property of Maurice Wesley Brown, Pentney on 5th January. Complainant deposed that at about 7 pm on 5th January he hung the gun up in a shed, which was divided from the cart horse stable by a partition, and he saw it was alright next morning. About 2 pm prisoner came and asked witness if he had lost anything, and went on to say that he had had a job with another man: he (prisoner) had his own gun, and the man with him threw the witnesses gun into a pit of water. If he (witness) would say nothing about it, they would get the gun; the other man had a large family. Witness then went into the shed and missed the gun and found the bottom half of the stable door fastened in a manner different from what it had been. Next day he gave information to P.C. George who brought the gun to him at 9.30 the same night.
    Charles Welham, gamekeeper for Admiral Hamond, Westacre deposed that at about 1.30 a.m. he took the gun from the prisoner. P.C. George deposed that when he arrested prisoner, he said he was guilty. He was further charged by Charles Welham, with entering a wood at East Walton with a gun, for the purpose of taking game on 5th January.
    Complainant deposed that he was watching with his two sons and another man, and at 12.30 they heard two reports and then another and they went into the wood. Witness took gun from the prisoner but found no game on him.

Previous convictions having been proved prisoner was sentenced to 2 months hard labour for stealing the gun, and 1 month for night poaching. 3 months in all, and at the expiration of that term to be bound himself in £10 and two sureties for £5 each to be of good behaviour for 12 months.

Grimston Petty Sessions, January 1898, reported in the *Lynn Advertiser*

Those sureties must have been lost because ten months later, Fred was back in court again:

Charge of Assault

Frederick Rolfe of Marham, labourer was charged with assaulting George Thompson on 3rd October. Complainant said he was in the Greyhound public house on the night in question, and defendant who was the worse for drink came outside, struck him in the face and knocked him down. Witness gave defendant no provocation. Frank Peake corroborated. Defendant stated that he was dressed up like a nigger and they had all been having a bit of fun together. Complainant and his witness pulled hold of his (defendants) coat and "framed" in front of him, and he struck complainant in self-defence because he thought he was going to be struck himself. Fined 2/6d and 15/- costs.

Downham Market Petty Sessions, 3 October 189, reported in the *Lynn Advertiser*

And again:

Drunk and Disorderly

Frederick Rolfe of Marham labourer was summonsed by P.C. Bone for being drunk and disorderly on the highway on September 13th. P.C. Bone gave evidence and stated that defendant threatened to set a dog on him if he interfered with him. Fined 5/- and 9/- costs.

Downham Petty Sessions, 13 October 1898, reported in the *Lynn Advertiser*

And this:

A Dangerous Dog

Frederick Rolfe of Marham, Labourer was charged by P.C. Bone with being the owner of a dangerous dog which was not kept under proper control. William Billing said he went up defendant's yard about a month ago and the dog flew at him, but he managed to keep it off so that it did not bite him. Mary Pack said the dog ran for her about the middle of August when she lived next door to the defendant, and she ran into the house and shut the door. Defendant said no one had ever complained to him about the dog being dangerous. It lay about the yard, and children played with it. The bench made an order that the dog be kept under proper control, defendant to pay 12/- costs.

Downham Petty Sessions, 28 October 1898, reported in the *Lynn Advertiser*

In the Records Office at Norwich is a book headed 'Register of the names and places of abode of persons convicted of 1st and 2nd offences under an Act of Parliament passed in the 9th year of King George the 4th entitled An Act for the Effectual Prevention of persons going around by night for the Destruction of Game'. Needless to say, Fred appears twice. Do not think, though, that he was unusual in his constant appearances in court for poaching, Court records reveal dozens and dozens of men were regularly convicted of various poaching offences during this period.

On 17 March 1897, Fred's father John died of senile decay. Thankfully he and Fred seem to have been reconciled as the death certificate states that his son was present at the death. In *I Walked by Night*, Fred writes that his father is buried in a pauper's grave.

Did John's daughters come back for the funeral? His eldest, Mary Ann, was by now living in Wereham, Norfolk, with her husband, James Gilden. They had three daughters, Rebecca, Fanny and Catherine. In 1901, Rebecca was still living at home with her two illegitimate children, Frederick (born 1893) and Margaret (1899). Although Mary Ann's two other daughters had left home, by 1911 Fanny had returned to live with her parents at Flegg Green, with an illegitimate daughter, Florence.

On the 1901 census John's second daughter Rebecca and her husband, Richard Franks, lived in Gedney, Lincolnshire, with Richard's mother, Millicent aged 88. By then, their sons, Charles and Job (born in Holbeach) had left home. A third son, Richard, died in 1881 aged 3. Had they wanted to, the family were near enough to travel home. By 1911, they were living in Dawsmere, near Holbeach, Lincolnshire.

In 1901, Maria, John's third daughter and her husband, Daniel Wilson, were at Wiggenhall St Mary the Virgin (five miles SSW of King's Lynn), where he was a farmer. They too could have easily returned to Pentney. Their daughter Florence was still living at home and made a living as a dressmaker, having her 'own account at home'. Twenty-three-year old Bessie, their second daughter (name shown slightly differently on various records) married Frederick Chadd Piper of Saddlebow, a gardener aged 23, on 5 April 1899.

Florence too married a gardener: Edgar Harry Chenery, aged 33 of Wiggenhall St Germans, on 19 October 1910.

John's stepdaughter Maria and her husband Charles Mitchell moved to Kingston-upon-Hull in Yorkshire in 1891, so it is less likely that they could have made the journey back. In 1901, they were living in Sculcoates, Yorkshire. The couple married in King's Lynn Register office in 1872, Maria having lied about her age. Perhaps she was forced to, being unable to get parental consent. On the 1871 census Maria was living with her Aunt Liza in Walpole St Andrew, about ten miles from West Bilney. Liza had been Liza Stacey before her marriage to Edward Corthorne, another West Bilney resident, so possibly the Stacey family took Maria in, when Elizabeth remarried and she was alienated from her mother, perhaps because John was such a cantankerous man.

Whether or not they wished to return for the funeral of their father, it is sad to think the daughters may never have got together again after they left Pentney. They could all read and write so perhaps they kept in touch with news of their children and grandchildren by letter.

The 1901 census shows Fred's mother Elizabeth was a widow at 74 and still working. By now she was living at 1 Lynn Road, Pentney, one of a row of cottages on the A47. She occupied the cottage nearest King's Lynn. The cottages are still there, only now they have been made into one dwelling. She lists her occupation as a midwife, one of the skills learnt from her own mother Ursula. With annual confinements in most of the cottages, midwifery was a much-needed skill.

In *Lark Rise to Candleford*, Flora Thompson describes the local midwife:

The only cash outlay in an ordinary confinement was half a crown [2/6d, about a quarter of a week's wages] the fee of the old woman who, as she said, saw the beginning and end of everybody. She was, of course, not a certified midwife, but she was a decent, intelligent old body, clean in her person and methods and very kind. For the half-crown she officiated at the birth and came every day for ten days to bath the baby and keep the mother comfortable. She also tried hard to keep the patient in bed for ten days but with little success........complications at birth were rare but in two or three cases where they did occur during her practice old Mrs Quinton had sufficient skill to recognise the symptoms and send post haste for the doctor.

105

In these more enlightened days the mere mention of the old untrained village midwife raises a vision of some dirty, drink-sodden old hag without skill or conscience, but not all of them were Sairey Gamps. The great majority were clean, knowledgeable old women who took a pride in their office. Nor had many of them been entirely without instruction. The country doctor of the day valued a good midwife in an outlying village and did not begrudge time and trouble in training her. Such a one would save him many a six or eight mile drive over bad roads at night and if a summons did come he would know his presence was necessary.

The Midwives Act came into force on 1 April 1905, when all midwives had to register. Only thirteen initially registered in Norfolk, so the practice of using an 'Elizabeth' must have continued for some time. The trained district nurses, when they came, were a great blessing in country districts but the midwife of old also had her good points, for which she now receives no credit.

. . . She was no superior being coming into the house to strain its resources to the utmost and shame the patient by forced confessions that she did not possess this or that, but a neighbour, poor like herself, who could make do with what was there, or if not knew where to send to borrow it.

Many locals paid into the Narborough Nursing Association, so that if they became ill or disabled a cottage nurse was engaged to look after the subscriber to the organisation. Long before the Welfare State, this cost 2/- a week. If non-members required treatment from the nurse, this would cost them double and only then, 'if she was at liberty'. In 1908 there were thirty-five Narborough subscribers, twelve from West Bilney and fifty-six from Pentney. Use was made of one of the village charities in special cases of financial hardship.

The invention of the bicycle is said to have done more to reduce infant deaths in rural areas than almost anything else, because the doctor could be summonsed much more quickly if things went wrong. Another interesting fact was that more middle-class than lower-class women died in childbirth, because they refused to use the local village midwife, insisting the local doctor attended them, but because doctors were not so used to doing deliveries as midwives, fewer women survived.

By 1898 Fred and his wife had moved back to Marham and were living at cottages by Lion House in Abels Row and by 1901 in a

106

cottage near the Fox and Hounds, Fred working as a planter of trees. Poor Kitty was having a dreadful time of it. Fred seems to have spent a great deal of his time either in the pub or in prison. Money must have been very tight and Kitty got no support from the neighbours. Meanwhile, Young Fred was causing difficulties and she was surrounded by her husband's former in-laws:

> *A year later while the Boer War was on, a couple moved from a distance and came to live near us. The man was a meek and mild creature, a mere apology for a man in fact. The woman was a big Juno like creature, none of the other women seemed to want to make friends with her, but I liked to be friends with all. I had to go to her pump for water anyway and we became friends, soon she was visiting our house and me at hers. She got to know my husband went out nights hunting, she dared him to take her with him. He objected at first, but she persisted, and of course in the end got her way. I thought I had enough to worry about him being out, without worrying about the two of them, but they were never caught.*
>
> *Then I found I was to have another baby, when I told my husband, he was pleased, he had always secretly longed for a son. He thought he would be able to teach him his trade. He had a son by a former wife, but he didn't care for hunting at night although he was a good shot.*
>
> *When the baby came he was a boy, fair-haired and blue-eyed like his Dad. He made a great fuss over him so did my new neighbour, she had no children of her own. My stepson told me a lot of yarns, and set my husband and me to quarrelling. And caused me a lot of trouble. But of course he was young and thoughtless, and didn't realise what he was doing.*

Fred and Kitty called their new son Joubert, a most unusual name for them to have chosen because it does not appear as a Christian name anywhere. The most likely explanation for their choice is that their son was named after Petrus Jacobus Joubert, a commandant general in the South African Republic, who died in 1900 just before the end of the Second Boer War. Sir George White who defended Ladysmith during the war described him as a soldier and a gentleman, and a brave and honourable opponent – perhaps that appealed to Fred.

Searches through the baptismal records in Pentney and Marham do not reveal that any of Fred's four children were christened, so he would not have had to withstand the clergy's possible disapproval of his choice of name.

A court case on 30 March 1900 is a pitiful example of the treatment Kitty endured. What she said to the bench, which allowed the case to be dismissed, remains a subject for conjecture, but her humiliation must have been dreadful. The journey from Marham to Downham is a long one, perhaps eight miles. Whether they got a lift with a carrier or walked, for there was no direct train service, is unknown, but with the witnesses all making the same journey, it could not have been a comfortable one.

Threat and Assault

Frederick Rolfe of Marham, labourer, was charged with uttering a threat towards Harriet Ketteringham on 17th inst. Complainant said that while she was standing on her door-step, defendant took hold of her, shook her and said "Now you—— old——, I've got a good mind to stick this knife into your——old veins". Unpleasantness had arisen through some water being spilt on defendant's door-step. She had moved into another house a distance off, but was still afraid defendant would do her some bodily harm.

Ellen Mason corroborated. Defendant (on oath) stated that complainant and her daughter came on purpose to abuse him, and he argued with them who was in fault, at the same time holding the complainant by the wrist. Mrs Mason struck his wife on the face. Emily Pearman said she heard some swearing but no threats. Mrs Ketteringham appeared to be frightened and ran away. Witness did not see a knife in defendant's hand. Further evidence was given by Catherine Rolfe and the case dismissed.

Defendant also charged with assaulting Ellen Mason, who stated that she went to assist her mother whilst she was being held by the defendant and he struck her on the side of the head and on the eye. In reply to a question by defendant, witness denied striking his wife. Maria Pearman corroborated but Eliza Pearman (called by defendant) said she did not see anything of the assault.

The bench convicted, and the defendant was fined 5/- and 20/- costs.

Downham Court, 30 March 1900, reported in the *Lynn Advertiser*

Mr David Steeles Carter, Fred's first wife's great-nephew, lives in Marham. He cannot add anything about Fred but has helped to complete the family tree, which shows that Anna's two brothers remained in Marham, and took over the family wheelwright and coach-building firm from their uncle. The first mention of them in old Post Office directories is 1858, so the family have been in the village at least 150 years.

A respectable family, as theirs seems to have been, must have despaired at Anna marrying feckless Fred. The salt must have been well and truly rubbed into the wound when he brought Kitty to the village and continued to commit crimes while they raised Young Fred.

Frederick Rolfe
Frederick Rolfe of Marham who was summonsed for using a snare for taking a pheasant on 25th ult, said he took the pheasant out of the snare but did not set it. He was caught in the act by Robert Peamian (sic), a gamekeeper.
He was fined 10/- and costs 25/-.

Downham Court, 5th October 1902

One night my husband was out, he came home much earlier than usual, and he was very much upset, his dear old dog, who had been his helper for years, had picked up some poisoned meat and died before he could do anything for him. We all loved dear old Sam. He was a wonderful dog, could do everything but talk, and knew every word we said to him. My husband missed him terrible, he trained another dog, but never seemed to get him as good. He seemed to be getting better, then one night he killed himself by running his head against a tree and breaking his neck.

It is odd that both wives tell the story of the dog with the broken neck, or perhaps Emily has confused the details in her mind, after so many years.

In *I Walked by Night*, Fred explains his next actions:

After a little while the place got too warm for me, and I decided to move, and I kept on moving from place to place. As sone as one got to hot I moved to another, and so I shifted about Norfolk, but always carried the Game on to some extent.

109

CHAPTER 10

The Agricultural Reformers

Disappointingly, Pentney Parish Council records reveal almost nothing about the dispute Fred outlines at length in *I Walked by Night*, when he took on the village's great and the good. He was convinced they were not distributing the proceeds of a number of ancient charities, in the form of coal and blankets for the poor, the elderly and widows, as they should. According to the book, this caused quite a rumpus and it is odd that it was not documented in some way. Fred relates that at a village meeting he had the audacity to ask why the charities were no longer functioning. Not beholden to any employer, he would have been able to challenge the toffs in a way that men with one employer and a tied cottage could not. He tells of a lawyer, almost certainly Mr J. J. Coulton, doing most of the talking.

Coulton appears to have been on every committee in the village and is the only lawyer listed in Pentney on the census returns. Joseph Arch, M.P., may have made Fred aware of these rights. Arch advocated that charity lands should be used by villagers for allotments and wrote that labourers must have 'the pluck to move for themselves'. He also instigated ways to make villagers aware of the charities in their own particular neighbourhood. In the autumn of 1882, the *English Labourers Chronicle* ran a series of articles detailing the charities available in the various counties in England and advised how labourers should proceed to take advantage of the new legislation.

The Secretary of the Charities Trust confirmed the bequests Fred wrote about are still administered by the village, having recently been amalgamated into the United Charities. There is nothing definite to pinpoint when Fred took up the villagers' cause. A series of minutes from the Pentney Parish records offer a few possible clues. On 14 March 1898, a large attendance of parishioners is recorded and in the parish meetings thereafter are various references to charities, culminating in the clerk being asked to write and thank Mr Coulton for his kindness to the parish in securing money for the charity. It must have rattled the Church and farmers: they offered to pay Fred's passage to Canada, desperate to be rid of him, but he refused to be driven out:

> that did not sute me at all.

In the Record office in Norwich, there is a book called *An Account of the Different Charities belonging to the Poor of the County of Norfolk* (1811). Under the entry for Pentney, the charities are listed and then it states:

> *. . . but in consequence of the person in whose hands it was placed becoming a bankrupt, and no composition paid, these said donations were quite lost.*

Thanks to Fred it seems they were regained.

Fred was remarkably well read for a man of his background and upbringing. He talks in *I Walked by Night* of the cleverness of Thomas Paine and Charles Bradlaugh, both men with strong views about the freedom of the individual, and particularly the working classes. He may have been strongly influenced by them. Fred was also interested in their views on religious belief; he, like them, believed in a Supreme Being but not life after death.

Joseph Arch

Fred's greatest influence came from the men such as Joseph Arch who rose from desperately poor agricultural backgrounds to rally the agricultural workers. Joseph Arch was born in Barford, Warwickshire, in 1826. Unusually, he was born in a cottage owned by his family. In 1835 his father refused to sign a petition in favour of the Corn Laws and was subsequently thrown out of work for four months. His mother kept the family by working as a laundress. They were able to manage because they had no rent to pay. Although still desperately poor, Hannah's pride would not allow her children to eat the soup provided free at the rectory.

Arch went to school from the age of 6 until he was 9. He then started work bird scaring at 4d a day for a twelve-hour day. Throughout his childhood, he continued to work in agriculture, his mother encouraging him to further his education at home in the evenings. She also took him to listen to the Methodist preachers who toured the area. He married Mary Ann Mills on 3 February 1847 and the couple went on to have seven children.

Arch then took a huge gamble to work on his own account as a jobbing labourer. He could only do this because he was still living in the family home. Whatever happened, they had a roof over their heads and a large garden to support them. He became a skilful hedger and won many prizes for his craft at agricultural shows. His reputation led to him gaining plenty of work at high wages. He also organised gangs to undertake large contracts. Because of this, and the fact that he travelled round the farms, he was in touch with a large number of the workers and witnessed their hardships first hand.

By 1866 attempts were being made to improve the lot of rural workers and several associations and unions were formed, but without leadership and an effective nationwide administration, they had little power. The isolation of villages and the strength of the farmers meant dissent was almost impossible.

Joseph Arch came to prominence on 14 February 1872 when he was asked to head a meeting of over two thousand Warwickshire farm labourers angered at the plight of a young waggoner. When too ill to work, he was sacked and thrown out of his tied cottage. Shortly afterwards he died, leaving his wife and children destitute.

The men agreed to strike for higher wages, a nine-hour day and to form a nationwide union. Arch's rousing speech gave the men, broken by hunger and toil, the courage to speak out. He took his message all over the county, using his great oratory skills, learned as a Methodist preacher. On Good Friday, 29 March 1872, a meeting was held in Leamington to hear Arch and others rallied to the cause encourage the strikers and propose the conditions of membership for those wishing to join the Warwickshire Agricultural Labourers Union. Men tramped for miles on one of their few days off to get to the meeting. Feeling the pressure, many farmers gave way and agreed to the new conditions; those not reinstated following the strike were found work elsewhere and some received assistance in emigrating to Canada, Australia, Brazil, New Zealand or South Africa.

A long, hard battle ensued and Arch led an ever-growing number willing to part with a few hard earned coppers to keep the union going. This, however, was to be a double-edged sword: as the men's conditions improved, they left the union again. Although the by-then nationwide union eventually faltered, it was the beginning of a movement that George Edwards rekindled and took forward at the beginning of the twentieth century.

In 1885 Arch was selected as Liberal candidate for north-west Norfolk and stood against Lord Henry Bentinck. His manifesto included the abolition of the Game Laws, Payment for Members of Parliament, disestablishment of the Church of England, free secular elementary education, Sunday closing for pubs, arbitration to settle world disputes and free trade for all food. He gained a 640 majority and his joyous electorate hauled his cart through the streets of King's Lynn. On his train journey to Swaffham, a huge sign was hung from the carriage window, proclaiming 'Arch MP'. Going through Pentney the news would have quickly spread – but not immediately to Fred who by then had absconded to Manchester.

In Parliament, Joseph Arch MP continued to wear a tweed jacket and billy cock hat. His maiden speech campaigned for allotments and he asked, '. . . whether the time has not come when these thousands of industrious and willing workers should no longer be shut out from the soil and should have the opportunity of obtaining a fair freehold and producing food for themselves and their families?' The farmers were against allotments for they felt their workers would go slowly during the day to garner their strength to work for themselves in the evenings.

On 10 July 1886 Arch lost his seat by twenty votes. It is thought to be because the farmers had had time to lean on their workers, having been taken by surprise in 1885. He hoped for an early return to parliament when his successful opponent Bentinck was put on trial for breaching The Corrupt Practices at Elections Act 1883, but he was cleared.

By 1890, falling numbers meant the union could no longer pay sickness benefit to its members. This hastened the number of men leaving the Union and so the downward spiral continued. Following the 1888 Local Government Act, Arch was voted onto the first Warwickshire County Council. He did not re-stand in 1892, telling a Liberal meeting in Rougham in Norfolk, 'a greater farce he never knew', but he spent a good deal of time in Norfolk speaking to the labourers to regain his seat. This he did, beating Bentinck again in 1892, this time by 1,089 votes. In his autobiography, *From Ploughtail to Parliament*, Arch recalls that:

> . . . *when the High Sheriff saw the figures he was so much annoyed that he refused to declare the poll and the Under Sheriff had to do it. I then*

held out my hand and thanked him for the very able way in which he had conducted the count. He shook hands with me, then deliberately pulled his handkerchief out of his pocket and wiped his hand.

Arch won again in 1895, with an increased majority. The Liberal *Norfolk News* wrote happily of the Triumphal Arches put up for him. However, union numbers continued to drop and difficulties arose over Arch not being paid enough to survive on. To support him, the Liberals raised funds. Also at this time, there were spreading rumours that despite having taken the pledge, Arch was drinking heavily. His wife Mary Ann became ill and died in Barford at this time. Frances, Evelyn 'Daisy' Maynard, the Countess of Warwickshire (1861–1938), took an interest in him and published his memoirs – 'The story of his life as told by himself' – which helped financially. Of course this fraternisation did not endear him to his supporters. By this time he rarely spoke at Westminster and although he sat on the Royal Commission for the Aged Poor, he contributed little. It was here he met the Prince of Wales and they struck up a friendship.

In 1899, Joseph Arch announced his intention not to re-stand for election. Now 70, he was in failing health. On 27 December of that year he married his housekeeper and at the dissolution of Parliament returned permanently to his cottage in Barford, wishing he had done more about cottages and sanitation. He must have taken satisfaction in the fact that by now George Edwards had the National Union of Agricultural and Allied Workers up and running. He remained at Barford until his death aged 92, on 12 February 1919.

George Edwards
Leading campaigner George Edwards, a man much admired by Fred, is another shining example of how a child born in abject poverty can rise to influence a generation. While he struggled to the top, thousands of intelligent, uneducated men among the rural poor, including Fred, did not.

Edwards was born in even more dreadfully impoverished circumstances. His father Thomas had been a soldier for ten years, when he came back from fighting in Spain in the 1840s. Unable to gain work, he was once reduced to surviving on blackberries. Eventually taken on as an agricultural labourer, he was paid less than the other men; having been a soldier, he was considered less able to work on the land.

Thomas married a widow, Mary Stagman, whose husband had died of consumption, leaving her with three children. The couple went on to have four more children. George, the youngest, was born on 5 October 1850, in Marsham near Norwich. To feed his starving family, Thomas stole five turnips in 1855. He was caught and sentenced to fourteen days' hard labour.

Mary and her seven children were taken to the Aylsham Work-house, where 5-year-old George was separated from his mother. On Thomas's release, the family spent the rest of the winter at the work-house – no farmer would employ a thief. At 19, Edwards was snaring hares and rabbits, leading the adoring mother on whom he doted to fear for his future if he was caught. Fortunately, he went to a Primi-tive Methodist meeting and was 'saved'. He wanted to be a preacher but was unable to read. Charlotte Corke, who became his wife in 1872, taught him to memorise parts of the Bible and hymns and then to read. To buy books, he gave up his weekly 6d, put aside for two ounces of tobacco. Following this, he began preaching around the villages each Sunday.

Edwards also became an active member of the Agricultural Labourers Union. After work, he walked many miles in addition to those walked on Sundays to address meetings, his preaching taking precedence over everything else. Local newspapers began to carry columns of Union news and the word spread. At about this time, he met Joseph Arch and was much enthused by him. When Norfolk workers asked for a pay rise from 11/- to 13/- a week, they were awarded it and thus became motivated to even greater efforts.

Edwards had been working as an agricultural labourer, but as an activist it was difficult to find work, so he turned to brick-making, having first negotiated the right to a breakfast break.

Arch's Union petered out, but in 1889 the men of Norfolk again began agitating for a Union and Edwards was foremost in its renewal. Throughout the close of the 1800s and the beginning of the 1900s, he worked tirelessly to improve the lot of the rural poor. Meetings were often held in Cozens Hotel, King's Lynn – a temperance hotel, where delegates were paid their train fare, lunch and 2/- for lost earnings.

In 1893 he gave evidence to a Royal commission inquiring into the Administration of the Poor Law. Edwards was asked to speak on the practice of Out Relief, usually given in flour and money to paupers living in the area of the Union as Fred's mother had been before she married John. He was asked to comment on the quality of the flour and the amount permitted, and to question whether people should be compelled to support their aged parents. To prove the poor quality of the flour doled out, Edwards took a sample with him. The board was so appalled they asked him to have his wife bake one loaf from a sample of the poor-quality flour and another using good flour. This made the difference even more apparent and the Prince of Wales, a board member, expressed his shock at the poor standard of food supplied to the needy.

Edwards went on to state cases of poverty known to him. One, for example, being a widow with four small children, who only received support for three of the children, being expected to support herself and one child; this meant she received 1/6d and 21 lb flour a week. Edwards' own mother received 2/6d with no flour allowance and he was called upon by the Board of Guardians to contribute 1/3d towards the sum allowed to her. One man with eight children was summonsed before Cromer Magistrates by Erpingham Board of Guardians to show cause why he should not contribute to the main- tenance of both his elderly parents. When published, the evidence caused a real stir and was instrumental in hastening the District and Parish Council Act.

After he spoke at a meeting in 1895, Edwards' employer came to him and asked if it was true that he had been speaking out at a Liberal meeting (the Labour party was not formed until 1906). When he admitted this was so, he was told that if he wished to stay in his employment he would have to desist. Edwards refused, saying he gave satisfactory service and what he did in his free time was no concern of his employer. In his autobiography, *From Crow Scaring to Westminster*, he recalls that he said he would complete his contract for one hundred thousand bricks and then go, but his employer insisted he should go at once. When Edwards threatened to sue for breach of contract, the employer had to agree to him seeing out the contract.

The employer then victimised him further by going to the guard- ians at the workhouse, where he was a member of the board, and persuading them to reduce the allowance received for his mother- in-law, who lived with the family, from 2/6d to 2/-. When it became known how he had been treated, he was offered work with the Liberal party. This he refused but then had to take work six miles from his home, meaning a long daily walk.

In 1908 Edwards was asked by the East Winch Branch Secretary of the Union to hold a Sunday meeting on the Common, about half a mile from The Lodge. He only consented on condition the meeting be conducted on religious lines. It was advertised as follows.

Eastern Counties Agricultural Labourers and Small Holders Union

A camp meeting will be held under the auspices of the above on Sunday on the Common, East Winch. Services to commence at 2.30p.m and 6.30p.m. Addresses will be given by C Reynolds, George Edwards General secretary and others. West Acre Brass band will be in attendance. Sankey's hymns will be sung.

In his autobiography, Edwards describes the meeting:

> It was a beautifully fine day and the services were attended by over 2000 people. Such a sight had never been witnessed before in the village. The singing was most hearty, accompanied by the band. I took as my text in the afternoon The Labourer is Worthy of his Hire, and in the evening my text was Thy Kingdom Come.
>
> The evening discourse was fully reported in the Lynn News. This caused a great stir. Some denounced it as mixing up politics with religion, others said they had never heard the gospels preached like it before, and demands for Sunday meetings came in rapidly.

In a long letter to *The Lynn News*, justifying the meeting being held on a Sunday, Edwards' explanation includes the following:

> Christianity strives for the salvation of the world; so does the Labour movement. Christianity believes in the sacredness of the human body and soul, and endeavours to uplift all, to give all the opportunity to live the best of lives, so does the Labour movement. We are all endeavouring to remove the stumbling blocks to the higher life, to stop robbery, oppression and greed, and to make all feel that we are members of one another. So it matters not under what name we may hold our meetings to advocate our views; our motives, hopes, and depth of human love and will are one. When we say that that the individual must be an end in himself, and not a willing slave and tool of someone else, we are only uttering one of the great thoughts of Christ; therefore when we denounce a system or law that hinders the development of the human soul as anti Christian, we are saying what is true, because it is anti human and we justly claim that our movement or organisation fulfils in the highest sense the ideals of Christianity as taught by Christ.

A few weeks later the press reported a meeting held in Gayton, about three miles away: '. . . the village was *en fête* that day the occasion being the first anniversary of the Gayton branch of the Agricultural Labourer's and Small holder's Union.'

A tea was held in the Rampant Horse public house and a procession round the village was 150-strong. There followed a speech urging men to elect those in sympathy with their interests onto the new Parish, District and County councils. The band played at intervals.

On the same day a meeting of the Union took place at South Creake. The chairman said that it was melancholy for every man who had sons to think the best they could do was go to the towns. He suggested instead they lobby for allotments so that they had an opportunity to keep people in the country on the land, urging them to let the land keep them. The chairman was also glad the Church of England was in sympathy with the movement and the vicar had shown his support by lending them the room in which the meeting was held.

The meetings must have proved successful for local subscriptions increased by four in East Winch, sixteen in Middleton, Marham one, Gayton two and Pentney one. In 1910, George Edwards became the first Labour member on the Council of Freebridge Lynn.

During the First World War the cost of living rose sharply, but wages did not increase. Workers informed the Union they would strike unless things improved. Negotiations took place, with the men asking for 5/- on top of the 15/- they earned; a compromise was reached when they settled for 3/-.

In 1920, George Edwards became Labour MP for South Norfolk, entering Parliament in a suit borrowed from an opponent. Then, in 1923, the National Union of Agricultural and Allied Workers (NUAAW) won a major victory when Edwards led a strike against threatened cuts, which resulted in employers guaranteeing wages. Against this background, in 1924 he played a central role in the establishment of the Wages Board, which set a minimum wage. In recognition of his contribution to public life, he was awarded the OBE and in 1929 became the first farm labourer to be knighted.

In December 1933 George Edwards died, aged 83, at his home in Fakenham. His funeral was one of the biggest ever seen in Norfolk.

In *I Walked by Night*, Fred says of him:

His name and his memery will live for ever in the minds of the Working man. He knew the wants of the Worker, none better as he had been one of them himselfe.

Fred, it would seem, was not influenced by non-conformist religious preaching, but greatly admired the men who gave their Sundays so freely to spread the word. His childhood was steeped in religion, learnt from his father and at the parish church, and he knew his Bible well, but while he believed in a supreme being, he had no belief in the afterlife. Having heard the parson say that labourers should be content with their lot and make the most of what they had, he believed Church of England priests allied themselves with the 'nobs' and valued money for themselves, not what it might do for the good of others. Perhaps too he did not embrace non-conformism because of the abstinence from alcohol!

A poster published by the Agricultural Labourer's Union Movement entitled 'Cases heard at one sitting of a County Court Bench 1873' shows various vignettes of the plight of the agricultural worker and highlights what they saw as particularly outrageous injustices. George Major was fined 6/-, with 9/- costs for unlawfully leaving his work. The defendant said he could not live on his wages. His wife, a delicate-looking young woman with an infant in her arms, described their cottage as being in a miserable state and she had caught her death through it. As protection from the winter, they had to hang up three old grass bags.

Henry Ballard was fined 6d and 5/6d costs for trespassing in pursuit of game. The defendant said he hoped the bench would be merciful as he had but 11/- a week to support thirteen children besides himself and his wife. His wife was consumptive and she very much wished for a rabbit. The 'merciful' bench allowed a fortnight for payment.

A certificate, ornately decorated with a picture of Joseph Arch, plus scenes of farming life and the tools of the labourer's trade, was given to each man who joined the Union. It was perhaps one of the few things of beauty owned by farm labourers.

Having lived through this turbulent time, it is easier to understand why Fred behaved as he did: the agricultural workers had been repressed for so long that they used any method at their disposal to fight back, and the likes of Arch and Edwards gave them the skill and confidence to do so.

CHAPTER 11

1903–16 The Lost Years

Fred had decided that his usual haunts had 'got to hot' and felt the need to move on. The 1904 electoral register records that the family first moved to Tottington, a village just a few miles south of Watton, Norfolk. It no longer exists, having been enclosed in the Stanford Battle area in World War II as a training area for the troops, when it was mostly blown to smithereens. By 1905, the family had left the village. Kitty's biography notes:

> My husbands boss moved to a new district near Watton and took us with him that fall. I never saw Marham again. Without the dogs we could not do as much night work, he got the occasional pheasant though, my girl would watch them go up in the trees and tell her Dad where they were. But I am glad my boy grew up too scared to follow in his fathers footsteps. My girl now left home and went into service. And I found it hard to make friends in the new district we were now in. The man who employed my husband had bad luck and committed suicide, so we moved again to another district near Walsingham and Fakenham.

Exact information over the next twelve years has been difficult to find. The next factual piece of evidence shows that Emily (20) gave birth to an illegitimate daughter Bertha on 20 July 1909, at Walsingham Hostel, Great Snoring; this was part of the workhouse. On the birth certificate, Emily is shown as being a domestic servant at Toftrees, which would fall into the Walsingham Poor Law Union catchment area, being about six miles away. Although there is no father named on the certificate, it was said by the family to be a man called King, who was in shipping. There is reference to mother and daughter in the Minute books of Walsingham Workhouse, dated 9 July 1909:

> *Re: Emily Rolfe. This woman, now an inmate of the Union House, appearing to have a settlement in the Freebridge Union, the Clerk was directed to endeavour to arrange for her removal to the Freebridge Lynn workhouse without a removal order.*

In 1834 the Poor Law Amendment Act was passed. Until that time each parish cared for its own poor according to Acts dating back to Elizabeth I. During the Napoleonic Wars labourers were so poor it became the custom of Justices of the Peace, who administered the old laws, to add to the wages of the poor according to the price of corn and the number of children in the family. This meant farmers felt no need to increase wages. The costs of supporting poor families fell on the whole community and not those employing them, hence the Poor Law Unions were formed. These were groups of villages which joined together to build workhouses and offer outdoor relief. There were thirty-six parishes in the union that included Pentney and West Bilney.

Conditions in the workhouse were made deliberately harsh to discourage all but the destitute and it was proposed to abolish out relief for the able-bodied. This never transpired because the Boards of Guardians found it cheaper to give outside relief than keep people in the workhouse. In 1846 there were 1,331,000 paupers in England, of whom only 199,000 were to be found in the workhouse, leaving over a million in the community, of whom it is estimated a quarter were able-bodied, so the workhouses became in the main a home for the old, the young, the sick and the mentally ill. Tramps also used them as overnight accommodation and were housed and treated in a different way. Over time the regime softened, though the horror and stigma did not.

At the Freebridge Union Workhouse the Board of Guardians met weekly and recorded in their minutes: 'Outdoor relief was allowed to the under mentioned able-bodied male persons on account of sickness, or infirmity as reported by the medical officers'. On 30 March 1860, Robert Wing, brother of John Rolfe's first wife, was given relief, being unable to work because of a frozen hand. It is not recorded whether he received any help the following week so, presumably to feed his family, he had to return to work.

James Shaftoe, Fred's maternal uncle, applied successfully four times between 1860 and 1864 for rheumatism, a bad cold, his boy being unwell and bronchitis. By then he had six dependant children (two more were lost in infancy). Other applicants received relief for having boils, a wife being unwell, a wife confined and a rupture, among other ailments.

The minutes show fewer pleas for support in the summer and it was rare for a person to receive money a second week. Other snippets portray a kinder side. The workhouse minutes also reveal trips to the seaside for the children, the infirm and imbeciles, plus gifts of flowers, snuff, books, tea and tobacco. The Sandringham Estate sent over hampers of rabbits. Ironic, really, when quite possibly women were in the house because their husbands were in prison for poaching rabbits and the Royal estate sent unwanted rabbits to feed them.

In the 1980s Downham Market workhouse spent 2/- a week on wine, and brandy was regularly purchased. It was said, though, that if the workhouse gave you brandy you had less than three hours to live. On the inventory was a gallon of cod liver oil and oakum for picking, value £5 2s 3d. At Downham abstainers at a meeting of the Board of Guardians tried to argue that the half a pint of beer given to the inmates after Christmas lunch should cease. There followed a long debate, during which it was pointed out that non-alcoholic beverages were also offered and that a half pint of beer was hardly likely to lead to unruly conduct. After a vote it was decided that the Christmas tipple could remain.

Poor Eliza Barlow's case was reported in the local paper in 1891. She threw a stone at another inmate, which did little harm. Despite being described as a half-wit, who had spent thirty of her forty-one years in the workhouse, she was sentenced to ten days' imprisonment. In the *Magisterial Formulist*, which sets out the Forms and Precedents needed by magistrates, their clerks, attorneys and constables, more than thirty offences in workhouses were listed in 1876. They included not being allowed to play cards, climb the boundary walls, refuse to wash or pretend to be sick.

The Master of the House had some powers of punishment himself. At an inquest into the death of Eliza West, 71, of Wisbech Workhouse, it was reported she was constantly rude and disruptive. As a punishment, she was made to spend time alone in the refectory, where she had a meal of bread and water. Clearly this did not calm her for one day soon after her day in solitary confinement, she was again found in a violent temper. She was placed in the vagrant's ward to spend the day alone and there she hanged herself.

The coroner called for rules governing the masters' powers and found that Article 30 under the Consolidated Order gave the master power to punish a pauper subject to certain conditions – for example, to be confined alone for a maximum of twenty-four hours. The jury returned a verdict of suicide while temporarily insane. The master, though, was always answerable to his Board of Guardians and in one set of minutes the master at Downham asked if the weekly stock take could be moved from its regular Friday spot to another day, Friday being Christmas Day. After debate it was agreed that the master could do so late on the Thursday evening: Christmas Eve.

There are many reports in local papers at the time of the elderly killing themselves. The future must have looked very bleak when their health started to fail, particularly if they had no family to support them. Even if they did have family, these young adults would quite likely have large broods of their own to feed and clothe, so would have nothing over to support their parents. If the parent went to the workhouse, the family was still expected to contribute to their upkeep. James Wallis of Gayton was brought before Grimston Bench summonsed by Mr Maltby, Relieving Officer for Freebridge Union, for non-payment of maintenance for his mother. He was ordered to pay 1/- a week and 20/- costs (about two weeks' wages). The defendant produced his father's will and endeavoured to prove to the court that his brother was the one who should be sued.

It is amazing to discover how recently people had the right to Parish Relief and it was only finally abolished in 1948 when the National Health Service began. In a case at Grimston Court in 1905 against Richard Hammond, the Overseer for West Bilney, he was summonsed for neglecting to pay £68 10s to the Treasurer of the Freebridge Union, being the half-yearly levy made by the union on the parish and collected on their behalf by Hammond. The Magistrates Clerk stated the case had been settled, the money having been paid previous to the court opening. Hammond was ordered to pay 10/- costs. *Kelly's Directory* for 1908 reveals that Richard Hammond was the general smith and grocer. In 1901 the population of West Bilney was 178, so each villager contributing to the upkeep of the union faced a sizeable cost.

The House also acted as a labour exchange: if a local farmer or tradesman wanted a lad to train up, they would go the workhouse and pick a suitable boy. Similarly, girls would become servants. Often children with no family to watch over them were harshly treated. As the regime softened towards the end of the 1800s, workhouse children were boarded out with families, who were paid for their upkeep.

The workhouse too was a place of confinement and in his novel *Far From the Madding Crowd*, Thomas Hardy tells the tragic tale of Fanny Robin. Fanny struggled back to the village of her birth to have her illegitimate child, so the parish had to take her into the workhouse and support her – 'She belongs by law to our Parish'. There are dreadful stories of overseers urging girls to keep trudging on to reach their own parish to spare their village any expense. Poor Fanny died in childbirth and was given a pauper's funeral. This paid for a coffin and 2/6d for the grave, but did not stretch to the bells being tolled because they were considered an unnecessary luxury.

Those who gave up agriculture to move to work in mills, pits and factories were incredibly brave. If things went wrong, the only place they could look to for support was their home village and most would not have had the means to return and take advantage of the system.

In 1890 a Miss Warne arrived at Freebridge Union at 4 am. Her son was born one hour later. When the workhouses first opened in the 1830s, pregnant, unmarried girls had to bear the ignominy of wearing a distinctive uniform. At Swaffham, they were forbidden to join the Coronation Dinner. Soon after their confinement the women and girls were put to heavy work. But if workers struggled on in life, they longed for dignity in death. In his book, *The Victorian Undertaker*, Trevor May states:

> *The greatest festival of all is perhaps the funeral. The poverty of the family makes no difference to their eagerness, and the little nest egg which a man has provided to help his wife through the first months of widowhood is often lavished within a few days of his death. I have known a woman have a hearse with four horses and a carriage and pair for the funeral and within two weeks have to apply to the Guardian to feed her children.*

To apply to the Guardians of the Poor for assistance was one thing, to suffer the indignity of a pauper's funeral was quite another. To escape from fear of this, many joined burial clubs or paid weekly premiums to one of the large insurance companies specialising in the work. In 1900 the Prudential had twelve million policies with an average weekly premium of two pence and an accumulated insurance fund of £17 million.

Returning to Emily Rolfe, the Walsingham Union persuaded Freebridge Union to take back their own, as can be seen from the following minute:

> Re: Emily Rolfe, Referring to the minute on Folio 489 the Clerk reported that an order had been given for the admission of this woman into the workhouse of the Freebridge Lynn, Union.

On 4 August 1909, Emily left Walsingham Workhouse with 2-week-old Bertha. Workhouse record books give no mention of her going to Gayton, so she must have gone straight to Fred and Kitty. In 1910, they were living in Swaffham Road, Toftrees. Whether they were living there when Emily was working locally is not known. The family had moved again to Moor End, Stibbard, by 1911.

Sixteen months later, on 30 November 1910, Emily gave birth to another illegitimate child. His birth certificate states that David James was born at 1 Old Swaffham Road, Gayton, the address used to save the children from the embarrassment of having been born at the Freebridge Union Workhouse in Gayton. The child was baptised on 13 January 1911 by F. Hicks, the workhouse chaplain. Emily and her baby must have remained until at least Sunday, 2 April as they are recorded as workhouse inmates in the 1911 census taken that day. Later, Emily left David in foster care in Gayton village.

Village school records do not reveal anything about David, but a number of entries give an interesting insight into life then:

14 January 1914
Mr F S Warnes, Master at the Workhouse, kept the workhouse children away as there was another case of scarlet fever in the village. There were so many cases of scarlet fever, seventy-one out of 106 pupils, the school was closed for eight days.

16 June 1914
Several of the children from the Workhouse have been boarded out, thus decreasing the number on the school register.

14 July 1914
Treat given to inmates of the Workhouse at Hillington Hall, consequently children from that Institution are absent today.

<u>March 1918</u>
Several children absent, sticking in the woods.

Perhaps Kitty at 40 did not think she could take on another child, or maybe they could not afford it: Joubert was by then 10 and with the toddler Bertha to look after too, Fred might have put his foot down.

In a letter dated 1988, Bertha wrote:

> *We lived in a small village called Stibbbard in Norfolk near Fakenhan.*
> *My Great Grandmother died in 1914. We had most of the furniture, it was very good quality, some oil paintings, two large Bibles, leather bound, with gold leaf inlaid on covers. In one of them, written all the names of the past generations. Everything was sold when Gran died, My Great Grandparents, lived in the next village which may have been called Egam, or Stiffkey. I heard the names mentioned.*
> *Also, I was told my Grandfather, who I was brought up with from 6 weeks old, was a black sheep of a large family, he ran away from home, as he hated so much talk of religion. He married twice, his first wife died in childbirth, leaving a son which he disowned. . . . we moved 5 times, before settling in Bungay. . . .*

David must have retained contact with the family for he recalls in correspondence to his son, also written in 1988:

> *If great Gran lived in the next village to Stibbard I feel that it is unlikely to have been Stiffkey, as by my map the two places appear to be about twelve miles apart, although it would have been possible for a journey by pony and trap. . . . to have a days visit given the right time of the year. Bertha would have been about 6 in 1914. I remember one occasion when I was taken to visit an elderly relation, whether mine or of the family I was boarded out with at the time I am not sure, the thing that sticks in the mind was the difficulty lighting the candle lamps on the trap for travelling after dark.*

He also remembered that as a very young child he fell into some water – possibly a pond – and was rescued from drowning by his sister Bertha. David recalled only ever seeing his mother once, and not surprisingly comments that they were not close.

David's night time journey may well have been to see his great grandmother Elizabeth, either in the workhouse on the outskirts of the village where he was fostered, or at her home in Pentney, about three miles away, for she died at the workhouse in 1915, when David was 5. Did Elizabeth enter with feelings of shame and fear, or was the bronchitis, senility and heart problems from which she would die, too advanced for her to be aware of her circumstances?

She was laid to rest on 14 November 1915 in Pentney churchyard, where both her husbands and her infant son Robert are buried. In *I Walked by Night*, Fred says that she was 97 when she died and he helped support her during her later years and buried her himself. In truth she was 88 and, like the rest of the family, she has a pauper's grave.

It was the responsibility of the workhouse to return the body to the parish paying the relief. However, Dr Humphrey, lecturer in Anatomy and licensed teacher of Cambridge University in the latter part of the nineteenth century, asked that bodies with no known relatives be given for anatomical investigations. The request was usually granted, with the overseers happy to be spared the expense of a parish burial.

When Bertha speaks of visiting her great grandparents nearby, this seems unlikely unless they were her paternal relatives, for the bibles and furniture belonged to Elizabeth. Although there is no evidence, it seems likely the family lived in Elizabeth's cottage at Pentney for a short period. This conjecture is born out by the recollections of Miss Towler, an elderly Narborough resident who tells of her grandmother moving into one of the row of cottages in which Elizabeth lived after World War I. Miss Towler has clear recollections of her family talking about Fred having lived there. For many years, the family had a washstand, which had been left behind in the cottage after yet another of the Rolfe flits.

There is much more evidence to support Bertha's recollection that they lived at Stibbard for a while. First, Fred's name appears on the Electoral Register there in 1911 and 1915. The Universal Franchise was finally extended to all men in the 1884 Third Reform Act. Before that, farm labourers were denied the vote, which effectively meant most of Norfolk couldn't vote. Until the 4th Reform Bill 1918 when the property qualifications for men were abolished, if your rent was less than £10 a year or if you were receiving poor relief, you were not entitled to vote, so perhaps Fred couldn't do so at times during this period. Steeped in the works of Arch and Edwards, he would have been keen to vote in the new Labour Party and keep the 'toffs' out.

Everything changed in 1918, when all men got the vote – along with women over 30. Extensive searches of the north Norfolk records and newspapers offer no more information about where the family were. It is hard to believe Fred had given up poaching; perhaps he was simply getting better at not being caught, as there are no court cases about him to be found.

Secondly, Fred's son Joubert's name crops up in the minutes of the Stibbard school manager's meeting on Friday, 4 June 1915, when it was recorded Mrs Hignett spoke of the frequent absences of Joubert Rolfe and it was decided to write to Mr Tuck, the attendance officer. Of the outcome, nothing is recorded, but as Joubert was by then already 14, he was probably taking work as and when he could get it.

A 90-year-old Stibbard resident recalls her father telling her about Fred Rolfe being a rat catcher in the village, especially at harvest time. When Fred moved into one of the cottages opposite the school, it is said he tipped the furniture over the hedge rather than take it piece by piece into the cottage.

Another resident remembers her mother talking of Fred Rolfe when he lived in Stibbard. One day, the village policeman came after him for a poaching offence and Fred escaped out of one of the windows at the back of his house across Mr Ashworth's fields.

Mrs Esther Green, a very sprightly old lady, confirmed that the Rolfe family lived in the row of four cottages in the village and painted a lovely vignette of the inhabitants. For instance, Walter Hutchinson – a baker who lived at the opposite end of the four to Fred – stank of noxious tobacco. Mrs Toll next door was little and fat, and next to her was a forces wife, with two little girls. The cottages were demolished in the 1950s and the rubble used to fill the village pond. Mrs Green also recalled another cottage out of the village at Moor End and she remembers her father telling her that Fred had lived there at one time (corroborated by the 1911 census). The cottages have recently been done up and received an award for restoration.

Perhaps during this period Kitty at last found a little contentment:

> Here the people were of a more friendly nature and we got along better. My little boy was now going to school. My husband secured a job as a yardman for a farmer. But he did not care much for the job, but managed to stay for a few years.

In 'Norfolk's Poaching Philosophers', Essayist D. England gives a generous mention of Fred when he lived in Stibbard:

> . . . *a man who knew him recalled that he was a dead shot with a cata-pult. He could knock the bowl off a clay pipe held in a man's mouth. A noiseless dexterity that was to serve him well.*

John Bromily, who has a keen interest in hunting dogs, poaching and folk lore in Norfolk, spent considerable time researching the life of Frederick Rolfe in the 1980s, including questioning a number of old men who remembered Fred. A friend of Bromily remembers going to Stibbard with him and poking about for information. There, he met a lady whose father had served with Joubert in the Army. She showed him a photo of Joubert and her father, but sadly he did not obtain a copy.

While the family were in north Norfolk, Young Fred remained in Marham.

> My other son, the son of my first wife, lay some were in France . . .

In fact, Young Fred never went to France as Fred led his readers to believe, but spent much of that time in Downham Market Work-house. The first entry in the workhouse Admissions and Discharge Book for Downham Union 1914/1915 bearing his name was on 1 June 1914, when he discharged himself from the workhouse. Only a week later he was back. Listed as Frederick Rolfe, a blacksmith from Marham, his religion noted as Primitive Methodist. On 21 August he again discharged himself, only to return a week later, destitute and sick. There he remained there right through to 21 May 1915, when on his own notice he left once more.

On 4 June he returned to the workhouse, under the column by whose order admitted are the initials RC and the note 'sick' once again. Was 'RC' a doctor or the overseer, perhaps? Young Fred left on 10 September 1915, again on his own notice, to return to Marham. On 19 November 1915, RC again sought his readmission and then tantalisingly the book ends and the next one is missing, so it is not known whether he remained at the workhouse until his death aged 32.

On 13 October 1917, Young Fred died in the workhouse. His death certificate reveals that he died of peritonitis and phthisis, like his mother Anna. *Webster's Medical Dictionary* defines phthisis as: . . . *a wasting disease, or consumption of the tissues. The term was formerly applied to many wasting diseases, but it is now usually restricted to pulmonary phthisis or consumption.*

He is buried in Marham Churchyard, a sad, neglected place. Many of the gravestones are completely covered with ivy, others illegible, the soft stone crumbled away. Even in the unlikely event that he was given a tombstone, there is no way of discovering where he lies or whether he left a grieving widow. Only two ancestors of Anna's relatives have legible gravestones: her grandparents, Garrod and Ann Steeles. In some censuses Garrod is listed as Garwood, just to add to the confusion.

It is surprising there were not more Steeles buried there – they are a family who lived in Marham for generations. Unfortunately, unlike death certificates for women, those for men do not show whether they were married unless the wife registers the death. In England, thirteen Frederick Rolfes married between 1901 and 1917, but none in Norfolk and only one Frederick Walter. Further research reveals he is not the same Frederick Walter.

Did Fred return for his son's funeral? Emily's manuscript says that when the family left Marham for Watton, Kitty never saw Marham again. The fares may have been more than they could afford. Perhaps Kitty did not want to go; Marham, Fred's in-laws and Young Fred had, after all, caused her nothing but trouble. It is sad to think Young Fred was buried in the churchyard when he gave his religion as Primitive Methodist. The chapel is still there in the village, but is now a private house. If Young Fred did not marry and have children, then sadly Anna has no descendants.

So was Fred misinformed about his son fighting and dying in France? As a blacksmith, Young Fred's services would have been desperately needed, so was his father yet again embroidering the truth?

CHAPTER 12

1917–18 Keepering Again – Briefly

In April 1917 the family moved from Stibbard to Flixton in Suffolk so that Fred could take up a keepering job on the Flixton estate. The logbook for Flixton County Primary School records that on 16 April 1917, Bertha Rolfe aged 8 was admitted from Stibbard School knowing 'absolutely nothing'.

Their grandson David joined his grandparents on 5 November 1917, having been left there by his mother Emily, who had failed to keep up the payments to his foster parents in Gayton and been forced to remove him. All his life, David had lived in Gayton. It is hardly surprising that by December of that year he was already in trouble with the teacher, who recorded in the punishment book:

> Clifford Brewer and David Rolfe continued playing and laughing, after repeated warnings, when teacher's back turned. Three and four behind slight.

Presumably this means he was lightly walloped on his backside four times!

The owner of Flixton Hall was Sir Robert Shafto Adair and Fred was employed as his underkeeper. Fred, Kitty, Joubert, David and Bertha lived in a semi-detached cottage on the estate called Wood Farm. Sadly it is no longer there.

Peter Catling, who now farms in north Norfolk, remembers his father Percy, a tenant of Sir Shafto Adair, being ordered to leave the army during World War I, 'to go home and grow food' on his father Henry's farm. Mr Catling also recounts the story of a shooting party held by Shafto Adair, at which Percy was present. The party was shooting South Africa Wood, part of Fred's beat on the Catling farm. It was his responsibility to place the beaters and see that all went well, with plenty of birds. However, Fred had been poaching the birds, so they were in short supply.

131

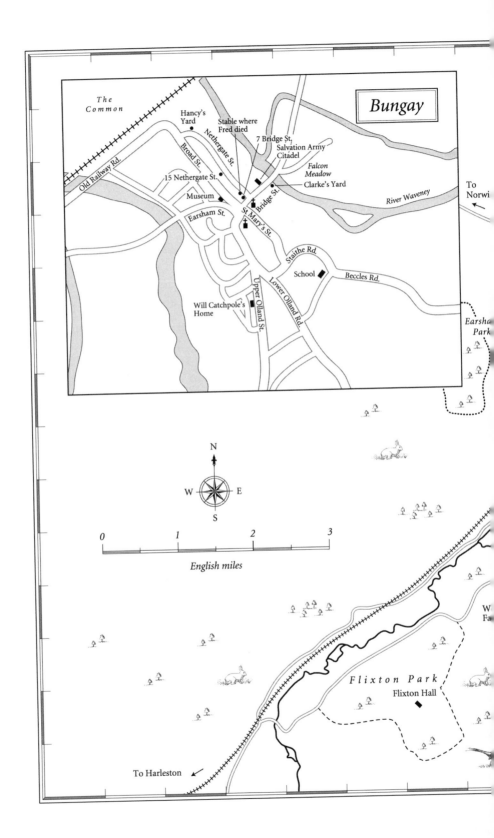

Bungay

The Common

Hancy's Yard

Stable where Fred died

7 Bridge St.

Salvation Army Citadel

Nethergate St.

Broad St.

Old Railway Rd.

Falcon Meadow

Clarke's Yard

15 Nethergate St.

Museum

St. Mary's St.

Bridge St.

River Waveney

To Norwi

Earsham St.

Staithe Rd.

School

Beccles Rd.

Upper Olland St.

Lower Olland Rd.

Will Catchpole's Home

Earsha
Park

N

W — E

S

0   1   2   3

English miles

Flixton Park

Flixton Hall

To Harleston

W
Fa

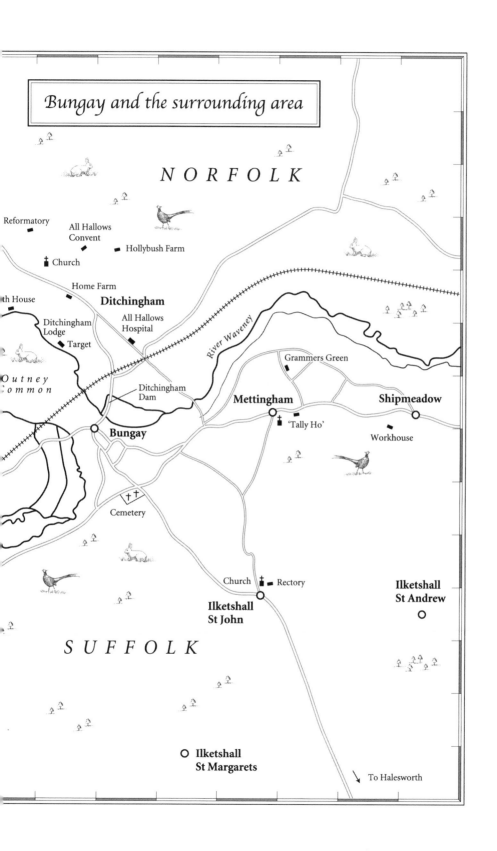

Bungay and the surrounding area

NORFOLK

Reformatory

All Hallows
Convent

Hollybush Farm

✝ Church

Home Farm

th House

Ditchingham

Ditchingham
Lodge

All Hallows
Hospital

Target

Outney
Common

Ditchingham
Dam

Grammers Green

River Waveney

Mettingham

Shipmeadow

'Tally Ho'

Bungay

Workhouse

✝✝

Cemetery

Church ✝ Rectory

Ilketshall
St Andrew

Ilketshall
St John

SUFFOLK

Ilketshall
St Margarets

To Halesworth

Sensing trouble but trying to prevent the finger pointing at him, he said in a loud voice: 'Where are the pheasants, Catling?'

'You have sent the beaters in the wrong direction,' was Percy Catling's reply.

To which Fred retorted, 'You know more than I do! Where should I have sent them?'

Percy yelled back, 'You should have sent your beaters around Bungay to beat the butchers' shops!'

The gentry paused to listen to this outburst and then moved on as if nothing had happened. That same night, gamekeepers from the estate caught Fred, at the bottom of the hill below the Hall, laden with pheasants on his way to Bungay. He got the sack, but met Mr Shafto Adair again, as he was a prominent member of the Bench, at Bungay and Harleston.

This event must have occurred in January 1918 because the Flixton school log records the children leaving the school on 7 January 1918, adding, 'gone to live in Bungay'.

Norfolk researcher John Bromily records that at this time Fred once again:

> Donned his crepe mask and his two game bags and calling his home-bred lurcher to his side, he set off on his nocturnal sojourns, this time in the company of new found friends, Charlie Hancy, Skill Biddle (in fact Bedwell) and Billy Catchpole.
>
> He was apparently resented by the townsfolk, partly for being an outsider and because his reputation as a poacher had followed him. He was to find himself before the Bench on many occasions for his trespasses, on one occasion offering to pay the fine when the pheasants came into season again.
>
> The old folk of Bungay do not remember him as being particularly well known for lurcher keeping, but say that the spaniels he bred and trained were second to none. This is not surprising as a gundog would be more useful in the retrieving of the higher priced pheasants than running down the lower priced game. Fred was also known to breed the occasional litter of lurchers, though. He always chose the Smithfield bitch as a foundation with a stolen mating from a greyhound dog, and unless otherwise requested would only keep the male pups as he considered them stronger and less temperamental than the bitches. It has been said recently that such a cross would be too slow for today's hunting methods, true enough maybe, but before the development of the spotlight, the poacher's dog was

134

only required to shepherd the quarry into a gate of longnet, or to retrieve silently to hand the odd shot pheasant or partridge. Charlie Hancy tells me that the best poacher dog in the Bungay area in his memory was a Smithfield cross Airedale owned by Billy Catchpole, who could outwit any quarry and most men besides.

John Bromily also related some other stories he heard told about Fred. It transpires the local gamekeepers found him easy to fool. They cut out some rough pheasant shapes and placed them in a tree, then hid. At dusk Fred, supposedly seeing the pheasant roosting, took a pot shot. When it failed to fall to the ground, he opened the second barrel of his .410 and they promptly arrested him.

Charles Hancy, who lived in Nethergate Street, Bungay (where Fred later lived), was born in 1901 and used to cart hay for his father – often to the barracks in Norwich, fifteen miles away, in huge wagons on his own at the age of 13. He often left at 1 am and because there was no traffic on the road and the movement of the cart was soporific, he fell asleep.

Mr Hancy says his only problem was with the police: he wasn't very old and they were always standing about, waiting to catch him asleep in the wagons. He was summonsed seven times in one year for being asleep while in charge of horses. On one occasion he and another lad had to attend court; he had just 12 shillings and his friend no money at all. Both were fined a pound. The next day he had to go to Beccles for a similar offence, but having no money left, he was forced to ask the judge for time to pay and granted fourteen days' grace.

He must have come across Fred, who was constantly in and out of court, according to *I Walked by Night* and local informants. In his book, Fred says that court appearances were all part of being a poacher – it seems he earned enough to pay his fines.

A successful poacher might catch a dozen or more pheasants a night. Provided the local carrier could collect them unnoticed and take them to the local town without being caught, the money was good. A cock pheasant would make 2/6d, a hen 2/– and so a night's work could prove very lucrative. Carriers were rarely caught as they became skilled at hiding the birds and avoiding police or keepers.

Fred had a pale lurcher and used to wrap it for work in black crepe. Spotted in the distance and questioned whether it was his dog, he could deny it and show his own light one. He is also said to have used the old trick of walking backwards so the keepers followed his tracks in the wrong direction and he wore white when there was snow on the ground to be less conspicuous. On one occasion he wriggled down a foxhole while pursued by the gamekeeper and his dog. The keeper, thinking the dog had smelt the fox when it nosed round the hole, called the hunt off and Fred waited for the coast to clear and then went home. He must have stunk!

Poor Kitty, each time things began to look up for her, Fred ruined everything. Yet again, she had to move, her own children, Emily and Joubert, were making new lives for themselves and now she had two illegitimate grandchildren in tow. Then Fred went off to war.

CHAPTER 13

1918 Fred's War

Little evidence of Fred's time in the Army during World War I exists other than that recalled by him in *I Walked by Night* and that is inaccurate because he says that he joined up in 1916, when in fact it was after he lost his job at Flixton in 1918, when he was 56.

> In 1916 wen they called for Volenteirs, I Joyned the 5th Suffolk Regment, being one of the first to offer myself for the Coast Defence Duty. They sent me with a lot of others to Bawdsey, Sir Quilter's place, and there made me rat Distroyer to all the Troops round Flextow (Felixtowe) and Walton, though I think I got as much game as rats.
>
> They were some of the best months I ever spent in my Life . . .

Kitty's biography reveals:

> *Then we moved again this time to Bungay. My girl was at this time in London, she could not get home very much, about once in two years for a week. But she wrote home regularly, sent us help when she could. My boy left school and went to work. Then along came that awful four years of war. I had taken a little girl to adopt by this time, she was a great comfort to me in my lonely hours. My husband was no coward, he joined the home defence corps, although he was over fifty years of age.*

Correspondence with various regimental historians and local museums confirms that the troops were camped in the grounds of Cuthbert Quilter's home – Bawdsey Manor, Suffolk – but no additional information could be found. Medals were only issued as a result of overseas' action and because Fred was in the Territorial Army and therefore could not be forced to serve abroad, no clues as to his time in the Army can be found in the lists of those who received a medal.

In *I Walked by Night*, Fred quotes some doggerel about a storm when all the tents blew down:

> Our Mr. Huddle the Clergyman
> Was in a dreadful Stew
> He found his sute case gone,
> His Gown and Wiskey too.
>
> Rawle the Rat man struggled hard
> Against the wind and rain
> To find his Boots wich he had lost
> His serch was all in vain.
>
> He had his blanket and his bed–
> But alas no place to lay his head.

A Reverend Huddle is listed in *Crockford's Clerical Directory*. It seems likely that this is the right man, as Crockford's only lists one. Alfred Huddle held the living in King's Lynn from 1907 to 1910 and from 1915 to 1924, he was at Ilketshall St Margaret, a village close to Bungay. Possibly the local vicars took it in turns to serve with the Territorials. Later, he became vicar of Ilketshall St Andrew and Ilketshall St Lawrence, again both near to Bungay. Further information seemed impossible until a letter arrived, giving the complete poem:

> The Storm at Bawdsey Camp
> (September 9th, 1918)
> by Rolfe the Rat-man
>
> *One night while we were in our tent*
> *– We thought secure and warm –*
> *We heard the moaning of the wind*
> *That heralded a storm.*
>
> *The ropes did break, the pegs flew out*
> *And all one side was slack*
> *Then Rowe on to the pole did cling,*
> *And tried to hold it back.*

But down it came, and flung him on
The boards of our wrecked 'home',
Prior through the door did fly
And out into the gloom.

Rolfe, the Rat-man, struggled hard
Against the wind and rain
At last he found the boots he sought—
His search was not in vain.

With blankets, bed, and pillow too
Another tent sought he.
There shelter for the night he found,
And fairly dry could be.

And Charlie Earl the signalman
Was forced abroad to roam,
To find a shelter in the huts
For he had lost his 'home'.

When in the morn we looked around
We saw an awful sight
For tents, marquees, and work-shops too
Had fallen in the night.

Here's luck to all the volunteers
And to our soldier boys.
Who would prefer a soldier's life
To home and all its joys?

                              But—
No volunteers nor country's call
Shall cause me more to roam
If after these three months I get
Quite safely back to home.

Pte F. Rolfe, 3rd Vol Batt., Suffolk Regt.

The source of this information is Geoffrey Earl, the son of Charlie the signalman, mentioned in the poem, who served with Fred. He came across the poem, which his father had jotted down in a note-book, when his mother died and it was passed down to him. It is extraordinary to think that Fred Rolfe, born 150 years ago in such humble circumstances, leaves such a paper trail of his life, and even more amazing that people have kept hold of these nuggets, which have enabled a picture of him to emerge. The two versions of the poem vary only slightly, and Fred was writing from memory as an old man nearly twenty years later when he wrote *I Walked by Night*, so the variation is hardly surprising. He must have changed his name to Rawle to protect his anonymity.

Geoffrey Earl said he had a photograph of his father and a group of his friends at Bawsey Camp. At the time Charlie Earl was 18, while Fred was 56. He remembers his father describing Fred as one of Bungay's old characters. Once the photograph arrived, it offered two possibilities as to which man was Fred, and it was not immediately obvious which was him; the answer did not lie in the men's faces, but in what they held in their hands. Fred, on the right in the picture, had a gin trap and ratting stick.

A poaching expert with knowledge of Fred, to whom the photo-graph was sent, replied:

> *The photograph is almost certainly Fred – the eyes are exactly the same as in the picture with the dog, and that almost shut-eyed, squint expression is so distinctive. The 'hook' in the picture is, I think, a hair on the glass plate when the picture was taken; I have looked through a magnifying glass and can see no connection between the stick and the hook.*
>
> *'The short stick would be hazel, and would have a knob on the end in his hand; this would make an ideal weapon for close-quarter rat control – light enough to swat rats with, and sturdy enough to probe the holes to make the rats bolt. Interestingly, the gin trap in his hand is in the set position: this would be a rabbit gin; the rat gins are a lot smaller. That said, it would hold anything, from a fox to a rat.*

Military historian Taff Gillingham added some background infor-mation: Fred was in the 3rd Voluntary Battalion rather than 5 Suffolks, as he states in *I Walked by Night*, which makes much more sense, given his great age:

> *The history is a little complicated, but here goes. Pre-1908 the 3rd Volunteer Battalion, The Suffolk Regiment, were men from the Cambridgeshire Area and, in 1908, 3rd Volunteer Battalion became*

1st Battalion, The Cambridgeshire Regiment. The Volunteer Force was replaced literally overnight by the Territorial Force, of which 1st Cambs was part (1st VB became 4th Suffolks and 2nd VB became 5th Suffolks at the same time).

When the war broke out there was already a movement called the National Reserve – basically ancient warriors who volunteered to serve if the country needed them. This gradually transformed itself into the VTC – the Volunteer Training Corps; basically a Great War version of the Home Guard.

Originally dressed in lightweight khaki-grey uniforms, these old soldiers and youngsters drilled with shotguns and outdated weapons. The Suffolk VTC had their own cap badge but later wore the Suffolk Regiment cap badge. By 1917, they were equipped with proper khaki serge uniforms and the final recruits wore the lion and unicorn badge (worn by the soldier on the left in your photograph – all the others are wearing Suffolk Regiment ones).

The Ipswich detachment was the 1st Battalion, the 1st Suffolk Volunteer Regiment, which makes them distinct from the 1st VB, who were based in Ipswich until 1908. However, most other battalions seem to have called themselves 2nd VB, 3rd VB, etc., which can be quite confusing. The Volunteers were disbanded at the end of the War (or maybe just before) and, as far as I know, have never been properly researched or written about.

Photographs taken at Bawdsey in about 1918 show men, not hard-pressed, being fed at long rows of benches, with tents behind, in a very relaxed atmosphere. Perhaps that is why Fred was so happy there – it seems strange for a man who so loathed authority to take to military life, but perhaps good food, warm clothes and companionship made up for having to toe the line, at least in part, for he admits himself in his book that he went on poaching while there.

Charlie Earl's diary of the three months he served in 1918 is punctuated with the food they had, which certainly met with his approval. For many poor rural lads it must have been the first time in their lives that they got three square meals a day. They also received medical treatment, warm clothes, hard beds and training.

The *Norfolk Register of Honour*, listing all the Norfolk men who died in World War I, has an introduction by Sir Henry Rider Haggard, a very moving piece in which he pays tribute to the 12,000 Norfolk men who gave their lives; tribute is also paid to '. . . all the crippled; all the sick and, what is sometimes worse, all the wrecked in mind.' Rider Haggard states that one in fifty-seven soldiers throughout the UK died during the fighting, but in Norfolk it was one in every forty-two. The piece was written on Christmas Day, 1919. What a poignant day that must have been – peace at last, but so many homes in mourning for those who would never again share in the joy of a family Christmas.

CHAPTER 14

1918–25 Bungay with Kitty

While Fred was away at war, Kitty set up home at 7 Bridge Street, Bungay, where she was to remain until her death. No. 7 was between the Post Office on the junction with Broad Street and the turning into Nethergate Street, about thirty yards down the hill. There were several shops and a barber's in that short row; their cottage was the last before houses in Nethergate Street.

My daughter came home for a short visit telling us she was engaged to marry a Canadian soldier. She intended to make her home across the seas after the war. After thousands of young lives were wiped out, leaving many young widows and orphans and sorrowing mothers the dreadful war came suddenly to an end. We couldn't believe it at first. But the fact that there was no work for young lads soon forced the truth home to me, my idolised young son ran away and joined the army. He was sent to Ireland for some months, then to India. Letters came at infrequent intervals. I worried so over him, I became ill. The doctor said it was my heart, and I would have to be careful.

My girl had married in London, then shortly after sailed for Canada. She sent letters telling of the wonders of a foreign land. Her soldier husband was a farmer, and she said women worked nearly as hard as the men, but she was happy. I can't say I missed her, as she had been away for several years earning her living. But my boy, my pride and joy in those wilds of India among the black devils, he was away so long I began to fear I would never see him again. He was in India six years, but at last word came he was on his way home. I was almost happy when he came, but knowing he would not stay long I had to make the best of it. My boy had become a man. He was stationed in England a year.

One day he came home and told me he was going to get married. He brought a nice girl to see me, we took to each other at once. Soon they were married they had a baby the first year. Then he was sent to China, he left his wife and baby with me. He was gone a whole year. Then he was sent to India without coming home at all. His wife joined him in India but I could not go. They has been gone three years now. I hear they will be coming home soon. Dear God let it be soon.

Fred and Kitty's son Joubert enlisted in March 1919. His military record gives a history of his entire career and includes the only description there is of him. The following is an extract.

Born Marham, Swaffham, Norfolk – General labourer. 5'6"; 123 lbs, chest girth when expanded 36"; range of expansion 3"; complexion fresh; eyes blue; hair brown; Church of England; scar from abscess on right-hand side of neck. Next of kin (until marriage) Frederick Rolfe, No.7 Bridge Street, Bungay.
SERVICE NO: 1036351

1919	5 Mar	Enlisted Norwich aged 18 years. 153 days as a Gunner, Royal Regiment of the Artillery. Signed for 6 years with the Colours and 6 years in the Reserve.
1919	6 Mar	Woolwich
	15 Mar	Driver
1920	19 Jan	Left England.
	20 Jan	En-route to India.
	10 Feb	Arrived India.
	29 Sep	3rd Class Certificate in Education
	30 Sep	Joined 2nd Norfolk Regiment at Lucknow
	28 Oct	Terms of service varied on transfer to 7 years before the colours, 5 years Reserve.
1921	31 Mar	28 days detention
	1 Nov	Iraq
1921		**WAZIRISTAN 1919–1921 Indian Service Medal and Clasp**

1923	24 Mar	En-route to Mesopotamia & Aden at Sailkot.
1924	9 Jan	Home.
1926	12 Feb	Extended service to complete 12 years Colours.
	6 Apr	Appointed unpaid Lance Corporal.
	16 Jun	Married Ellen Turner, English Spinster at Colchester Registry Office.
	19 Aug	Brought on establishment; paid Lance Corporal.
1927	13 Aug	Deprived of stripe for neglect of duty when in charge of a tent.
		Stella Rosemary born 28.7.1928
1928	28 Sep	China.
1929	13 Nov	India.
1930		Re-engaged at Sailkot to complete 21 years service.
1931		Exam passed 2nd Class.
	1 Feb	In civil custody in Guard Detention.
	2 Feb	Guard Room awaiting Disposal.
	3 Feb	Guard Room awaiting Disposal.
	5 Feb	Guard Room awaiting Disposal.
	6 Feb	Released into open arrest.
	27 Mar	Tried by District Court Martial and sentenced to undergo detention for 21 days for the following offence – Sec 40 AA to the prejudice of good order and Military Discipline – in that on 1st February 1931 carried firearms for sporting purposes without being in possession of a shooting pass. Confirmed C R Lerrott, Brigadier, Commander 2nd (Sailkot) Cavalry Brigade dated 27.3.1931. Sentence – placed in suspension under Section 57AA. Authority GOC Lahore District 16.4.1931.
	10 Apr	Released from Guard Detention Room.
	17 Jul	Sentence to be reviewed.
1933	22 Sept	Taken into Civil custody at Dalhousie on Commitment Order.
	19 Oct	Transferred to Gurdaspol.
1934	11 Jan	Acquitted and released from Civil Custody at Amritsa.
1937	2 Mar	Gibraltar.

		Long service and Good Conduct Medal (with gratuity).
1939	*31 Jan*	*Return home from Gibraltar.*
	1 Sep	*Mobilised.*
	11 Sep	*Made Will.*
	20 Sep	
		Embarked Southampton.
	21 Sep	*Theatre of War, Cherbourg.*
1940	*14 Oct*	*Posted to 8th HD Bn Royal Norfolk Regiment. Transfer to RASC – 46 Division.*
1943–1945		*Served in UK in various locations taking courses related to motor mechanics. Rank – Private or Driver.*
1942–1945		*8 Courses in vehicle maintenance and driving including on 3rd Oct 1943 a vehicle waterproofing course.*
1943		*Transferred to REME Posted to 7th Holding Company in rank of Craftsman.*
1944	*26 Mar*	**Entitled to award of 1939/1943 Star and Defence Medal.**
1945	*16 Jan*	*Refused inoculation.*
	29 Mar	*Permanently attached to 1st Bn DCLI*
	15 Jul	*Notification of Impending Release.*
Trade on enlistment		*General labourer.*
Service trade		*Vehicle mechanic class ii.*
Military conduct		*Exemplary.*

"this man has served with the colours for 26 years during which time has proved himself hard-working and very reliable. He is an expert in his present job (see above) and is an excellent motor trade mechanic. He is sober and trustworthy".

| *1945–1953* | *19 Sep* | *Reserve. Lived at 3 Colchester Road, St Osyth, nr Clacton on Sea.* |
| *1953* | *3 July* | *Military service complete.* |

Various things spring out. First, that Kitty would have seen Joubert shortly before her death in 1925, as Emily says in her tale. But she must have been wrong when she states that Joubert's wife and daughter lived with Fred and Kitty as Joubert and Ellen (Nellie) were not married until 1926 and Stella, their daughter, was not born until July 1928.

In 1988, David Rolfe wrote to his son, David Junior, about his uncle Joubert:

About Joubert a little more detail, he would be about eight years older than I. Joined the Norfolk Regt 2nd battalion early in 1919 spent a considerable time in India his wife Nellie and daughter were given passage there possibly about 1930, as at home at the time (I) was able to see her off. I recall some talk with a member of the Regiment who knew him, but not personally, he was apparently a bit of a regimental character, had a stripe once but managed to lose it, spent most of his spare time fishing, was sent home from India 'he shot a wog' the soldier said, apparently a not uncommon thing at the time. Name cropped up again in an article in the 'People' he had persuaded a queue jumping officer to return to the back of the line, it seems that he used the sharp end of a rifle, this was during the evacuation of Dunkirk.

The last I heard of him he was living at St Osyths, Essex, possibly working as a motor mechanic, I heard of Nellie's death sometime ago, through Bertha possibly about twenty years ago.

On 21 January 1965, Joubert died in Clacton-on-Sea, Essex. Bearing in mind that he had been court-martialled for having a gun without a shooting pass, plus the comments in David's letter, one wonders if Joubert had something of his father about him.

In *I Walked by Night*, Fred talks of going to Ireland in 1919:

I was tellergramed for as my son, that was the son of my second wife, was verry ill on the Currar Camp with newmonia, and they did not think that he would live.

A Royal Military Museum librarian confirms this is likely to be correct as The Curragh was the location for a summer camp for the Royal Artillery in 1919. Fred enjoyed his stay in Ireland after Joubert's recovery, looking up old haunts – he had spent time in Ireland while on the run in the 1880s.

Three weeks after Joubert joined up his sister Emily married Albert Roy Bulman, of Bradford Ontario; he was a soldier aged 28. The wedding took place on 3 April 1919 at All Saints Church, Battersea, London. At the time she was living at 7 Roydon Street, Battersea, and the marriage certificate lists her as having no occupation. It also gives her age as 28 – two years younger than she really was, and she has given herself a middle name: Frances. Fred's occupation is given as a gamekeeper. Roy's father is named on the marriage certificate as Jack Bulman, a farmer.

Albert Roy Bulman joined the 177th Overseas Battalion on 11 April 1916. His enlistment papers describe him as fit 5 ft 8 in tall with a dark complexion, blue eyes and dark hair; his religion listed as Methodist and he had no distinguishing features.

Emily told her children that she would send for them when she was settled in Canada, but despite them waiting excitedly for many long months and years, she never did. The Bulman family (traced by the kindness of chief librarian Liz Fenwick at the Bradford West Gwillimbury public library in Bradford, Ontario) are living in Cookstown, Ontario. Brian Bulman and his aunt, Marguerite Watson, both descendants of the Bulman family that Emily married into, were able to supply other information about the family and the life she lived with them.

Marguerite remembers that Roy (as he was known in the family) and Emily lived on the east side of Beeton in a farm on the south side of the road. Brian knows the farm still exists as he passes it when taking his daughter for swimming lessons in Beeton. On the marriage certificate Roy refers to his father as Jack, but Brian suggests that perhaps this should have been Zack for Zacharias because Roy's parents were Zacharias Bullman (1859–1951) and Sarah Ann Canham (1861–1934).

The couple came from Wicken in Cambridgeshire, England. There, they had been used to farming in the wet Fenland area and found farming on the marshes around Bradford very similar. Brian knew that Roy and Emily married in England and that they are buried in a cemetery in Newton Robinson (a small town west of Bradford). Bradford itself was quite prosperous – the railroad stopped there and the Holland river allowed access to Lake Simcoe and from there to the Great Lakes. After World War I, the marsh on the south and east of Bradford was drained and canals are now used for irrigation.

Roy was born on 4 July 1890 and he and his nine siblings grew up on the family farm where his father had an abattoir. He and Emily had no children together. Emily died on 3 January 1942 but unfortunately Canadian death certificates do not provide cause of death. Roy died in 1967.

The family then sent photographs and David Rolfe was able to see for the first time what his grandmother looked like; it was agreed there was a similarity between Emily and her father. Unfortunately it is not possible to tell if she had red hair, like many of the members of the Rolfe family. It was difficult to ascertain whether or not the Canadian family were aware of Bertha and David's existence, or whether they thought the family in England perhaps did not know and they were being diplomatic.

On being asked if he would like to hear about Emily's background, Brian replied: 'I think the skeletons and family warts are what make history interesting,' and so he was told all about David and Bertha, and a bit about Fred.

Game Case

At the Police Court, Bungay on Thursday, before Sir H Rider Haggard KBE Sir R Shafto Adair, Bart. Mr J Bedingfield, Mr J A Bezant, Mr R C Mann and Sir John Twigg KCIE.

Frederick Rolfe of Bungay, rat catcher was charged with two cases of game trespass, killing game on Sunday, and killing game out of season. Defendant pleaded not guilty to all four cases and denied being on the land. William Crickmore, gamekeeper to Mr Edwards, the tenant of Upland Hall shooting, stated that defendant had no right to shoot on that estate.

Alfred Wiskin, agent to Messrs W D and A E Walker, also proved that defendant had no right of sporting on their land. George Fairhead of Trinity Farm Bungay said he saw defendant deliberately shoot partridges on the land in question. Sgt Firman said he asked defendant if he had a game licence and he replied "No." He said he had a right to shoot vermin on Mr Greenacre's land. The bench decided to convict. P.C. Farrow stated that Rolfe used to be in the employ of Sir Robert Shafto Adair [he did not sit on this case] as gamekeeper. It was discovered that he was taking Game to Bungay. Witness stopped him one night and took four rabbits away from him.

Defendant was now fined £2 and 33/6d costs.

16 September 1919, *East Suffolk Gazette*

By 1920 it must have been obvious to Fred and Kitty that Emily was not going to send for their grandchildren and so they applied for David to be taken into Dr Barnardo's. Documents supplied by Barnardo's provide the following information:

David Rolfe

Admitted – *20 April 1920*
Age – *9 years, 4 months*
Date and Place of Birth – *30 November 1910, at Gayton Union Infirmary, Norfolk*

149

Religious Denom of Father – *unknown*
                    Mother – *Church of England*
If Baptised – *Unknown*
Full agreements, signed by Grandparents

PHYSICAL DESCRIPTION
Colour of hair – *red*
Colour of eyes – *grey*
Height – *4ft 3in*
Complexion – *fair*
Vacc – *4I.a*
Weight – *62 lbs*
Condition of body – *good*
Remarks by Medical Officer – *Vermin bitten. Teeth bad. Grade 1*

Application for the admission of this illegitimate boy was made by the maternal grandfather, Frederick Rolfe, 7 Bridge Street, Bungay, Suffolk, and the facts of the case were investigated by one of our officers.

The mother Emily Rolfe was a domestic servant and while in service in Great Yarmouth was seduced by a man named Frederick King. She gave birth to a girl in Walsingham Union Infirmary, and brought the child to the grandparents who kept it without payment ever since. Very soon after that she again got into trouble, and on November 30th 1910 gave birth to this boy in Gayton Infirmary, Norfolk. Nothing is known of the putative father. After this she went into service in London and boarded this child out with some people there, paying them 5s per week until 1918, when the foster mother said she could not keep him any longer. The mother then took the child to the grandparents, and for about a year paid them 5s weekly. She then married a Canadian soldier named Roy Bullman [sic], and went with him to Canada. He promised to adopt the boy as soon as they were settled.

Early in October 1919 the mother sent 5 dollars to the grandparents, but since then they have heard nothing from her though they had written several times. The grandfather was a vermin destroyer, and his earnings averaged £2 5s 0d weekly, the rent on his cottage was 5s 6d. He was quite willing to continue keeping the girl, but said he could not afford to maintain both children as he feared the mother meant to throw them both on his hands. He did not want to send the boy to the workhouse if it could be avoided. Many of the grandfather's statements were contradictory but our representative thought this was due more to ignorance than any wish to deceive.

Both grandparents were very illiterate people. They could not produce the

150

mother's last letter, or say where she was married or from which port she sailed. The vicar of Bungay, the Rev. Hawtrey Enraght, was interviewed but appeared to have little personal knowledge of the family though they had been in this parish for two years.

David was said to be a strong, healthy boy, and to have had no illness but measles. Application has been made to the Salvation Army Home, but they have no room for the boy.

<u>Relatives</u>
Mother – Emily Bullman [sic], married, last address RR 3 Bradford, Ontario
Father (putative) – Name and address unknown
Half-sister – Bertha Rolfe (10) with grandparents
Grandparents – maternal Frederick Rolfe 59 and Catherine Rolfe 55, 7 Bridge Street, Bungay, Suffolk
Uncle – maternal Joubert Rolfe 18, driver 257662 RHA India

Two uncles were killed in the late War.
David's reference number 90640.
His time in Barnardo's was spent as follows:
Admitted 20 April 1920
Margate 24 April 1920
Salmon Lane 25 September 1920
Boys Garden City 26 January 1921
Russell Cotes Nautical School 16 February 1921
To Southampton for Mercantile Marine 20 September 1926.

Barnardo's report states that David had two uncles, who were both killed in the First World War. Perhaps Fred invented them to increase the sympathy vote!

At first it seems unbearably harsh of David's grandparents to send him to Barnardo's, but Fred was by then 59, earning very low wages and already supporting David's sister Bertha. He and Kitty had obviously given thought to his future and being keen to keep their grandson out of the workhouse, they approached the Salvation Army but without success. In attending Barnardo's, David gained a career in the Merchant Navy and afterwards as an engineer, thus he was able to break out of the poverty stricken background, with its inevitable health issues. He went on to marry Kate May Banks in 1935 and the couple had two sons, David (b. 1937) and Richard (1943–2001).

Both sons had children of their own and all have been most helpful in revealing information about the family, many of them as red-headed as David himself.

David recalls his father saying that while at Barnardo's he visited two older ladies on Sunday afternoons and they could have been 'aunts'. He remembers they fed him better than Barnardo's did. Whether or not they were real aunts is unknown.

Reading through the Head Teacher's Minute Book for Wingfield Street Primary School, Bungay, the school that David and Bertha attended after leaving Flixton, this shows how commonplace abject poverty was at the time:

10 December 1914
Mr Watkins came in the afternoon – I complained of the great coldness of the school – he had on a thick overcoat & wrap & was warm & considered the temperature too hot. My little babies are many of them thinly clad and under-fed & a temperature of 46 degrees (8 degrees centigrade) is not right for them. The highest the temperature reached before they broke up for Christmas on the 18th December was 48 degrees. Buns, nuts, oranges and sweets to the value of £1 3s 8d.

21 January 1915
Susie Catchpole came to school yesterday without any dinner and bringing her little brother, as the sister was out all dinner time the child was crying alone. I sent the boy home with another child & kept Susie at school giving her some dinner. The sister came up to school and tried to get Susie away, threatening her with a thrashing. This morning the child came to school with a bruised eye. I left Miss Salmon to open school and took the child straight round to her father at Mr Botwrights. He denied all knowledge of the girl's cruelty and said she had never let him read the numerous notes I have sent.

I have burned the child's clothes and given her new. I have beseeched the big girl to see after her better. I have bathed her in school time because she smelt so unpleasant no one could go near her. This morning after receiving her father's permission I cut all her hair off, undressed her and found her clothes filthy and insufficient and her body extremely dirty and flea-bitten. The child does not remember being bathed twice. I did so in July. She is developing morally in a very sad manner due to her sister's bad influence & it is time something were done to remove these two young children from her care. Three sons are in reformatories.

8th February 1921
Florence Raven died of diphtheria after only 2½ days' absence from school.

Disease was constantly mentioned in the Minute Book. Then, in 1922, the school closed due to an outbreak of diphtheria and then came nits, scabies, impetigo and ringworm. Fire drills took place regularly throughout the period of World War I and the teacher felt the boys to be particularly unruly as their fathers were away at war. In 1918 a half-day holiday was declared to let the children gather black-berries: 9 cwt (1008 lb) were picked, which were sold at 3d a pound for a war charity.

Miss Larner was mentioned in 1914 and she was still teaching there when the author attended the school in 1956. David was admitted to the school on 8 April 1918 and withdrawn on 16 April 1920 with a note in the school log – *To Canada*. Did the poor little soul still think he was going to join Mum and Roy in Canada, when in fact he was on his way to Barnardo's? There was no mention of Bertha in the school log.

The family say that David only remembered hearing from his mother once, while he was on board a ship. He did not recollect the contents of the letter, but he did say that he had to lie about being illegitimate to save himself from ridicule and unkindness. The family also recall that he always referred to his mother as 'that woman'.

One of the good things about moving to Bungay must have been that it gave Kitty her first taste of town life since leaving Manchester twenty-eight years earlier. Bungay is not a large town – at that time it had a population of just over three thousand – but to return to streets with lighting and shops close at hand must have been a real treat for her. Bertha and David were at school, so perhaps for once she had some time to herself. However, although the house in Bridge Street looks quite small, Electoral Registers show that during the period from 1919 until her death in 1925, she always had lodgers – some years as many as three.

It was unlikely much money was coming into the house, although Fred would have had steady wages while in the Army. Whether or not he sent money home is another matter. On leaving the Army, he had various occupations including mole catching, a shop, gun repairs and tooth pulling. In 1925, he was listed in *Kelly's Directory* as a tinman – someone who mends pots and pans, and enamel washing-up bowls, etc. – and of course there was always poaching. It would seem he would turn his hand to anything to make a few extra coppers.

Bridge Street is the main route through to Norwich, so there would have been constant comings and goings. There were lots of shops, barbers, pubs and the Salvation Army Citadel, which was down a loke (an East Anglian word for lane or alley) only a few hundred yards from Kitty's home. Every weekday evening, services were held at 8 pm and there, she tells us, she found great solace.

Much of Bungay's history is associated with Outney Common, which lies within a kink of the River Waveney and it is where Fred poached.

Steeple Chase meetings were held on the common, every spring from 1888 to 1957. Everyone in the town turned out and certainly Fred would have been among them. In 1937 Lilias Rider Haggard wrote in her book *Norfolk Life*:

> One of the few lovely days this spring (they can be counted on one hand) and a very good day's racing at Bungay, marred by Intruder dropping dead in front of the stand. He was galloping queerly up the slope, and as he jumped the hurdles a local light, most wise in the ways of horses, shouted out, 'Get off him—he's a dead 'un!' a prophesy fulfilled within twenty yards.

Common Bailiffs included George 'Friday' Everett, the first bailiff, who took up his post in 1897 and who did the job for seventeen years. Alfred Barber was next, coping through the First World War while the common was used for Army manoeuvres and a Zeppelin dropped bombs, missing the Army encampment, but killing and injuring many cattle.

John 'Broomy' Baldry took over in 1931 and retired from full-time work in 1951 but carried on part-time until 1961. His journeys during the latter period were made in a cart pulled by a white pony called Tom. He was to prove very kind to Fred as he became older and less able to cope. The common was once divided into 'goings', which were rights to graze stock and originally allocated to each principal house in the town; these were sold on until the goings were only held by just a few people. Over the years, there has been endless argument as to the ownership of the common and who could be on it and own what lay below it in the form of gravel. Only lawyers seem to have gained from the discord.

Uniquely the town is administered by Feoffees and a Town Reeve. The Butter Cross in the centre is unusual in that Justice, who surmounts the Cross, is not blindfolded and this is one of only three in the UK: the others are over the Old Bailey in London and in front of Yarmouth Toll House.

Stocks were kept fastened to one of the pillars and let down when required for the punishment of offenders. Some wrist irons are still fixed to a pillar. The cage for the detention of prisoners (formerly in the centre of the cross) was taken down in 1836. Twenty-seven years later the small dungeon beneath the floor was filled in. One feels certain that had Fred lived one hundred years earlier, he would have been found there from time to time.

During his latter years Fred liked to spend time watching justice being dispensed at the Bungay Magistrates Court, which until suffering bomb damage in the Second World War, stood behind St Mary's Street by the Castle Hills. There, he would have watched Sir Henry Rider Haggard preside over the proceedings until his death in 1925.

Once held in the streets, Bungay Fair has now moved onto the common, but these days it's much more of a funfair. Each year, primary school children were given 14 May off to attend. Lilias Rider Haggard, in her book, *A Country Scrapbook*, remembering that as well as being an auction when horses and cattle were sold, this was also a day when stalls filled the town with everything for the farm and home: food, kitchenware, harnesses and candles of varying quality. The upper classes could purchase Flemish cloth and furs from Germany, everything required for falconry, books and writing, and songbirds.

Things less familiar were ink made from the blackthorn bark, dog whistles, spurs for cocks and bundles of tally sticks, one of which each man in a gang would mark to indicate jobs done, no man being able to emulate the mark of another. There was plenty to entertain with wrestling, incredibly cruel bull and bear baiting, and most popular of all: cock fighting.

The locals have recently started to close the streets again for antique fairs and a spring garden market, thus renewing the old tradition.

In *A Practical guide to the Game Laws*, 1928, Mr Charles Row wrote:

> *One old poacher used to call on me on Christmas Eve for a Christmas box, always remarking, 'You know I'm one of the very best clients you've got.' He generally succeeded, but he has now, it is believed, given up poaching, so does not trouble me. He was not a 'bad client' as there were against him some fifty or sixty convictions, but he always reminded the magistrates (who, when adjudicating, always referred to*

155

the number of convictions recorded against him), by saying, 'Yes, yes, that's all right, sir but only one for felony. They were all game offences and I always consider there's more credit due to me for killing an old cock pheasant now and again than there is for breaking into a hencote and stealing the fowls. I always chose the lesser of two evils.

This old poacher joined up during the War [1914–1918], but, being too old for the fighting line, was appointed Regimental rat catcher to a Norfolk regiment, and used to take his gun, ferrets and dog to keep down the rats about the camp.

After the war he, like many others, could not get work, and being a little pressed one day, and possessed with some sense of humour wrote, it is said, to the squire of the parish asking, 'If he would be good enough to send him a brace of pheasants, and a brace for his wife, as both were very poorly, or he would have to come and fetch them.' I did not hear whether the pheasants were sent, but I hardly think so.

This cannot be a description of anyone but Fred! By then Charles Row had been secretary of the East Anglian Game Protection Society for thirty-two years. Landowners founded the Society so they could employ a specialist prosecutor when poachers were found on their land; the police prosecuted on public property, but on private land this fell to the owner. Charles Row undertook that role all around the area, which is why he must have attended so many different courts and knew Fred. He appears in old court records in Cromer, Fakenham, Grimston and Harleston.

Mr Row lived at 361 Unthank Road, Norwich, so whether Fred went there for his Christmas box or visited his office in 1 Redwell Street, Norwich, is unknown, but the office staff must have been pretty appalled by the sight of a smelly, shuffling old man on the scrounge.

The Poacher's Companion (1982) includes a chapter on dogs. It quotes Fred on his method of training the poacher's dog and in a footnote, editor E.G. Walsh states:

I think that this is the best description of training a working lurcher I have ever come across, either in word or print. The King of the Norfolk Poachers knew his job.

So as Fred, by now very lame, whiled away time on some scam or other, hopefully Kitty would have enjoyed good enough health to stroll around the streets of Bungay, wisely spending the little money

156

that came in and then enjoying companionable evenings with the Salvation Army, trying not to worry about Joubert.

Since he has been gone this last time I have been going to Salvation Army Services. They have taught me the blessed assurance that although we may meet no more on earth, we will surely meet in heaven. With Jesus to reign ever more. There will be no parting there. So if I have to go before my boy returns I can go happy and in peace, trusting in the Everlasting Arms. I will now close my story with a few words of a favourite song:

Memories, memories, dreams of a bygone day
Though you left me alone
Still you're my own
In my beautiful Memories.

Yes, Dear Reader, she lived to see her boy and his family return.

Even the final five weeks of her life, which were spent at the Shipmeadow Workhouse, were tainted by Fred's seeming inability to get things right. The following entry is in the Minute Book for the Workhouse:

<u>Katherine Rolfe</u>
The clerk is directed to write to David Rolfe of Bridge Street Bungay informing him that the Guardians require him to contribute 2/6d a week towards the cost of maintenance of his wife Catherine Rolfe, an inmate of the workhouse.

Presumably the use of David's name is a clerical error. It was the only such appeal asking for support from any family included in the book. Fred didn't put his hand in his pocket to support his dying wife. Catherine, Bertha's daughter and Kitty's granddaughter, thought Kitty had died due to an accident using the mangle when it swung back and caught her head. In fact, her death certificate states she died from valvular heart disease, but perhaps the blow to her head was the catalyst that led to her death. In *I Walked by Night*, Fred describes this sad time:

Well, I finished the War there, and in time I come back to Bungay and not so long after I lost my second wife. She had borne me two Children – a Boy and a Girl, she was a good wife to me and I had her

157

for nearly forty years. After I come back the children left home. The girl married a Canadian solger and went to Canadia with him and is there now. As evry one know there was no work for the young men after the War and so the boy enlisted and is now serving in his Magistey's Army in India. . . .

It was after all that and we were left alone, that my wife fretted and I saw the change in her – she lost all intrest in life and just pined and died. The Doctor said it was hart trubble, and I think it was, but not in the way he ment for I think she died of a broken hart fretting for the children.

Kitty died on 13 March 1925, the death certificate recording that Fred was in attendance. The death certificate states she was 60 years old, but from evidence in earlier records it would seem she was younger than that, probably about 56. As yet, it has not been possible to trace Kitty's birth certificate.

Mrs Hart, an elderly lady who grew up in Mettingham, about three miles east of Bungay, remembers the inmates of the Shipmeadow Workhouse as she went to school with some of the children. They were dressed and treated differently; labelled paupers, whose parents could not, or would not support them out of ill health, fecklessness or criminality. How could the Board of Guardians justify such unkindness, which makes one fearful of the treatment Kitty received during her time there?

Almost everyone who talked about Shipmeadow Workhouse had a tale of ghosts or the supernatural. One person recalled that before its conversion to apartments, the building had been used to house pigs and one day the room went very cold and the pigs became terribly agitated. Another remembered that although a staircase was no longer there, footsteps were heard hurrying up them, and history tells that it was a girl sneaking in to take food to her grandfather on the top floor. Yet another recalled that the builders felt uneasy working there after dark and reported tools going missing. Another felt she was being watched and someone else told of singing heard in the chapel.

Kitty is buried in an unmarked grave in Row 42, just on the right side of the left-hand path after it turns to go up the hill in Bungay Cemetery. Malcolm Bedingfield's *The Way We Lived Then: Bungay in the 1930s* (1994) describes how the grave would be loved and tended in a way that Kitty was almost certainly never cared for in life:

One man was employed full time in the cemetery cutting the grass and keeping the graves tidy. His duties included digging the graves and taking whatever steps necessary to control the rabbit population. On Sunday mornings, although his day off, he would shave, trim his bushy moustache and stand at the top of the cemetery hill dressed in his Sunday best. With a clean white collar, boots polished, watch chain stretched across a buttoned waistcoat, a trilby hat on his head, and with hands behind his back, he would nod and greet the people who regularly visited and tended the graves of loved ones at this time. Men took their work very seriously in these days no matter what it entailed and loyalty and dedication was evident.

Bless him!

CHAPTER 15

1925–38 After Kitty

In 1988, in a letter to her cousin David Rolfe, Bertha's daughter Cath wrote:

> *Bertha could not talk of her Gran without a tear in her eye by the way she was treated all her married life. My great grandfather was no saint.*

Bertha told Cath that Great-gran (Kitty) hardly ever opened her mouth as she was abused sexually by Fred and much browbeaten. She described her as melancholic and told how she hated to remember the 'dark days', referring to her time in Bungay. Cath also remembers being told that her mother went to a séance and made contact with Kitty, who told her that she had forgiven Fred; also that Bertha left home when her grandmother died, but David's letter to his son in 1988 (when young David was inquiring about the family's past) says:

> *Bertha and Grandad were still living there in 1927 when I had a week with them between trips, I did not see any Bibles with family trees at any time I was with them.*

Bertha still being in Bungay at that time is borne out by a local press report:

No cycle lamp
Complainant John Goodrum. Bertha Rolfe on November 4th. Riding a bicycle on the highway at Broome at night without a lighted lamp. Miss Rolfe did not appear.
Convicted. Penalty 9/- costs 1/-. In default distress or seven days imprisonment.

Town Hall Loddon, 23 November 1927

There is no evidence to show whether or not Bertha settled the fine. At that time, she was working for Clays Printing Works in the town, but left to work in London, probably in 1928.

Fred was still at 7 Bridge Street in November 1928. Mr Fred Bayfield, a remarkably sprightly man of 91, has clear recollections of Fred Rolfe. When shown a photograph of him, he said that the gun Fred was holding was not his usual one (he had a 12-bore hammer action), while the photo showed a single-barrel .410 hammer gun.

Born in 1912, on the Elvedon Estate, Fred Bayfield was raised in a keepering family. His father started his career in Bradenham, where he was employed at the Hall by then-owner F.G. Nicholls (it was the home of Sir Henry Rider Haggard as a child). The Bayfield family then went to Elvedon, a very famous shooting estate, once owned by Duleep Singh (a favourite of Queen Victoria and Prince Albert), who spent a fortune on the Estate and Shoot, and slaughtered game on an extraordinary scale. Keepers went with their master to all the other shooting parties, where they were needed to act as loaders. Fred's father went with Lord Iveagh, owner of Elvedon, at that time.

On one day in Stanford Norfolk in 1889, Lord Walsingham shot: 39 pheasants, 5 partridge, 1 red-legged partridge, 6 gadwall, 4 pochard, 1 goldeneye, 7 teal, 3 swans, 1 woodcock, 1 snipe, 2 jacksnipe, 1 wood pigeon, 2 heron, 65 coot, 2 moorhens, 9 hares, 16 rabbits, 1 otter, 1 large rat and 1 pike.

A game book for a Downham Market shoot records four days in 1892 when 2,543 pheasants were shot, two days in 1893 when 1,135 pheasants were shot, another three days in 1894 when 1, 284 pheasants were shot and finally, three days in 1900 when 1,239 pheasants were shot. It is easy to see why estate owners, with their endless lust for shooting, needed large numbers of gamekeepers!

Mr Bayfield senior took over as head keeper at Earsham Hall, just outside Bungay, in 1922. He became the fourth generation to hold the position. At 16, young Fred Bayfield became keeper's boy, under his father and did all the rough jobs: caring for the dogs, ferrets and hens, of which large numbers were needed as broodies to hatch the pheasants eggs collected from the wild.

Fred Bayfield remembered that on 4 November 1928, the night before Guy Fawkes, his father went out on patrol. As children in Bungay were letting off fireworks, he felt this was a good night to catch poachers – they might hope their shots would mingle with the noise of the bangers. Mr Bayfield was quite lawfully carrying a truncheon. While going up a track in Bath Hills, Ditchingham, he met Fred Rolfe coming down towards him. As he tried to arrest him, there was a tussle and Fred's gun went off, blowing a hole in Mr Bayfield's hat. Having taken Fred to the lock-up, he returned home. On seeing the damage to his hat, his wife was naturally concerned and the next day went into labour, giving birth to twins on 5 November! The case was reported in the local paper and Mr Bayfield's memory, seventy-five years later, is almost perfect:

Labourer and Pheasant
Frederick Rolfe, Labourer of 7 Bridge Street, Bungay, was summonsed at Loddon on Wednesday for night poaching at Ditchingham. There was a further summons against defendant for killing game on a Sunday. He pleaded not guilty to the first summons and guilty to the second.

Wm Fredk Bayfield gamekeeper to Mr Oliverson, Earsham Hall, said that on November 4th when in company with Fredk Martin, an underkeeper he heard a gun fired in the direction of Bath hills. A few minutes later they heard another shot from the same direction. They proceeded to a footpath by the side of the wood and witness saw defendant come out of the wood on to the path. He was carrying a gun and looking up into the trees. Witness caught hold of the defendant and Martin took the gun away. Witness searched the defendant and found on him a freshly killed pheasant and six cartridges. Defendant said to witness 'I am unlucky it is the first time I have been out this season. I suppose I shall get a month for this.' Defendant then rode away on his bicycle. Fredk Martin the underkeeper, said defendant struggled to retain the rifle and his hand was near the trigger.

Defendant said he borrowed the gun and cartridges; he was out of work and wanted food. His intention was to try and get a rabbit. He did not go into the wood but was on the path.

The chairman reminded defendant that his record was none too good – A fine of £2, and 2/6d costs was imposed in the first case and 10/- in the second. Defendant was further summonsed for killing game without a licence. He pleaded guilty and was fined £1.

24 November 1928, *Norwich Mercury*

Fred must have paid the fine for there is no mention of him in the prison records. Costs, at that time about 3/6d, were awarded to the gamekeeper. After a case, Mr Bayfield described how keepers and poachers alike would drink at The Angel in Earsham Street, Bungay and bear one another no animosity. In this day and age, Fred would probably have been charged with attempted murder, but Mr Bayfield must have seen it as one of the shortcomings of his job and so subsequently he was not even charged with assault. Mr Bayfield still has his father's account books, and one from 1925 is full of fascinating snippets that evoke the period and lifestyle: Mr Bayfield senior earned £3.12.0 a fortnight and received £6 a year for his clothing; beaters and beer for a day's shoot cost £7 16s; two bottles of whisky, use unspecified, were £15.

Dogs and their needs crop up regularly, their health and wellbeing obviously hugely important, and Mr Bayfield senior received an allowance of 15/- a fortnight. This must have all been spent for you see listed: wine for Bess 4/6d, distemper pills for Bess 1/-, embrocation for Bess 1/3d, 2lbs of beef fat for Bess 1/- (surely if the dog ate that, it would be ill). Perhaps that was what was wanted, the amount of poison purchased! Seven pounds of arsenic and Rodine rat poison constantly appear in the accounts. On the credit side were large numbers of rabbits sold for 1/3d, hares 2/6d, woodcock 1/3d and eggs (presumably pheasant) at 3/6d a score. It was obvious the books had to be balanced each fortnight and presented for audit. Skins and feathers were sold to Horace Friend at Wisbech.

Soon after the court case in 1928, Fred Rolfe gave up 7 Bridge Street. He lived as a lodger with Mrs Jessie Redgrave at 46 Bridge Street, part of Clarke's Yard, near the River Waveney. It was part of the coal yard owned by Manning Clarke, who also hired out rowing boats. Number 46 fell into poor repair after Fred and Jessie moved out and was eventually demolished.

Pauline Brunton, who is Jessie Redgrave's granddaughter, recalls that she was born Jessie Godfrey in 1885. She married Charles (Charlie) Redgrave, a widower with three children, and they went on to have three more: Herbert (Joe), Elsie (Mettie) and Edith. Charlie died shortly after Edith was born, leaving Jessie to rear all six. The family were desperately poor and Fred's money must have been most welcome.

One of Mrs Redgrave's stepsons, Charles, was out with Fred one night poaching when they met up with a gamekeeper and had a fight. As a consequence, Charles fled to Australia in 1928 at the age of 20, where he remained for the whole of his life. Pauline, Joe's daughter, recalls being told that Fred and Mrs Redgrave argued, following which Fred moved out and went to Mettingham. The family were not pleased when she fetched Fred back, saying her first thoughts should have been for her daughter Edith. It is hard to know what to read into that statement: perhaps Edith simply did not like him or would have to give up her room. Other snippets of information suggest that for some reason she may have been afraid of him. Of course, this could all be put down to teenage petulance, with Edith unconcerned about her mother missing Fred's company and the money he gave her.

Fred's leaving Clarke's Yard for a time would tie in with the recollections of a number of people, and also with the Electoral Registers, proving that he was lodging with Mrs Redgrave in 1930. He was with her between 1931 and 1932, but the following two years he does not feature. Electoral Registers for the period do not indicate his whereabouts, but a number of people remember him in Mettingham.

By 1935 he is back with Mrs Redgrave and he then remained with her first at Clarke's Yard and then at 15 Nethergate Street until his death. While in Mettingham, he scribbled down his memories. In *I Walked by Night*. The preface reads:

> What is written here was born of an old man's loneliness, as he sat in a little cottage perched high on a hill, overlooking the Waveney Valley with no company but his dog.

The first page of Fred's handwritten manuscript is dated 15 July 1929, when he was 67, which implies he started earlier and perhaps continued his tale later. Maybe he lived at Mettingham before he went to lodge with Mrs Redgrave and feeling lonely and bored, while not in good health either, he started to write down his memories. Several people have said that by this time he used his bike as a crutch to lean on, rather than pedalling it.

After living with Mrs Redgrave he certainly went to Mettingham when they quarrelled. When she fetched him back and Lilias Rider Haggard was shown that first manuscript, he was witnessed sitting on the riverbank in Clarke's Yard writing, presumably by then with Lilias's encouragement.

As a lad, John Pearson used to walk across Ditchingham Dam and the Falcon Meadow to school. He remembers Fred Rolfe sitting outside a cottage in Clarke's Yard and being a short, stocky man, slow of gait:

> *He had a trilby hat, moustache and always had a pipe in his mouth. He had a Jack Russell dog he had taught to walk on its hind legs. He lived*

there with Mrs Redgrave. When he sat outside the cottage he always seemed to be writing, scribbling in a book. He was considered a rogue, a loveable rogue [Pearson's voice had a laugh in it when he said this]. *He seemed to be remembered with affection, he was well known in the town and spent a lot of time in the Magistrates court watching the cases of the day. Mrs Redgrave couldn't read or write. She and Fred used to go to the cinema together.*

Although Talkies had arrived by then, Mr Pearson remembers Fred reading out the sub-titles and people getting annoyed with him chattering away to Mrs Redgrave, telling her what was going on. In *I Walked by Night*, when philosophising on the declining standards of the younger generation, Fred mentions going to the cinema, a case of the pot calling the kettle black:

So it has come about that the young Generation both males and females have lerned the ways of the world. We se plain proof of that evry day. They run the streets at night and get in all sorts of compney, and not good Compney mostly. Then there is the Cinemars and Dance halls, they are all Hells kitchen and another great hinderance to the young and enexperenced mind. I am not condeming those places of entertainment, but some of them places are to tempting for the Young people, they are not the places morality to find, as I have noticed myself.

Pearson also recalled his mother going to work across Ditchingham Dam one day when she met Rolfe on his bike.

'Morning, Mr Rolfe you're about early,' she said.
'The early bird catches the worm,' was his reply.

Too true – a few days later he was up in court for taking coal from Ditchingham railway yard before it opened one morning.

Prison for Coal Theft
Fredk Rolfe, labourer of 7, Bridge St., Bungay was found guilty at the police court on Wednesday of stealing 5 stones 6lbs of coal, the property of Messrs Rutter and Co., at Ditchingham, on February 14th, and was sentenced to two months Imprisonment with hard labour.
PC Masters said that at 2.45am he saw defendant coming from a coal heap carrying something that he placed on the wall before climbing over into the road. When he caught sight of witness, defendant mounted his bike that had been against the wall and rode off, but he was overtaken. A lump of coal

165

was found on the wall. William Prentice, maltster's foreman of Ditchingham, and PC Collins also gave evidence.

Defendant said he could not plead guilty to the charge as he had not taken anything off the premises. He had only done two days work since Christmas.

5 March 1927, Norwich Mercury

Poor man, the punishment seems very harsh for someone of 65.

'*You know he came to a sticky end,*' Mr Pearson said. '*He never struck me as a man like that.*'

Mr and Mrs Buck, who lived in Mettingham during their youth and are still greatly involved in the church there, knew that Fred had lived at Grammers Green in Mettingham. Mr Buck remembered that Fred, when he lived there, kept a hedgehog that he called Sam in a box under his chair. The chair was placed outside his door and much to the delight of children passing by, he would get the hedgehog out to feed it bread and milk.

Mr Buck has compiled a book of recollections of Mettingham sold in aid of church funds. A charming ramble through the history of the village, it shows that poaching was not at all uncommon; one lady wrote that her mother told her the tasty meal they were eating was chicken – with pretty feathers.

At the Tally Ho public house in Mettingham, a photograph of Fred hangs on the pub wall, so he is obviously remembered as living locally. Mrs Norton, who now lives at Grammers Green, was so kind and helpful. Set on a hill overlooking the Waveney Valley, her lovely house is just on the outskirts of the village. Originally it was four cottages with a brew house attached and it was there that Fred lived. The brew house has since been demolished, but the marks on the wall where it was once attached to the side of the house can still be seen.

Mrs Norton has a picture of the cottages as they were originally and this was painted by a neighbour, a Mr John Reeve, who was inspired to capture the scene himself, having seen a painting of the valley in a book of prints by Edward Seago, who illustrated *I Walked by Night.*

The people who had lived in Grammers Green at about the same time as Fred appear to have been a gloriously eccentric lot. Among others was a Russian émigrée who didn't wash too often, had hundreds of cats and wore enough jewellery to buy every house in the village. When the old boy living in Fred's cottage before him died, they were unable to get his body out before rigor mortis set in and subsequently had to break his legs to get him through the door. Best of all was Miss Pulford, a Madam, who kept brothels along the coast at Great Yarmouth and Lowestoft. In the autumn she brought the prostitutes to one of the cottages in the row by donkey cart, much as ponies and donkeys are brought from the beach to overwinter and then taken back again in the spring for the summer season. Mrs Norton was also familiar with the hedgehog story. She said there was no policeman or gamekeeper in the village, so Fred and others must have been able to poach with a degree of confidence.

Alec Boast, a Bungay man in his eighties, proved a mine of information as he remembered Fred well. His recollections of him entirely fit in with the period after Kitty's death. Mr Boast moved to Mettingham in 1929 and left in 1936. He remembers Fred living in the cottage at the end of the row, just up the hill from Low Road; he identified the spot and described the tiny cottage just as Mrs Norton had.

He described Fred as always wearing a hat, even indoors; he had the air of an aristocrat, which he said he was not. Fred rode a bike with a double-cross bar, with his gun strapped to the lower bar; his dog ran behind. He was a vermin killer on piece work, meaning either so much a field, or so much for a mole, rat, etc. Mr Boast also said Fred was a 'well behaved' man (in his manner towards other people). During corn cutting, he was there all the time, waiting for the last cut when the rabbits were forced to flee. Boast remembers him gutting a pile of about thirty rabbits in five minutes. He got out his pocket knife, held the rabbits head up, made two swift cuts, pulled the guts out and linked the back feet together by passing one through a cut in the leg of the other.

'He hung himself, you know,' Mr Boast told me. When I asked him if he knew why, he said that he knew the rumours – but people didn't believe it. 'I was in his company a lot – I liked him. He was a bit aggressive; he was not a drinker.'

Asked about Fred's cottage, Mr Boast laughed:

He was not tidy, he lived a bit rough; he got a good living – he got 9d a rabbit when a day's wage for a working man was 5/-. He limped, he fascinated me with his mannerism. He was a Romany type, a loner.

He remembers Fred telling his father, 'I don't know, Stanley. I feel like putting a bullet through me' To which Stanley replied that it would be a waste of the 2d that the bullet would cost. When he was shown Fred's photograph, Mr Boast said he must have dressed up to have it taken for he remembered that usually he had a large red-spotted handkerchief tied as a cravat.

Mr Boast's sister Lucy can remember the hedges near Fred's home festooned with moleskins that were hung up to dry before being sold. In those days, moleskins were particularly prized for waistcoats and fetched 2½d each during the 1920s. Mole catchers received a farthing an acre for clearing the moles and were able to keep what they caught to sell on. The skins are pegged out within twelve hours and stretched to between 4½ and 6½ sq in. In his book, *Sixty Years a Fenman* (1966), Arthur Randall wrote that mole catchers would have 100 to 150 skins stretched and ready to sell at any one time. In 1905, twelve million moleskins were exported to the United States for clothing.

Mrs Elsie Treanor was born in Bungay in 1917, one of thirteen children born to Robert and Ellen Flegg, nine of whom survived to maturity. The family lived in Nethergate Street, close to Fred and Mrs Redgrave. Mrs Treanor told me that as children they knew when their mother was having another baby – not by her changing shape, which they failed to notice, but when she got the battered old pram out again. Not as you might suppose to put the new baby in, but to carry the vast numbers of loaves her mother prepared. The children pushed them to the bakers to be cooked in their large ovens. They were then fetched home, so there was enough bread to keep the entire family fed while their mother was confined. Mrs Treanor said she always associated the smell of new baked bread with the introduction of a brother or sister.

She remembers Bertha, but assumed she was Fred and Kitty's daughter. Once, on one of Bertha's visits home from London, she thought her too heavily made-up: 'My mother thought she must keep bad company. I just thought she looked like a clown.'

She and others recall Fred's bike was always leaning against the wall of his house in Bridge Street, so PC Stammers might assume he was at home, while Fred had slipped out the back door and was up to his tricks.

Another elderly Bungay resident, who had a straw hat on back to front and a glorious twinkle in his eye when interviewed, remembered Fred. From a shed packed full of old farmyard implements he produced a gun, which he broke in half to show it could be hidden inside clothing. This was Fred's original poaching gun which, since his death, the elderly man had owned.

He recalled that when he first had it, the gun still had a cocoa tin packed with wadding attached to the barrel to act as a silencer. As a lad he used to talk to Fred, who with his dog Patch, was always out and about on Bungay Common. He said that although by then Fred was very lame and none too clean, the kids liked him and used to sit and enjoy his observations about the wildlife around them: 'Fred knew a rook from a crow,' he said, in a way that made it clear that he held Fred's authority on the ways of the countryside in the highest esteem.

Fred's other guns are held in Bungay Museum despite the fact that he left them to his son in his will. In fact, Fred gave the guns to bailiff John Baldry, who left them to his son Alfie. In turn, Alfie left them to his son Andrew, who then presented them to the museum.

Part of a letter given to me by a member of the Baldry family reads:

> *The gun was given to Pop by old Rolfe the poacher himself as a small token of gratitude for helping him out in so many ways, such as keeping his nails and hair trimmed, etc., things that to some people would mean nothing at all, but to Rolfe it meant a lot for which he was grateful.*
>
> *As far as Alfie can remember he was about 10 years old when Rolfe gave the gun to Pop. When Pop died, Nana said Alfie was to have it.*

John Baldry was the Common bailiff. He lived in Outney Road and was always to be seen on the Common with his white pony and trap. He lived to be 93, and Andrew, his grandson, guesses he was about ten years younger than Fred. The family wonder if John was the younger man with whom Fred poached, as mentioned in *I Walked by Night*. Mr Baldry certainly poached, Andrew said.

When he came out of the Army after the First World War he made a living by doing this and that, kept six cows and sold milk round the town, a penny a pint. There were never any problems over payment as in those days people were not allowed 'tick' so there were no debtors. Mr Baldry also kept pigs. He lived almost at the bottom of Broad Street, where it joins Nethergate Street. He had a game licence so all the poachers could bring their ill-gotten gains to him to sell legitimately.

It would seem more likely that the poaching pal that Fred refers to in the book was, in fact, Will Catchpole:

I have had one good frend since the days I have been telling about. I met a man that had come home from the war, and him I seamed to take to more than any other man I have ever met. He told me after a bit that he wold like to lern all that I could teach him, and the ins and outs of the Game as I knew it. Well teach him I did, and I found him a verry apt scholler, and consider him one of the Cleverest men that there is on the Job to day, and one of the best Palls.

I have had a verry tryen year this last one and have been onder a verry severe Opperation in Norwich Ospital, and he have stuck to me throw it all and have helped me in evry way that laid in his power, and that is the man that I can eprecate.

Despite his kindness to Fred, comments about Will Catchpole are mostly unfavourable. Various sources describe him as mean, a skinflint and a person who would trade in anything second hand to sell at a profit. Catchpole sold mole and rabbit skins, which were pegged out to dry in a shed behind his tailor's shop.

Mr Catchpole had been a sniper in World War I and was a keen cyclist. He died at 91, his obituary stating among other things that he had been a tailor, like his father before him. He had sat cross-legged to work, stitching to the highest standard. Tailoring, however, was not his first love: 'I went into shooting day and night, forty years I had on the estates and was never caught. It was a marvellous time. I enjoyed every part of it.'

In his garden shed was all the paraphernalia of a poacher, including rabbit nets, snares and salmon hooks. Perhaps the snares came from the 'snare factory' in Bungay. They were made by local girls above Gibson & Balls, the ironmongers, who sold them guaranteeing 'Bungay rabbit snares are best'. The obituary also states how his poaching tales formed the basis for the bestselling book, *I Walked by Night* by The King of The Norfolk Poachers. This is incorrect, as is clearly borne out by a letter in the correspondence columns of the *Eastern Daily Press*, following Will Catchpole's obituary appearing in the paper:

Memories of Poacher Will
Sir – I refer to the "EDP" letter of November 5th and 11th and letters "Poacher Will". I was the village policeman at Ditchingham from 1932 to 1936 and knew Frederick Rolfe very well, as he resided at Bridge Street, Bungay.
He often took a walk along Ditchingham Dam, and I often chatted

with him. He had given up poaching then as he had very bad legs, due he told me, to injuries whilst poaching. I also knew Miss Rider Haggard very well, and George Baldry of Ditchingham, who Miss Rider Haggard assisted to write his book The Rabbit Skin Cap. *Whilst at Ditchingham, I was told personally by the late Mr Dixon Longrigg of Ditchingham House Farm how the book* I Walked by Night *came to be written. Fred Rolfe did odd jobs for Mr Longrigg on his farm, and one day in conversation Rolfe told Mr Longrigg he had an old exercise book at home in which he had written, as they occurred, many of his night poaching episodes, and asked if Mr Longrigg would like to read it. Mr Longrigg took it home and almost forgot about it until one evening Miss Rider Haggard came to spend the evening with Mrs Longrigg. During the evening Mr Longrigg saw the old exercise book, handed it to Miss Rider Haggard and said, "I think this might interest you, Miss." On reading some of it, Miss Rider Haggard replied: "It certainly does", took the exercise book with her, later contacted Fred Rolfe, who I believe she had never met before, and that was how* I Walked by Night *came to be written.*

Although I was the policeman at Ditchingham, and quite a lot of night poaching was done in the woods at Ditchingham and Earsham, I personally never heard of Will Catchpole being connected with poaching in my district.

Yours faithfully
T.H. Makins

That Will Catchpole did poach was remembered by a Bungay man: one winter's night, he was spotted by a gamekeeper and a policeman on Bath Hills, a steep and wooded area on the Norfolk side of Bungay Common. They had been keeping an eye out as he was known to be a regular poacher. Seeing them, he swam the river with the pheasants he had shot on his back and pedalled off, dripping wet, on his bicycle – which he had left hidden by the river's edge.

The policeman had to contact the Suffolk Constabulary because Will, by crossing the river, had crossed the county boundary. By the time the Suffolk Police arrived the pheasants had been pulled up the chimney of a local cycle repairer, Percy Harmer, by a chain until they were out of sight. Early the next morning, Will rode to London on his bike to sell the pheasants, well out of harm's way. The informant also told me that Mr Harmer had only one arm, but was literally a dab hand at doing repairs.

The last court case found which refers to Fred has some novelty value. Heard at Bungay Magistrates Court on 19 December 1928 for poaching before Brigadier General Abbott, it was unusually dismissed.

John Gray, another elderly gentleman who kindly agreed to tell me what he knew of Fred Rolfe, lived as a child at Valley Farm, sometimes called Holly Bush Farm, in Ditchingham. William, his father, was a tenant farmer, who grew apples. The landlord took the land back in 1932 and the family were forced to leave; they had been there since 1927.

William Gray told of Rolfe coming as casual labour when the thrashing machine arrived, probably in 1930. The family owned a cross-bred whippet, usually chained near the back door; it barked when people came and was a useful animal. The dog went missing, but its collar and chain remained. Somehow Mr Gray was under the impression that a greater crime was being committed if the collar went too and whoever took the dog would know the ropes regarding this. He felt that whoever took the dog must have known dogs to get that near, as the dog appeared unapproachable.

P.C. Charlie Marsters was informed. His police house was close by, at the All Hallows junction. The dog was found shot on Bungay Common. P.C. Marsters surmised Fred had taken it, the dog being one that showed promise for helping to net rabbits, but when he found the dog was more trouble than it was worth, he shot it. Mr Gray has no idea if this was true – it was simply Fred's reputation that made him the most likely candidate. No action was taken against him.

John also told the following delightful yarn. Two Ditchingham boys wanting to make a go-kart stole the wheels from the road mender's tar pot. They were caught, and with their fathers appeared before the magistrates. Either Mrs Mead or Miss Carr was in the Chair; the first child's case was heard and a fine of 2/6d imposed, similarly with the second child. This father objected, saying he had had to take a day off work with loss of wages and all the other difficulties ensued, and it was hardly worth it for the small size of the fine. The chairman agreed that it was a derisory fine after all his inconvenience, and to make it worth his while she'd double the fine to 5/-.

It is quite possible that Fred heard this case, as his obituary included the following:

Right up to the last, Rolfe was a regular habitué of Bungay Police Court – not as a defendant but as one interested in the cases, which came before the Justices there. Practically every court he was to be seen sitting there listening intently to the business that came up.

Charles Cunningham, a lively 81-year-old, who remembered Fred, described him as short, with a long drooping moustache, wearing canvas boots, corduroy trousers and a trilby, always a trilby. He remembers him walking up Bridge Street, where he lived, using a walking stick and also recollects speculation and gossip that Fred sired a child in his seventies.

CHAPTER 16

The Books

As Constable Makins mentioned in his letter, Fred Rolfe's story first came into Lilias Rider Haggard's hands in the early 1930s when one evening she called in to see Mrs Longrigg, a farmer's wife. Two years earlier, Fred, who went mole 'catchen' on the farm, had given Mr Longrigg a dog-eared exercise book in which he had written his early memories, thinking they might amuse him. When Lilias and her neighbour were talking, she suddenly remembered the book and fished it out of a drawer, thinking the contents might be of interest. In the preface to *I Walked by Night*, Lilias says:

> The Farmer's wife only half approved of the old man and his literary efforts, partly because her innate respectability was outraged at his reputation, and partly from an inborn distrust of one who had mysteriously cured her son of warts when all other remedies had failed. Had she not spent more than enough upon the chemist's nostrums, with no result, until one day, when singling beet, the old poacher's eye fell on the boy's hands. He dealt with the warts and they vanished with no further ado; but the boy's mother was a Londoner, and did not hold with such ideas as 'charming', which to those who dwell in East Anglia seems to this day a most rational remedy. Still she was a kindly soul, and cherished a soft spot for the charmer, even after reading the shocking revelations set forth in the exercise-book.

Lilias used Fred's jottings as a basis for articles in her weekly column in *The Eastern Daily Press* and pieces she contributed to *Country Life*. Realising how much interest they generated, she cajoled Fred into writing down more of his memories. While Lilias was well paid for her articles, it is questionable what Fred received besides a glass of beer, which locals say she gave to him at her back door when he turned up with his stories, written in his large, neat handwriting.

Over the years it has been questioned whether or not Fred wrote *I Walked by Night*, or whether, in fact, Lilias was the author. However, there can be no doubt that he wrote the first exercise book full of his memories as they are in his own handwriting and came into Lilias's hands via a known route.

On the flyleaf of a first edition in 1935, Lilias wrote on a copy she gave to Mrs Longrigg: 'With grateful thanks to you to whom "I Walked by Night" owes its existence.' In the work, she makes it clear that she encouraged Fred to write more and says that he enjoyed recollecting the people and places of his past; she merely tidied up, making small alterations where necessary, and put the pieces he wrote into chronological order:

> When I get hold of a pen and begin to rite I feel I can go on Just as long as I can hold it. Thoughts come to me that have laid dorment for years – I see old faces and the places that I have forgot . . . the tears come into my eyes wen I write of my first wife, and the things we did wen we were young.

The book is so detailed and accurate about Pentney and surroundings in particular that even if Fred had talked to Lilias about his memories, however skilful a writer she might be, she would have been unable to capture the flavour of Norfolk in the late 1880s with the poacher's authenticity. His love of the countryside and the tricks he learnt shine off the pages, the phonetic spelling and the use of the Norfolk dialect only adding to the work. Sadly, while the descriptive parts seem very accurate, he greatly embellished his personal life.

In her book *A Country Scrapbook* (1950) Lilias wrote:

> *In my time I have produced two books, which were the life stories of local characters. For their truth and the existence of the authors within a mile of my door I had, I thought, completely and convincingly vouched in the prefaces. But year after year comes the regular query: 'It isn't really true, is it?' Patiently I explain it was, and is, and that there is such a thing as literary integrity still abroad upon the earth in spite of the fact that I was once entertained by a cheerful young bachelor on the proceeds of an article he had sold, entitled 'What to Do when Baby Refuses His Bottle' by a Mother.*
>
> *Apart from any private convictions one may have that it should be respected (for all good craftsmanship is honest) from a business point of view it is the best policy. The public, contrary to general belief, is*

175

extremely difficult to hoodwink. Invariably some enquiring mind checks a statement, and filled with righteous joy at discovering an error, post haste puts pen to paper in order to reveal it in all its horrid nakedness.

Fred must have spun his yarn well, for clearly Lilias believed his tale and presumably none came forward with evidence of falsehoods, though clearly some had doubts. Whether he sought legal advice over how he should be paid for his part in the book is not known, but it seems unlikely. Certainly Lilias made sure everything was cut and dried.

> *Ditchingham House*
> *Bungay*
> *May 8th 1934*
> *Received of Lilias Margitson Rider Haggard the sum of £20 (twenty pounds) in full payment and satisfaction of all my rights of whatsoever description in all manuscripts in her possession relating to my life and experience, and in particular to the book of Recollections which she is about to have published.*
> *Dated this day 9th of May 1934*
> *Frederick Rolfe*

This was signed across two one-penny stamps; in pencil on the agreement, Lilias had written, 'sign here across the stamps'. As a journalist, Lilias would have been aware that it was essential to tie up all the legal ends carefully.

By then, the old age pension was 35/- a week, so £20 would be about twelve weeks' pension, which doesn't seem a great deal. However, it may have allowed Fred and Jessie Redgrave to move from Clarke's Yard to the better house in Nethergate Street.

For many years Lilias wrote a weekly column, 'Country Woman's Week' in the *Eastern Daily Press*. Describing her columns, her obituary states she had '. . . an unrivalled knowledge, they revealed information she had built up about the district. She wrote of the big houses and families who occupied them.' Henry Williamson (1895–1977), author of *Tarka the Otter*, who moved to Norfolk just before the Second World War, described them as 'the best thing of its kind in contemporary literature'.

In 1943, he edited a selection of her work in a book titled *Norfolk Life*. Three years later, *A Norfolk Note-book* appeared and then, in 1950, *A Country Scrapbook*. Lilias modestly described her columns as being 'the ordinary events which happen to every one of us, all day and every day. Rather to my surprise many people write that they enjoy the notes. For that I am very grateful, for they have brought a great deal of pleasure to their parent.'

She also penned a biography of her father, Sir Henry Rider Haggard, called *The Cloak that I Left* (1951). Henry Rider Haggard was no scholar and, as a young man, his father packed him off to Africa in 1875 to work as unpaid secretary to Sir Henry Bulwer. There, he ended up farming ostriches. On his return to England in 1880, his brushes with the Boers and the Zulus gave him exciting material from which to write his very popular adventure books.

Henry served on many committees, including All Hallows hospital where Anna had died, and also stood unsuccessfully for Parliament. Following the death of his only son Arthur ('Jock') from measles, he became increasingly concerned that writing 'romances' was not enough, while altering the lot of the underprivileged was paramount. He advocated giving men smallholdings so that they might benefit from their own labour and he also joined in with the work of General Booth of the Salvation Army in taking the poor from London's pitiful East End and training them in camps to go out and colonise the new world. In 1912, he was knighted and appointed to a committee to report on the health of the British Empire, which was interrupted by the First World War.

Lilias (1892–1968) was the youngest of Henry's three daughters and born the year after the death of Jock while Henry and Louisa were in Mexico. Henry was disappointed when his youngest turned out to be another girl.

During the First World War, Lilias served with the Nursing Auxiliaries in France and was awarded the MBE in 1919. A Norfolk County Councillor, like her father, she served on a number of committees in the area and never married. Much of her time was spent at The Bath House at Ditchingham and, after her father's death, she would take it in turns with her sister Angela in caring for their mother at her home nearby until her death in 1943. The tale of her mother's family, the Margitsons – *Too Late for Tears* – by Lilias was published posthumously in 1968.

The list of illustrations in *I Walked by Night* stated that the image on the frontispiece was the author, suggesting it was a likeness of Fred, which it certainly was not. The picture is misleading and he never reveals his name in the book. Did he and Lilias deliberately try to put people off the scent when it came to his identity? It seems unlikely as his photograph appeared in the local newspapers at the time of publication. Shortly after the book was published, the review in the *Eastern Daily Press* (4 October 1935) reads: 'A remarkable autobiography'.

As well as including quotes from the book and the tale of how Lilias came to edit it, the review states that the poacher was in his early teens when he was awarded a month's imprisonment in Norwich gaol – so the misconception began immediately. Interestingly, it also talks about Fred's life away from Norfolk, a subject not often touched on:

> *The book gives a wonderful insight into the rustic life of Norfolk . . . but even more remarkably reveals the character of one who, though he was an outlaw according to the laws of his time, was a philosopher and a loyal lover and student of Nature. His life story even when it tells of existence among the mill chimneys and the murky streets of Lancashire, in the market places and the fields of Ireland, is informed with an unquenchable love of the wild things of the fields and the woods to which he inevitably returned. . . .*

The Norfolk artist Edward Seago's illustrations in the book are delightful, many of them simple black-and-white sketches in pen and ink. In the 1935 edition, some illustrations appear in colour. Seago lived in Brooke, a village halfway between Bungay and Norwich, about six miles from Ditchingham, where Lilias lived. Their families were well known to each other. In some of the early editions of the book, a note from her appears in the front:

> *It is a matter of some satisfaction to me that this book is a local product. The Author, Editor and Illustrator live within a radius of seven miles. I am indebted to the courtesy of the Editor of Country Life for permission to republish certain portions, which have appeared in articles. Also my warmest thanks are due to many friends who have always found time to help me with notes on the text, and copies of Norfolk and Suffolk rhymes and sayings; and last but not least to the Author, who has suffered so patiently under my incessant questions.*

Having been very cosseted by his mother throughout childhood because of illness, Seago spent a great deal of his time drawing and painting. He was taken under the wing of the famous artist Sir Alfred Munnings (1878–1959) and his first London exhibition was held in

1929. Later, he became fascinated by the circus and even travelled with one in the 1930s, sketching their acts and way of life. These sketches became vibrant paintings, some of which were later hung in the Royal Academy Summer Exhibition.

While with the circus he fell in love with Tommy Baker, eldest brother in a riding act. Together they travelled with the circus and he remained by Tommy's bedside when, after an operation for appendicitis, he contracted peritonitis and died. For the rest of his life, Seago wore a signet ring that had once belonged to Tommy. He later became equally obsessed with the ballet. In 1934, in correspondence with Poet Laureate John Masefield (1878–1967), Seago wrote:

> *Dear Mr Masefield,*
> *Thank you so much for your letter and thank you also for dropping some of the formalities. I do so wish you would go further and use my Christian name.*
> *Your suggestion for a year of Country Life appeals to me enormously. If I can manage to tide myself over for a month or so financially there is nothing I should like better. For the moment, I have had to abandon the idea of joining the circus and start on a set of illustrations instead – the story of a poacher – it's a frightfully interesting book written by himself.*
> *We had a great hunt with the staghounds yesterday – a 17-mile point.*
> *Yours very sincerely,*
> *Ted Seago*

Later, he collaborated with Masefield on a book titled *Country Scene* and then, during the Second World War, they produced another work, *A Generation Given*.

Seago liked to hob-nob and, as a camouflage officer during the war, he went painting with General Auchinleck and General Alexander, who arranged for him to be in Italy with them, although his history of ill health meant that he should not have gone near the front line. During this time he lived happily with Bernard Clegg, a pilot, who was tragically killed in a bombing raid.

Seago mingled with royalty and he encouraged Prince Charles to paint, but remained bitter because although all his pictures, particularly landscapes of Norfolk, sold instantly at exhibitions, he was never made a Royal Academician. After the war he purchased the Dutch House at Ludham on the Norfolk Broads, where he lived with Peter Seymour until his death in 1974.

In *Peace in War* (1943) Seago mentions several times that he had visited Lilias Rider Haggard at her holiday cottage on the north Norfolk coast and painted there. There is also a charming story of a picnic, which took place on a cold March day:

> *Lilias arrived to go with us, with sundry extra coats and a sheepskin hood, and a large basket containing lunch. My mother protested that the picnic was already packed, that really, Lilias shouldn't have brought anything at all and that she mustn't think of bringing anything, really . . . Lilias protested too. Honestly she hadn't brought rationed stuff, just some homemade things which one could get quite easily. . . . Together they twittered their duet of protest. My mother caught sight of some homemade scones and a jar of homemade jam in the depths of Lilias's basket and weakened slightly.*

The party motored to an unnamed estuary and ate their picnic huddled behind a hedge, sheltering from the howling wind. With the sun trying to come out, Seago set off to paint.

> *Finally I set down my traps, opened up my three-legged stool, and unpacked my paints. The wind blew straight off the sea. And I couldn't even keep my box still when I lodged it on my knee. Lilias appeared. "But you can't sit there, my dear!" she screamed. "You'll get pneumonia in an hour!" "This is where I am going to paint," I said, "so this is where I am going to sit." The others arrived; my mother full of ideas for preventing the prophesied pneumonia. "Tie your scarf round your head, dear, and you must have a rug round your knees!" My red neckerchief was duly tied, pudding basin fashion, around my head, and eventually I was left, looking rather like a chrysalis of some weird moth, to start my work.*

The picture he painted that day was 'The Rain Cloud'.

Four years after *I Walked by Night* was published, Lilias edited a second book, *A Rabbitskin Cap*. It is the story of George Baldry, who lived on the river Waveney in Ditchingham. Both books were republished in 1974 when, after some preamble about Lilias's literary background, the review in the *Eastern Daily Press* goes on to say:

> *. . . and perfectly brought together by Miss Rider Haggard so that a rich piece of English countryside should not be lost forever.*
> *There can be no doubt about the need for these new editions. For years*

the first editions and later impressions have been extremely hard to find and a lot of people have been disappointed, for no Norfolk or Suffolk bookshelf should be without these volumes.

They are attractive in their new dress, the covers being decorated with a reproduction in colour of M.E. Cotman's 'Britcher's Boat-house', but generally speaking they do not equal in quality the first editions and one cannot expect it at their price. The text is well set out though the margins are narrow and Edward Seago's beautiful black and white illustrations have lost none of their charm on this less substantial paper, a number of his full page drawings now being too heavy in tone. One also feels the loss of the coloured frontispieces, omitted as an outcome of a request made by Mr Seago before he died. Unfortunately the frontispiece has not been deleted from the list of illustrations given in I Walked by Night, which may lead some readers to suppose erroneously that their copy is defective.

Some confusion exists as to whether or not Seago wanted the frontispiece removed. Boydell and Brewer, who published the 1974 edition, say it was taken out because it was in colour; however, the frontispiece appeared in colour on the Oxford University Press paperback edition, published in 1982.

Reading University hold the archives for many of our publishing houses and archivist Mike Bott was able to supply information about the number of times *I Walked by Night* has been reprinted and by which publishers.

There is always the danger of confusing two Frederick Rolfes because in 1934 A.J.A. Symons published his book *The Quest for Corvo*. This 'experiment in biography' describes how Symons researched the life of the writer Frederick William Rolfe (1860–1913), author of the novel *Hadrian the Seventh* which was later turned into a successful stage play. Among Rolfe's other writings is a series of letters, known as 'The Venice Letters', published posthumously in 1974, in which he recounts for an English acquaintance, true or imaginary, homosexual exploits with young gondoliers. He styled himself 'Baron Corvo'.

An unusual man, but not to be confused with the poacher.

I Walked by Night has been reprinted eleven times in the United Kingdom since the first edition came out in 1935 and once in the USA by Dutton (1936). Last reprinted in paperback in 1986, it was reissued as a cheap edition in 1946 on poor-quality paper, presumably when paper was short after the war, bearing a note, 'Printed in full conformity with the War Economy Agreement'. There were also reprints in 1948, 1949 and 1951.

The 1974 edition cost £3 25s and 7,500 copies were printed. A sales record from 1974 shows that between October 1974 and July 1976, 3,755 copies were sold. The Boydell edition was reprinted in 1974, 1975, 1976 and 1977.

There is no evidence on the files as to what fee Seago received for his illustrations. More frustratingly, it has proved impossible to find out where the original drawings are.

Terry Coppin (yet another kind person who took the trouble to get in touch during the research for this book) recalls that about twenty years ago he was at Noel Abel's Auctions in Watton, Norfolk when an old pine bookcase full of books came up for sale. Among them were a number by P.G. Wodehouse and a copy of *I Walked by Night*, in which Edward Seago had sketched five pictures on the flyleaf. Mr Coppin and another collector both bid for the lot, the woman seemingly interested in the P.G. Wodehouse books. She made the highest bid and his recollection is that the lot went for between £60 and £70.

Mr Coppin approached her and offered £5 for the Rolfe book, without letting on why he wanted it. She declined to sell. An old dealer nearby said, 'You did wrong there. You educated her, you should have offered 2/6d.' Mr Coppin thought the lady was a local, so does the gem containing Seago's doodles still sit on a bookshelf somewhere in the area?

Sections of *I Walked by Night* have been used repeatedly for articles on aspects of the countryside. In 1980, Geoffrey Humphrys wrote about Lammas Day and the harvest traditions, quoting Fred's memories of how the Lord of the Harvest oversaw the negotiation of wages, the organisation of bringing in the crops and all the surrounding traditions. Delightful, rustic stuff.

Lammas took place on 1 August and marked the start of harvest in the rural calendar. Community land was known as 'Lammas' land. Often it was let to individual farmers so the winter corn growing on it had to be harvested by 31 July so that the land could be re-let on 1 August. Loaves were baked from the flour made from the first cut and were taken to church to be blessed. Lammas Day was originally a pagan festival, a day of celebration and hope for a successful harvest.

Fred is given as an example of the acceptable side of poaching. He received sympathy for his lifestyle from D. England, writing in

Norfolk Fair (1980) in an article titled 'Norfolk's Poaching Philoso-phers', which states that there was a tacit agreement to live and let live. England also tells of a man named Culley, caught poaching on the Hoare estate at Sidestrand. The squire, Sir Samuel Hoare, said to his head keeper, 'I'll have to send him to court, but here's a sover-eign, because I know he won't have any money to pay the fine.'

Kitty's story, written by Emily, the daughter of Fred and Kitty, is another piece of writing that much deserves a mention, although it has never been published or even seen by more than a handful of people until now. Emily has enabled a much fuller picture of Fred and his life to emerge. Although Lilias Rider Haggard does not name the woman, the following letter appeared in her book, *Norfolk Life* (1943):

> *A glimpse of how other people live. In my post today is a letter from Canada, from a woman who married a Canadian soldier after the war and went with him to his father's farm.*
>
> *"We have had very poor crops for several years. Two years in succes-sion the winter wheat was a total loss, and last year we had such a hot dry summer we got about half a crop, and of the other grains a quarter the usual amount. We also had the misfortune to lose a fine horse and two cows. It does not matter how hard one works to try and succeed; one is helpless if Nature turns against one. My husband and I live with his father on 100 acres, which he owns. I keep house and my husband and another man do all the work. At very busy times our neighbours come and help us, and we help them in turn, also feed them in the house. My husband's father is nearly eighty, came to this country as a boy of sixteen with one pound in his pocket, over sixty years ago, and has worked all his life to make himself independent in his old age. He is badly crippled with arthritis, but still manages to hobble round and feed his pigs, which are his pet hobby".*

It is very likely that this letter was written by Emily to ask Lilias if she was interested in seeing a manuscript setting out her mother's side of the story. A further letter followed from Canada:

> *Dear Miss Rider Haggard*
>
> *I wrote you some time ago, promising to write my mother's story. I thought maybe you could make a book out of it, sort of a comparison to my father's book I Walked by Night. I've written it from memories of things my mother told me about her early days. There were a few years*

*which I did not know very much about as I was not home much from
1912 to 1918. In 1919 I came to Canada. I have also written a few of
my mother's old songs that she loved to sing. Of course I don't know if
you can do anything with my manuscript or not. Maybe my father could
tell you any details that I have left out.*
I remain, yours very sincerely,
Emily Bulman

After Lilias's death, on 9 January 1968, many of her papers were
lodged in Bungay Museum. During the research for this book,
Emily's manuscript was found there in a large, shabby, brown enve-
lope, and is reproduced with the museum's kind permission. The text
has been altered very little, only where there were obvious mistakes
and odd punctuation. One or two words are illegible; otherwise they
appear in print for the first time, exactly as Emily wrote them.

Emily's memory of her mother's stories seems to be so accurate
that Kitty must have talked to her a great deal about her early life and
the siblings she lost touch with. Poor Kitty, lonely and isolated, she
must have talked to Emily for hours, in her broad Lancashire accent,
as she had no one else to talk to. Like *I Walked by Night*, the manuscript has songs and poems between the chapters. Kitty must have
sung them to her daughter and Emily recalled them years later as she
sat so many miles away in Canada, feeling homesick. Emily was born
in 1889, so she would have had fairly clear recollections of her own
from the mid 1890s. The text shows someone of intelligence with an
excellent grasp of English, spelling and punctuation; the handwriting
is well formed and only occasionally does Canadian slang slip into the
text. However, her memories do tend to become less accurate after
she moved to Canada.

Emily seems to have been very jealous of Joubert, calling him her
mother's darling boy, but perhaps as she sat remembering so very far
away, it is not surprising that her thoughts might have been embittered and miserable. Raised by a bullying, feckless father and a
cowed, often unhappy mother, she left behind two children with
whom she had little contact and never saw again, once she married
and went to Roy's family in Canada. So, perhaps guilt, too, played a
part.

Which member of the family it was who kept in touch with her
and sent Emily her father's book is not known; cynics might say that
maybe she was simply trying to ride on the back of Fred's success to

raise some money by putting forward her mother's point of view. Perhaps she was trying to raise enough money to come home and see her family one more time. How disappointed she must have been that the work was never published and that she never saw any of her family again after she emigrated in 1919. Nor did she receive any money from her father's will.

> *This is the last Will and Testament of me Frederick Rolfe of 46 Bridge Street Bungay, in the County of Norfolk made this seventeenth day of June in the year of one thousand nine hundred and thirty six.*
>
> *I hereby revoke all Wills made by me at any time heretofore. I appoint William Robert Hall of the Bank House Bungay, Manager of Barclays Bank Limited to be my executor, and direct that all my debts and funeral expenses shall be paid as soon as conveniently maybe after my decease.*
>
> *I give and bequeath unto my son Joseph Rolfe of the Second Norfolk Regiment and to my Grand-daughter Bertha Rolfe all cash securities and investments in my possession at the time of my death including any sums on deposit or on current account with my bankers together with any royalties due to me at the time of my death in equal share. To my said son Joseph Rolfe I give and bequeath my watch and chain my clothes my books my guns and any sums received from royalties accrued and due after my death. To Mrs Jessie Redgrave of 46 Bridge Street Bungay I give and bequeath my household furniture.*
>
> *Frederick Rolfe*
> *17 June 1936*

Obviously there was some confusion when the will was written as Fred's son's name was Joubert. Fred may have been confused because Mrs Redgrave also had a son and although his name was Herbert, he was always known in the family as Joe. Probably Fred saw far more of him than his soldier son and he muddled the names, but clearly he meant Joubert as he mentions his regiment.

In the files at Oxford University Press is a query from a descendant of Fred as to the legality of the agreement which Fred made with Lilias in 1934 *(see page xx)* and whether there were any royalties owing to the author. Under the terms of this document Fred assigned all his publishing rights to Lilias in return for a fee. There was no mention of future royalties. The publishers assured the relatives this was a legally binding document. However, Fred's mention of royalties in his will implies that he believed that earnings would come to him or his descendants and, presumably, his solicitor agreed.

After probate was signed on 6 May 1938, Fred left £35 13s 1d gross, which following deductions, meant that there was £24 2s 1d to be distributed. The recollection in the family is that Bertha received all of the money. Whether this is true, or how it came about, is not known. She petulantly said that after Kitty's death, Fred took up with another woman called Jessie, who took him for all of his money, or most of it. That seems harsh: Bertha herself received his money and Mrs Jessie Redgrave only had the household furniture after Joubert got the books plus Fred's clothes and watch. Fred had already given the guns to bailiff John Baldry.

Jessie had looked after Fred for many years and although the pair moved, possibly on the strength of Fred being better off, it was to his advantage as well. Regardless of the possibility of some impropriety with the Redgrave girls, clearly Fred and Jessie were companionable, going to the cinema together and such like. Later, when Bertha had inherited the money, she bemoaned the fact that Fred had so freely sold the rights of the book as she was left alone with her daughter Cath and very little money to keep them both.

CHAPTER 17

1938 A Sorry End

On 23 March 1938, aged 77, Frederick Rolfe committed suicide. He died on a Wednesday, the inquest was on the Thursday and his funeral took place the day after.

In their reports of the inquest the local *Eastern Daily Press* and *The Journal* recorded:

> *At 3.35 on Wednesday afternoon the celebrated character Frederick Rolfe, who lodged at 15 Nethergate Street Bungay was found hanging from a beam in a disused meal-house at 1 Nethergate Street. The discovery was made by Police Constable S.E. Dunnett who found life extinct. With the help of Police Sergeant D.J. Sawyer the body was cut down and removed to Rolfe's address.*

Fred had climbed into the hayloft of the meal house – formerly a stable – which was a few feet into Nethergate Street and almost next door to the old family home at 7 Bridge Street. He attached a snare to a roof truss and pushed himself off from the hayloft, dropping into the stable below.

Five-year-old Les Knowles, coming home from school that day, ran through the building. Fred's dangling boots hit his head, knocking him over and marking his face. Bruised and scratched from the kick and fall, he went home crying. Still crying when his father came home, Les told him that Mr Rolfe had kicked him. His father, not understanding through the child's tears what had happened, went across the road to where Fred lived to remonstrate with him. Mrs Redgrave told him Fred was not at home. Sadly, we know why.

The inquest itself was heard at St Mary's Mission Hall in front of the Coroner, Mr G.E.K. Burne. Fred was described as a retired warrener and old age pensioner. The newspaper report continued:

> *Mrs Jessie Redgrave, a widow living at 15 Nethergate Street, said the deceased had lived there for the last fourteen years. On Wednesday she*

came downstairs at about 7.45 a.m. and saw a note lying on the living room table. She was unable to read so she took it to her daughter upstairs. It was in the deceased's handwriting and after hearing the contents read she sent it to Sergt. Sawyer. At about 3.30 p.m. on the same day she was told by the Sergeant that Rolfe was found hanging in a shed at 1 Nethergate Street. Deceased had been worried since Monday night, when she had to talk to him concerning a matter of a rather serious nature. On Tuesday Rolfe told her he knew a way out of the trouble. She last saw him alive at 9.45 p.m. that day when he went to bed. He stopped at the door and said "Goodnight mother [a Norfolk way of addressing a woman], this is the last time I shall bid you goodnight." She told him not to be so silly. After that she heard no more of him. He had enjoyed good health recently.

Harold William Coleman, Yarmouth Road, Broome, Public Service Vehicle Driver, said that on Wednesday at about 5.58 a.m. he was cycling to work at Bungay when he saw deceased standing at the junction of Nethergate Street and Bridge Street, smoking his pipe. As witness passed deceased turned to go down Nethergate Street. When witness said "Good morning", Rolfe mumbled something in reply. Witness could not understand what he said. He had known deceased for several years and saw nothing unusual about him that morning. However, he had not seen deceased about as early as that before.

P.C. Dunnett said that on Wednesday he went with Sergeant Sawyer to look for the deceased. At 3.35 p.m. he went to the premises in Nethergate Street and in a disused meal house saw Rolfe hanging by a piece of wire from a beam. They released Rolfe, who had been dead for some hours. He was fully dressed and his trilby hat was lying nearby.

P.S. Sawyer said it was evident that the hanging was a determined effort. There was practically nothing of value on the body, but in a leather wallet in the jacket pocket he found a note (produced), which he knew to be in Rolfe's handwriting.

This note was not read out by the Coroner.

Witness added that in the course of his duties he had recently had occasion to interview Rolfe.

The Coroner said it was quite clear that Rolfe took his own life. He returned a verdict that death was due to asphyxiation by hanging, self-inflicted, whilst the balance of his mind was disturbed.

There was no post mortem.

A number of papers reported Fred's death and they were fulsome in their praise of him. Under a large photograph, the *Yarmouth Independent* reported that he had won fame as the Ex-King of the Norfolk Poachers and wrote a remarkable life story. The *Journal*, which covered the Bungay area, described a celebrated character found hanging at Bungay. A column covering the whole page talked of the inquest, but also at length about his fascinating book and the wonderful insight it gave into a day that was past. Even the *Lynn News*, fifty miles away in west Norfolk, wrote extensively about Fred, saying his book was a history told without reserve, with humour and philosophy.

In *I Walked by Night*, Fred mentions taking his own life:

> I have exausted my knolidge, Dear Reader, and have no more to rite, so I must bring this life Story to a close as I am thinking of bringing my Life to the same end, only I know I must make myself content to the finish.

Mrs Treanor, who as a child lived near Fred, had heard that when his constant companion Patch the dog had died, he talked of suicide then. He talked of suicide to Mr Boast's father, and he had also tried to drown himself. A local man told his son that he had been walking to the bottom of Target Hill on Bath Hills one day when he saw a body bobbing up and down in the water, and it appeared to be a man trying to drown himself. It seems that Fred's army greatcoat ballooned out, filling with air, which kept him afloat. This occurred shortly before he hanged himself.

Fred's inquest was heard by the Coroner appointed at the Liberty of the Duke of Norfolk: medieval dukes and earls often possessed rights of jurisdiction in areas of the country where they had their castle or seat, or where they owned extensive lands. These were known as an honour, barony or liberty. Most are now defunct, but in Bungay, the Duke has retained the power to appoint the Coroner since 1468. He is nevertheless a Crown servant. G.E.K. Burne, the Coroner in 1938, was with the firm of solicitors Lyas, Burne and Lyas at 2 Mount Street, Diss.

As the Coroner's report is not allowed to be opened for seventy-five years, the two suicide notes (one found downstairs by Mrs Redgrave and one in Fred's leather wallet) mentioned at the inquest would not normally be available until 2013. Inquiries of the current Coroner as to where the file would be held elicited the response that if the papers could be found, he would give permission for them to be opened immediately.

Usually, the Coroner held the papers at the office where he practised or at his home. A letter to the current solicitors at 2 Mount Street, Diss led to the information that all old documents had been filed with the County Records Office. Neither Norfolk nor Suffolk Records Office has a file for Frederick Rolfe, nor does Arundel Castle, the home of the Duke of Norfolk.

The Record Office says that almost all the Inquest files that remained with solicitors were destroyed. A Home Office Circular 250/1967 decreed that after fifteen years a coroner could 'weed' and destroy his records, so what was in Fred's suicide notes will never be known. It will not be known whether they referred to the statements made by Mrs Redgrave or the police sergeant that they had cause to speak to Fred on a matter of concern.

The rumour was that Fred Rolfe had sexually assaulted a girl in the coal yard behind Ditchingham railway station in the months before his suicide.

What was the likelihood of Fred having committed a sexual offence against a young girl? If he had, how would this have related to his suicide? A retired psychologist pointed out that beyond the policeman having spoken at the inquest of interviewing Fred, no firm evidence was presented that an assault had taken place. Very likely, an isolated old man with Fred's background would have become the subject of gossip.

The psychologist felt that if evidence arose to support the allegation, the first question was to determine whether such an assault was characteristic of Fred's past behaviour. On the other hand, was it so uncharacteristic as to suggest he might be ill? Was he usually impulsive and insensitive in his behaviour towards others or not? Such problems were less likely to result from an increase in sexual arousal than a loss of inhibition and a resultant impulsiveness. Alcohol and drugs were the most common cause of this, but it could just possibly relate to some forms of depression or senile dementia.

As to his suicide, an accusation of serious misconduct and gossip could well lead to anxiety and depression, but it is also possible that other problems such as ill health, loneliness and social isolation were more influential. Suicide is far from uncommon among those over 65, especially men, and depression is a common form of illness that carries this risk. Incipient dementias can also be accompanied by depression.

A chartered psychologist who specialises in sex offenders commented that there has been little research into very elderly men who offend in this way. However, impulsiveness is definitely a significant factor in many forms of offending.

The RM2000, the risk assessment used to measure sex offenders drawn up by Dr David Thornton, suggests the risk of sexual offending is reduced as men age, but risk is increased if sex-offending men have a history of violent crimes and burglary.

Although Fred had a long criminal record he does not appear to fall into the latter category, but that his behaviour was impulsive and insensitive to the feelings of others might be relevant. Elements within his life must also give cause for concern. There is evidence from his family and Mrs Redgrave's family too, that his conduct was unacceptable. Nonetheless, Fred is not here to defend himself. He was not found guilty or charged with any offence, so the maxim enshrined in English law must pertain: innocent until proved guilty.

So why did Fred hang himself? Even if he had committed the offence, he had served plenty of time in prison before and he did not seem concerned about being on the wrong side of the law. Punishments for sexual misdemeanors at that time could be light. For example, in 1935 a Norwich man was found guilty of indecently assaulting a 9-year-old girl. His punishment was two months' hard labour. Local papers reported a 1938 case in which a man was given one month's imprisonment for 'misbehaving' in the presence of three young girls.

Perhaps he had simply had enough of struggling with increasing ill health and the recent allegations? Maybe he felt he could not handle the shame, an emotion he describes with painful honesty after his first period of imprisonment. We shall never know.

In Brian Plummer's book, *Hunter's All* (1986), there is an article about John Bromily, a well-known name in the field of hunting dogs. He was also interested in the folklore of Norfolk and spent much of his time questioning old men who during their teens knew Frederick Rolfe. He says they remembered him as being an oft-convicted, belligerent recluse, detested by the natives of Bungay, treated as an outsider and ostracised. He talks of the treatment meted out to the crusty old man and considers Rolfe to have been mentally disturbed, stating that he attempted suicide twice, hanging himself with copper wire on both occasions.

In the first attempt he partially garrotted himself, rupturing his vocal cords. The second, successful attempt, nearly succeeded in severing Rolfe's head. However, there is no evidence to support the

191

statement that Fred had damaged his vocal cords or had previously tried to hang himself.

Despite Fred being a difficult, cantankerous character, he had undoubted prowess in breeding and training working dogs, so certain members of the Norfolk lurcher club intended to make a collection to place a gravestone over his last resting place.

He is buried in plot R.I. 58 in Bungay cemetery, a beautiful spot on a slight incline with views across the Waveney valley. His wife Kitty is buried not far away. Neither has a headstone to denote their whereabouts.

The following extract is taken from a letter that David, Emily's son, wrote to his own son David:

> Grandad came down to Richmond once to see us, must have been 1937 you were not then about. This was after the book was published. The next I heard was early 1938 or 1939 Bertha wanted me to go with her, to his funeral, as she had some expectations, I had none so was not disappointed. She collected about £25 which would have been about eight weeks wages for me at the time. However she did pay my fare.

The service was held in the chapel at the cemetery. Suicide, apart from being illegal at that time, is against the teachings of the Church, yet the vicar from St Mary's, Bungay, took the service. David and Bertha were the only members of the family present at the funeral. Mr Catchpole and Mrs Redgrave were also there and the *Bungay & Beccles Journal* reports they all stood in steady rain during the interment:

> Among others attending was the Rev. F.J. Kahn [Vicar of Mettingham] in which parish Rolfe had at one time lived. A bunch of daffodils from Mrs Kahn had tied to it a card bearing the words, "Happy memories. The heart of the eternal is most wonderfully kind".

Fred must have had something about him to make a clergyman's wife write "Happy Memories". What can they have been? The Rev. Francis Kahn was vicar at Mettingham with Ilketshall St John from 1933 to 1943, so he would only have been in office for a very short time when Fred lived there. Kitty died in 1925 in the workhouse close by, but she died too early for him to have been involved with her death and funeral. So where is the link with Rev. Kahn and, more strangely still, his wife?

The couple had moved to Suffolk from Bunny with Bradmore,

between Nottingham and Loughborough. Mrs Marjorie Buck, churchwarden at Mettingham, and her husband Colin painted a thumbnail sketch of the Kahns as they remember them from their childhood. The pair, who had no children, sound kindly, but rather from the upper drawer.

Rev. Kahn drove a big open-top car, a Sky Pilot, and used to take the local children in it when he visited his other parish, the vicarage being in Mettingham. To help the War Effort two girls sold bunches of violets tied to a pin around both parishes. When they sold some to Rev. Kahn, he told them that he could do magic and from out of his pocket conjured two small bars of chocolate. What a feat when sweets were so tightly rationed, and what a treat!

His parishioners must have thought well of him for the Parochial Church Council minutes of 12 May 1943 record that to mark his leaving, Rev. Kahn was presented with a cheque for eleven pounds subscribed by the parishioners. Mrs Nora Kahn was given a hymn book and a teaspoon by the Mothers Union, and Miss Sorrell, Nora Kahn's sister, who acted as their housekeeper, was given a bouquet and brooch from the Sunday school.

There are therefore some rather contrasting pictures of Fred's later life: a man who spent his days watching court cases and his evenings at the cinema; who so charmed a vicar's wife that she went to the trouble of sending flowers and a touching note to his funeral; and a man who was observed by John Bromily as being difficult and was possibly mentally unstable. Yet another point of view is set out in a letter received during the course of this research:

Dear Mrs Paton

Reference your letter in the Bungay and Beccles Journal dated 31st January of this year about Fred Rolfe, may I please add my contribution.

I am 87 years of age (born 1915) and lived with my parents in Southend Road in Bungay until I was 18. During this period Fred used to visit a friend of his called Bill Catchpole, well known locally as "Tailor Will", one of the last of the cottage tailors, as was his father before him. Bill Catchpole owned a large garden and Fred used to stay for hours as both men had a lot in common, meaning poaching. Fred Rolfe was a kindly man and my brother and I living next door used to go and see him and listen to his many tales of his life. To me, then aged about 10 or 11, I was spellbound by his tales and the hard life he had been pushed into. I always looked forward to sessions with Fred, he was a

193

good and kindly man, and he loved children and animals, which might seem strange, him being a poacher. A lot of the tales recorded in the book he told me himself, word for word. In the book a P.C. Stammers is mentioned. I knew Stammers when a lad and have had many a clip round the ear from him, which in later years taught me a lot. Again, Stammers was a kindly man who kept law and order as best he could, and his battle with Fred was a challenge.

May I wish you all the very best in your research into the life of one of the men I still remember so well at the age of 87.

Yours sincerely
Arthur Bedwell

What these contrasting views seem to show is that Frederick Rolfe was a complex, difficult person, who is described both as a bully and a kind-hearted man.

It appears that he was intelligent; a man who wasted his intellect by belligerently waging war on authority. Had he made use of the education and opportunities he was offered, he might have lived a very different, respectable life and then sunk into obscurity without a trace. Instead, his bloody-minded defiance has left us with a lasting legacy: a glimpse into the world of poverty and endurance suffered by the rural poor in the latter part of the nineteenth century and their attempts to defy the gentry and carve out a life for themselves; the life seen in *I Walked by Night*.

CHAPTER 18

Afterthoughts, 2009

I set out to find out if the King of the Norfolk Poachers once lived in my house. Although I cannot conclusively prove it, I think the information from his own book and Emily's manuscript goes a long way towards substantiating my theory. Evidence in papers, censuses and so on also make it more likely than not.

I find it hard to believe that it is six years since I embarked on this journey and that initially I did not even know that the poacher's name was Frederick Rolfe. Who would have thought – and certainly not me – all those years ago that I would write a book? What a lot has happened in that time: I've learnt to use a computer, gained a daughter-in-law, three step grand-daughters, two grand-daughters, and a lot of weight. We have also welcomed Christian and his two daughters into the family. Along the way, I have met some wonderful, kind and helpful people.

I have been staring out into the garden: it is a beautiful bright winter's day and already I can see the noses of daffodils pushing up through the leaves at the edge of the wood. Did Fred stand and stare at those same harbingers of spring and feel glad as I do, or did he regret that they meant the poaching season was over?

It gives me enormous pleasure to look at the same trees Fred would have seen and to enjoy the same flowers Emily picked as a child to send to Lynn hospital. I walk the dog across the fields that Fred must have walked both silently as a poacher and with swaggering bravado when he lived as a gamekeeper here.

I have just paused and walked round the wood, viewing it all in a new light – how tall in Fred's time were the beeches which are now so dominant? Was the old yew just as gnarled when he was alive? Was the noise of the stream full with winter rain and glimmering in the low afternoon sun, as he saw and heard it?

I am glad my immediate thoughts have been that Fred conjures up the joy of the Norfolk countryside and that his descriptions have given people so much pleasure over so many years. I have tried not to think of the darker side of his life.

Fred has also opened my eyes to the way many uneducated, but intelligent people with little opportunity or money aspired to know more, do more, see more and read more. They suffered dreadful poverty as well as the repression of those with power and money. They are an inspiration.

Social historian George Ewart Evans (1909–88) recorded in his books the oral recollections of East Anglians talking about their customs and working lives through the period in which Fred lived. Evans said that it was, 'Mainly the voice of a class of people that have had little opportunity to speak for themselves. They have left few letters, diaries or written accounts of any kind . . .' Well, Fred bucked the trend and left us a gem of a story that has delighted all who have read it over the last seventy years.

I also think Fred was a charmer, of more than just warts, but women too. Certainly, he persuaded both his wives to leave everything they knew to be sensible and throw in their lot with him. He charmed Lilias Rider Haggard and Mrs Kahn, while Mrs Redgrave wanted him to return to live at her house despite family opposition. He has also charmed me.

I am sure that, having read the book, people will come back to me with – as Lilias Rider Haggard said – righteous joy at discovering an error. Hopefully I shall find out more and, above all else, I would really like to know what Anna and Kitty looked like. I would like to find an original Seago illustration and also to carry out more research in Manchester to find out about Kitty's early life.

The final lines of *The Quest for Corvo*, the biography of the other Fred Rolfe by A.J.A. Symons, seem to apply equally to either man:

> *Nothing was left to be discovered, the Quest was ended. Hail strange tormented spirit in whatever hell or heaven has been allotted to you for your everlasting rest!*

I hope, Fred, that although your life was difficult and you did not make it easy for others, you do rest in peace.

Charlotte Paton
January 2009

Bibliography

Arbor, Annette, *The Norfolk County Goal*, thesis lodged at the Castle Museum, 1989.

Arch, Joseph, *From Ploughtail to Parliament*, Cresset, 1986.

Armstrong, Alan, *The Population of Victorian and Edwardian Norfolk*, Centre of East Anglian Studies, University of East Anglia.

Askwith, Richard, *The Lost Village*, Ebury Press, 2007.

Aubrey & Co., *Landed Gentry*.

Baldry, George, *The Rabbitskin Cap*, ed. Lilias Rider Haggard, Boydell Press (rev. ed.), 1974.

Bedingfield, Malcolm, *The Way We Lived Then: Bungay in the 1930s*, Morrow and Co., 1994.

Beeton, Isabella Mary, *Mrs Beeton's Book of Household Management*, Ward Lock & Co. (rev. ed), 1899.

Bennett, E.N. *Problems of Village Life*, Williams and Norgate.

Benson, John, *The Working Class in Britain, 1850–1930*, Longman, 1989.

Blake, Bull Cartwright and Fitch, *The Norfolk We Live In*, Jarrolds, 1964.

Blythe, Ronald, *Akenfield: Portrait of an English Village*, Penguin, 1972.

Buck, Anne, *Clothes and the Child*, Bean publishers, 1996.

Buck, Colin, *Memories of Mettingham*, booklet produced in aid of the Church.

——, *More Memories of Metttingham*, booklet produced in aid of the Church.

Butcher, Brian David, *A Movable Rambling Police: An Official History of Policing in Norfolk*, Norfolk Constabulary, 1989.

Butcher, David, *Waveney Valley*, East Anglian Magazine, 1975.

Callum, Frank, *Both Sides of the Fence*, Tyndale & Panda Publishing, 1987.

Carter, Michael J., *Peasants and Poachers: A Study in Rural Disorder in Norfolk*, Boydell Press, 1980.

Coles, Frederick, *Flixton, Countryside, War and a Boy*, Samundham Raven, 2001.

Coulton, G.G., *Fourscore Years*, Cambridge University Press, 1943.

Crockfords Clerical Dictionary, Oxford University Press.

Davis, Jennifer, *The Victorian Kitchen Garden*, BBC Books, 1987.

De Bootman, M., *Pentney Abbey, 1075 AD–1534 AD*, pamphlet photo-copied from the Abbey.

Digby Ann, *Paupers Palaces*, Routledge and Kegan Paul, 1978.

Diprose, Tony (comp.), *Lurcher Ways and Lurcher Days*, Diprose Publications.

Drakeford, Jackie, *Rabbit Control*, Swan Hill Press, 2002.

Earwaker, J. & Becker, K., *Literary Norfolk: An Illustrated Companion*, Aurum Press, 2003.

Edwards, George, *From Crow Scaring to Westminster*, proof copy in King's Lynn Library, 1922.

Evans, George Ewart, *Ask the Fellows Who Cut the Hay*, Faber & Faber, 1965.

——, *The Days that We Have Seen*, Faber & Faber, 1975.

——, *The Farm and the Village*, Faber & Faber, 1974.

——, *The Horse in the Furrow*, Faber & Faber, 1986.

——, *Where Beards Wag All: The Relevance of the Oral Tradition*, Faber & Faber, 1977.

Freeman, H.W., *Chaffinches*, Old Pond Publishing, 2001.

——, *Joseph and His Brethren*, Old Pond Publishing, 2003.

Gibson and Rogers, *Coroners' Records in England and Wales*, Federation of Family History Societies, 1997.

Gliddon, Gerald, *Norfolk Roll of Honour*, Norfolk News Company, 1920.

Goodman, Jean, *Edward Seago – The Other Side of the Canvas*, Jarrolds, 1990.

Goodwyn, E., *A Prison with a Milder Name*, Bidnells, 1987.

Greer, A.W., *Tubbs – A 19th Century G.P.*, Seagull, 1988.

Haggard, Henry Rider, *Rural England, Volumes I and 2*, Longmans, Green, 1906.

——, *The Farmer's Year Being His Commonplace Book for 1898*, Longmans, Green, 1899.

Haggard, Lilias Rider, *Norfolk Notebook*, Faber & Faber, 1946.

——, *A Country Scrapbook*, Faber & Faber, 1950.

——, *Norfolk Life*, Faber & Faber, 1943.

——, *The Cloak that I Left*, Boydell Press, 1976.

Hancock, David, *Old Working Dogs*, Shire Publications Ltd., 1998.

Hardy, Thomas, *Far From the Madding Crowd*, Warner Brothers (rev. ed.), 1967.

Harrison, Molly, *Children in History*, school textbook, 1959.

Hepworth, Philip, *Victorian and Edwardian Norfolk from Old Photographs*, Batsford, 1972.

Hogben, Julius, *The Life and Times of a Poacher*, draft for a possible TV programme, 1991.

Horn, Pamela, *The Victorian Country Child*, Sutton Publishing, 1990.

——, *The Victorian Town Child*, Sutton Publishing, 1997.

——, *Joseph Arch*, The Roundwood Press Ltd, 1971.

Howell, Shirley (ed.), *Stibbard School Log Book, 1863–1934*, self-published, 2003.

Howitt, William, *A Book of Seasons*.

Howkins, Alun, *Poor Labouring Men*, Routledge, 1985.

Ingram, Arthur, *Trapping and Poaching*, Shire Publications Ltd., 1994.

James, George, *The White Horse Gang and Others*, G. Harding, 1988.

Jessopp, Augustus, *Arcady: For Better or Worse*, T. Fisher Unwin, 1890.

Johnson, Derek, *Victorian Shooting Days, East Anglia, 1810–1910*, Boydell Press, 1981.

Jones, D.J.V., *The Poacher: A Study in Victorian Crime and Protest*, The Historical Journal 22.

Magistrates Formulist, 1876.

Mann, Mary, *Tales of Victorian Norfolk* (rev. edn), Morrow and Co., 1991.

Martin and Carter, *Histories, vols. 1–4*, Basil Blackwell, 1925.

Martin, Brian P., *More Tales of Old Gamekeepers*, David and Co., 1993.

May, Trevor, *Gondolas and Growlers: The History of the London Horse Cab*, Alan Sutton, 1995.

——, *The Victorian Undertaker*, Shire Publications Ltd., 1996.

——, *The Victorian Workhouse*, Shire Publications Ltd., 1999.

Mee, Arthur, *Norfolk*, Hodder, 1940.

Morrow, Peter, Reeve, Chris and Honeywood, Frank, *The Town Recorder*, Morrow and Co., 1994.

Nicholson, Shirley, *The Victorian Household*, Sutton Publishing, 1988.

Patrick, Charles, *Little Dobbin*, Charles Patrick, 1999.

Perrott, V., *King's Lynn, Boom and Prosperity*, Vista Books, 1995.

——, *King's Lynn, Life and Leisure in Victorian Lynn*, Vista Books, 1995.

Plummer, Brian D., *Hunter's All* (rev. ed.), Huddlesford Publications, 1988.

Popcock, Tom, *Rider Haggard and the Lost Empire*, Weidenfeld and Nicholson, 1993.

Randall, Arthur, *60 Years a Fenman*, Routledge and Kegan Paul, 1966.

Ranson, Ron, *Edward Seago*, David & Charles, 1987.

Read, C.S., *The Condition of Farmers in Norfolk*.

Reeve, Terry, *A Common Privilege*, Morrow and Co., 1996.

Richards, Paul, *King's Lynn*, Phillimore, 1997.

Ripper, Ben, *Ribbons from a Pedlars Pack*, Quaker Press, 1972.

Rodliffe, Rosemary and Stan, *Glimpses of Fiddamans Lynn*, Rodliffe Associates, 2000.

Seago, Edward, *Canvas to Cover*, Collins, 1947.

——, *Peace in War*, Collins, 1943.

Shooting Times magazine.

Sister Violet, 'Pamphlet on the History of All Hallows Convent and Hospital'.

Skipper, Keith, *Larn Yarself Norfolk*, Nostalgia, 1996.

Springhall, L. Marion, *Labouring Life in Norfolk Villages, 1834–1914*, George Allen & Unwin, 1936.

Storey, Neil R., *A Grim Almanack of Norfolk*, Sutton Publishing, 2003.

Symonds, A.J.A., *A Quest for Corvo*, Folio, 1952.

Thompson, Flora, *Lark Rise to Candleford*, Oxford University Press, 1945.

Troubridge, Laura, *Life Amongst the Troubridges*, Tite Street Press, 1999.

Turner, David, *History of Narborough*, Halsgrove, 2004.

Walsh, E.G., *The Poacher's Companion*, Boydell Press, 1982.

Whitmore, Richard, *Crime and Punishment From Old Photographs*, Batsford Ltd., 1978.

Wilkins, John, *An English Gamekeeper 1892: The Autobiography of John Wilkins* (rev. ed.), Sporting and Leisure Press, 1989.

Williamson, Henry, *The Story of a Norfolk Farm*, Faber & Faber, 1941.

Index

References to Fred Rolfe and his life are indexed under the relevant topics.

206

Other Books from Old Pond Publishing

Suffolk novels by HW Freeman

Chaffinch's
A moving novel that depicts the life of farm worker Joss Elvin and his struggle to raise a family on 19 acres of Suffolk farmland.

Down in the Valley
In the 1920s young Everard Mulliver leaves the town to settle in a quiet Suffolk village. He learns to fit into the countryside, acquiring a deep-rooted passion for the land.

Joseph and His Brethren
H W Freeman's novel follows the story of a Suffolk farming family through two generations in the late nineteenth century.

Hugh Barrett's sharply detailed memories

Early to Rise
Hugh Barrett's vivid account of life on a Suffolk farm in the 1930s. Living in as a farm pupil, Hugh learned to plough, build a stack, hoe beet and grind the pig food. His book, here in paperback, is accurate and humorous.

A Good Living
Managing Suffolk farms from 1938 to 1949, Hugh Barrett encountered a range of characters from gentlemen farmers to ex-miners of land settlement holdings, with wartime profiteers and downright rogues for good measure.

The Land Army

Charismatic Cows and Beefcake Bulls
Sonia Kurta's memories of farm work as a young girl are mostly set in Cornwall on the great Caerhays estate. She joined the Land Army in 1943 and stayed until it was disbanded in 1950.

Land Girls Gang Up
The group of 17-year-old London girls sent to pick potatoes in Cornwall in 1942 created havoc wherever they went. Pat Peters describes humorously their running battle with the local farmers and the long-lasting effects of her time on the land.

Land Girls at the Old Rectory
An entertaining account by Irene Grimwood of what it was like for a town girl to join the Land Army in 1939-45. She and her lively friends in Suffolk learned to hoe, build stacks and cope with livestock as well as American servicemen.

A Land Girl's War
Joan Snelling became a tractor driver during her wartime service in Norfolk. Her book recalls the dangers and tragedies of the period as well as its lighter side and her romance with an RAF pilot.

Photograph collections

Bells Beneath the Sea
For twenty-five years photographer Carl White has explored Suffolk's heritage coast from Felixstowe to Lowestoft. His evocative collection of photographs includes the sea, shoreline, reedbeds and landmarks that make this area so distinctive.

Suffolk Steam Railways
From the 1860s to the last days of steam, David Kindred's collection of photographs deals with the trains, the crews and wider activities of the railways. It shows the main lines, branches and lines now long gone – but not forgotten

Free complete catalogue:

Old Pond Publishing Ltd, Dencora Business Centre,
36 White House Road, Ipswich IP1 5LT, United Kingdom
Secure online ordering: **www.oldpond.com**   Phone: 01473 238200